TALKIN' BASEBALL

With *The Men of Autumn*, Dom Forker has
brought another world championship flag to the
big ballpark in the Bronx. He has captured
the aura and the mystique of the 1949–53 Yankees with uncanny skill and accuracy . . . with
impeccable insight, emotional restraint, honest
humor, and nostalgic charm. Each chapter is
a superb revelation of what it meant to be a Yankee, then and now, physically and spiritually.
As you turn the pages of *The Men of Autumn*,
you will be turning back the pages of time to
the summers and autumns when the Yankees
weren't just a team . . . they were family. Thanks
for the memories.

—Mel Allen
Foreword

An Oral History of the 1949–53 World Champion New York Yankees

"An action-packed oral history of the unbeatable
team that swept everything before them . . .
As Gerry Coleman once observed: 'Being Yankees was never our job. It was our religion.'"
—*The Book Reader*

The
MEN
OF
AUTUMN

An Oral History of the 1949–53
World Champion New York Yankees

DOM FORKER

FOREWORD BY
MEL ALLEN

A SIGNET BOOK

NEW AMERICAN LIBRARY

A DIVISION OF PENGUIN BOOKS USA INC.

SIGNET TRADEMARK REG. U.S. PAT. OFF. AND FOREIGN COUNTRIES
REGISTERED TRADEMARK—MARCA REGISTRADA
HECHO EN DRESDEN, TN, U.S.A.

SIGNET, SIGNET CLASSIC, MENTOR, ONYX, PLUME, MERIDIAN
and NAL BOOKS are published by New American Library, a division of
Penguin Books USA Inc., 1633 Broadway, New York, New York 10019

First Signet Printing, March, 1990

1 2 3 4 5 6 7 8 9

PRINTED IN THE UNITED STATES OF AMERICA

To all of those Yankee fans
who remember the player who hit the home run
off Cliff Fannin of the 1949 Browns
when the right-hander came into a tie game at Yankee Stadium
with the bases empty in the bottom of the ninth inning,
threw one pitch
—and got tagged with the loss!

Joe DiMaggio

CONTENTS

FOREWORD

I've broadcast Yankee games for six decades. There have been many thrills along the way—too many to mention. But if I had to zero in on a few, I'd single out Joe DiMaggio's 56-game hitting streak, Allie Reynolds' two no-hitters, and Don Larsen's perfect game.

DiMaggio was a treat to watch. You knew there was something special about him. Some players could do some things better than him. There was a razor-blade difference. For example, Ted Williams was a better hitter than Joe. But all-round no one compared with him. He was near the top of every aspect of the game. He could hit, hit with power, run, catch, and throw, until he hurt his shoulder. And he would take the extra base. He wouldn't do it often. Just when you needed it. He would always, it seems, rise to the occasion. Henrich and Phil Rizzuto once told me that when the game was on the line, in the seventh inning, they would invariably sneak a peak at Joe in center. That would give them a lift, they said. He exuded intangible qualities. Ones which never showed up in the box score. That's why the Associated Press voted him "Greatest Living Player" in 1969.

I remember one day Joe was on first base against the Indians when the hit-and-run was flashed from the bench. The batter missed the pitch and Joe was out by a mile at second. Jim Hegan's throw to Boudreau was right on the bag. But Lou hasn't tagged him yet. Joe started a hook slide, rolled over on his stomach, took his body away, went past the base, and hooked it with his hand. You should have seen the look on Boudreau's face. He couldn't believe what Joe had done to him. And we're talking about a Hall of Fame infielder.

Joe never talked about his accomplishments when he played. But a few years ago at an Old Timers' Day Game, he told me, "I hit the ball harder when I hit 46 home runs in 1937 than I did when I hit safely in 56 games in 1941. That's why I got that ulcer. I hit so many fly balls that were caught against the wall in 'Death Valley.' I honestly believe that in any other park that year I would have hit 75 home runs."

Two years later he batted .381. But it could have been .400. Not too many people know this. With three weeks to go in the season, he was batting about .415. But he got an eye infection.

Joe McCarthy, his manager, said to him, "Why don't you sit out for a while?"

But DiMag said, "No, I couldn't do that. They'd think I did it on purpose. I don't want to hit .400 by going in the back door."

That's the kind of guy he was.

Raschi, Reynolds, and Lopat—*there* was a great pitching staff. Vic had a good fastball, a good sinker, and great command of his pitches. Allie probably had more stuff than Vic. He had a great fastball and a great curve. When he came over from Cleveland, he was just a thrower. But Jim Turner taught him how to pitch. Eventually Allie matured and realized what he could do. Turner did the same thing with Bob Turley when he came up from Baltimore. He told Bob, "You're overthrowing. Take it easy. Relax.

Use the tools you've got. You don't have to win every game with us. It would be nice if you could win two of every three." He did the same thing with Reynolds. Allie was one of the best pitchers I ever saw. He was a big-game pitcher. I can't think of any other pitcher, offhand, who got off the bench and ran down to the bullpen in big-moment situations like he did. They say, "When the going gets tough, the tough get going." Allie Reynolds was that kind of pitcher.

Lopat, like Raschi and Reynolds, was tough in the clutch, too. No pitcher ever had a smarter head on his shoulders than Lopat. He would deliberately fall behind a hitter two-and-oh to get the batter on a pitch he wanted him to hit. He had so much confidence in his ability to throw the ball over the plate. And he could win the big game. Especially against Cleveland. And *every* game against the Indians was a big game.

Another reason that the Yankees of that era were so great was their double-play combination. They were so good up the middle of the diamond. Coleman was so elegant and graceful at second. He could get rid of the ball so quick on the double play. And Phil could do *so* many things.

I enjoyed giving nicknames to players. They were a popular part of the game at that time. The Cardinals of the 1930s were called the "Gashouse Gang." Lon Warneke was known as the "Arkansas Hummingbird." They were such descriptive names. A lot of people thought I spent all night thinking them up. I didn't. When I coined the "Springfield Rifle" for Vic Raschi, the phrase just popped into my mind. Nicknames were the norm in those days. Certain ones fit their character. For example, the Louisville and Nashville train went right through my town in Alabama. It was named "Old Reliable." When Henrich had that big year in 1949, it seemed only natural to call him that. Reynolds was the "Chief." When he pitched those two no-hitters, he became the "Super-chief." Frank Shea came from Naugatuck, Connecticut. I called him the "Naugatuck Nugget" because of the alliteration. Mickey Mantle was the "Commerce Comet" for the same reason. Ted Williams' name was the only one I didn't like. The "Splendid Splinter" just didn't fit. On the other hand, the "Yankee Clipper" was so natural for DiMaggio. Arch McDonald, whom I broke in under, coined that name in 1939.

I'm very happy that Dom Forker has decided to tell the story of the 1949–53 Yankees. It's an extraordinary story that deserves to be both told and read. Those Yankees were a unique collection of baseball players, products of Joe McCarthy and Casey Stengel, two of the greatest managers who ever lived. Between the two of them they won 18 pennants and 14 world titles with the Yankees. Yet their styles were as different as the dead-ball and the live-ball eras. McCarthy played a set lineup. Stengel fielded a squad of two-platoon players. But the results that they produced were similar. And their dynasties were buffered by Bucky Harris, the perfect transitional manager. He also won a pennant and world championship with the Yankees: in 1947, which was 23 years after he, as a 27-year-old playing manager, led the 1924 Washington Senators to their first-and-only World Series win. Bucky Harris was a "man of autumn," too.

Dom Forker has captured the aura and the mystique of the 1949–53 Yankees with uncanny skill and accuracy. He has done it with impeccable insight, emotional restraint, honest humor, and nostalgic charm. Figuratively speaking, he has brought another world championship flag to the big ballpark in the Bronx.

Take the chapter on the late Vic Raschi, for example. What a superb revelation it is of what it meant to be a Yankee, then and now, physically and spiritually. As you turn the pages of *The Men of Autumn*, you will also be turning back the pages of time to the summers and autumns of 1949–53, and you'll be ready to go to spring training again, as Vic Raschi said, *with the Yankees, of course.*

Mel Allen

ACKNOWLEDGMENTS

I would like to thank all of the 1949–53 Yankees I talked to for their time and consideration: Vic Raschi, Allie Reynolds, Eddie Lopat, Johnny Sain, Tommy Byrne, Bob Kuzava, Frank Shea, Tom Ferrick, Joe Ostrowski, Charlie Silvera, Yogi Berra, Joe Collins, Johnny Mize, Gerry Coleman, Billy Martin, Gil McDougald, Dr. Bobby Brown, Billy Johnson, Phil Rizzuto, Gene Woodling, Hank Bauer, Irv Noren, Cliff Mapes, and Mel Allen.

I also want to thank Mrs. Cora Rizzuto, Mrs. Jill Martin, and Mrs. Carmen Berra for their intercession on my behalf. I am grateful, too, to the many writers who down through the years have reported about Yogi; they include Ben Epstein, Ed Fitzgerald, Gene Schoor, and Phil Pepe.

Lou D'Ermilio, the Yankees' assistant director of media relations, has been of invaluable assistance to me. He patiently answered my inquiries, helped me to track down players, and gave me permission to use the Yankee photo files. Jim Ballweg, a personable and perceptive young man from Wisconsin who worked with the Yankees on a 1988 internship, helped me to cull the photos.

I am especially grateful to Dudley Jahnke at Taylor Publishing Company, who believed in this book from the beginning; and Jim Donovan, my editor at

Taylor, whose illuminating and insightful instincts have inspired and guided me.

Finally I would like to single out my three sons, Tim, Geoff, and Ted, who have supported me all along. They repeatedly expressed their confidence at times when my own faltered. They were the proper antidote to temporary adversity. They knew all along that I would prevail. They just didn't know when.

INTRODUCTION

This book is about the 1949–53 New York Yankees, the only team in the history of professional baseball to win *five* consecutive world championships. They were a unique group of baseball players performing a unique feat in a unique time. "The chemistry and camaraderie on the 1949–53 Yankees were great," says Dr. Robert "Bobby" Brown, now the president of the American League. Everyone got along with each other. There were no cliques. The Yankees didn't have bad guys. They had good guys. They got along with each other then. They enjoy each other now.

"It was an unforgettable and a great experience, not only because the team was very successful, but because they were great guys. And I think that we played during the peak period of baseball. We traveled on trains. That made us closer. And we had sixteen teams that were very competitive. It was just a delightful time to play baseball."

When Johnny Lindell, a Yankee outfielder of the '40s, died in the summer of 1985, I was just starting this book. I hadn't known that he was ill and had intended to call him very soon. When I heard the news of his death, I was very sad—because of his passing and because I truly wanted him to be a part of the story. But his death is what prompted me to put this book in drive. Most of the other players were still alive, and they had lived an extraordinarily successful sports story. It was time to put the story in historical perspective. Because it was baseball history at its very best.

That's why I wrote this book. The Yankees, from 1949 through 1953, were the best team in the history of professional baseball. They played team baseball. They had great pitching and defense. They could bunt well, hit behind the runner, and advance the runner. And they posed a long-ball threat at virtually every position. Compared to today's teams, they probably didn't have great speed (although Billy Martin contends that seven of those players had more speed than any baserunner the Dodgers had during that era). However, every one of those Yankees could go from first to third, or second to home. The Yankees gave away very little, and once they got an opportunity, or a break, they capitalized on it. But perhaps the greatest quality common to the players on those teams was their ability to play well in big games. They were clutch players.

The Men of Autumn took me three years and four summers to complete. I started it in May of 1985 and finished it in July of 1988. Most of the featured players who live on the East Coast were interviewed in person. With these men I taped the interviews. However, in no instance did the tape recorder intrude. Usually I placed it in a corner of the room while my subject and I talked. The players who live either on the West Coast or a considerable distance from my New Jersey home were interviewed by telephone. But it didn't matter whether my subject and I were across a desk from one another, or positioned at the opposite ends of a phone line. Why should it have? We were discussing one of the great passions of our lives.

I tried to avoid repetition, but there are exceptions. Joe DiMaggio's dramatic return in 1949, Tommy Henrich's sudden-death home run in the 1949 World

Series, Phil Rizzuto's squeeze bunt in the waning weeks of 1951, Eddie Stanky's "drop-kick" in the 1951 World Series, and Billy Martin's catch in the 1952 Series have beome legendary events in the history of the National Pastime. Described from different points of view, they become larger-than-life in this book, too. As with any event, the viewpoints vary slightly, but I think they complement rather than repeat each other.

Some of the Yankees talk about their former teammates more than others do. Joe Collins, for example, speaks about the "Yankee family." "The Yankees were a great group of guys," he says. "Everyone talks about Pittsburgh: 'Family, family, family.' But I don't think that any team had a greater group of fellows than we did." Those are my sentiments, too. The men in this text are "Yankee family" from the top to the bottom of the lineup.

Then there is Mel Allen. I talked with Mel Allen near the end of my task, hoping he would shed some extra light on the subject, because I had grown up with Mel. Much of my love of baseball and the Yankees, I'm sure, emanated from his baseball descriptions. Mel didn't come from the age of broadcast and telecast journalism; he came from the era of colorful commentary. "Old Reliable" . . . "The Springfield Rifle" . . . "El Toro the Bull" . . . "Hank Bauer, the Man of the Hour" . . . "The Naugatuck Nugget." He coined these and many other beautifully descriptive nicknames. When you listened to Mel Allen, you felt as if you were at the park. You knew which way a ball would land before the umpire's call. On a ball that was close to the third-base box seats, you knew whether or not Bobby Brown was going to make the catch. They say that catcher Bill Dickey never moved out of his crouch for a foul ball that landed on the backstop screen at Yankee Stadium. His instincts were that unerringly good. It was the same with Mel Allen. And he could subtly suggest those instincts through vocal nuance and intonation.

Mel Allen has been broadcasting games for fifty years, but he shows no sign of slowing down. He still does the Yankee games on cable television. He also narrates "This Week in Baseball," a weekly special. In addition, he does tapes for other shows, commercials, and features. I finally caught up with this Yankee of five decades at his apartment in Connecticut, on a hot summer evening in 1987.

At first Mel had difficulty recalling details of those Yankee seasons of almost fifty years ago. But soon he warmed up and remembered with precision Joe DiMaggio's bid for a .400 batting average in 1939, Bobby Feller's 1-0 no-hitter against the Yankees in 1946, and Phil Rizzuto's squeeze-bunting Joe home with the winning run in a big game in 1951.

And once again I was the boy, placing total faith in Mel's account, knowing that if he said a Joe DiMaggio "Ballantine Blast" was "going, going," it was gone. And I was happy.

Allie Reynolds

Many New York fans were upset when the Yankees made the trade for Allie Reynolds. That's because general manager George Weiss gave up Joe Gordon for him. Gordon was synonymous with the success of the Yankees in those days. In his first six years in the Bronx, "Flash" played on five pennant winners and four world champions. In his second year with the Indians, he played on another world title team. Joe Gordan was a winner.

But so was Reynolds. In six of his eight years with the Yankees, the Bombers won the World Series. In one of the years when they didn't win, they were eliminated on the next-to-last day of the season. In the other year they won 103 games.

Reynolds was a big-game pitcher. From 1949–53, he started the opening game of the Series four times. The one time he didn't start the first game was in 1950, when manager Eddie Sawyer of the Phillies surprised virtually everyone by opening up with relief pitcher Jim Konstanty. Casey Stengel wanted Reynolds to hook up with Robin Roberts, the Phillies' best. That match-up took place in

Game Two. Reynolds defeated Roberts in 10 innings, 2–1, on a home run by Joe DiMaggio.

Reynolds was good in World Series final games, too. In 1950 he saved the clincher for Whitey Ford. In 1952 and 1953 he wrapped up the Series with wins out of the bullpen. Overall, he won seven games in Fall Classic play. He saved four others. That's 11 wins. No other pitcher has equaled that feat in World Series play.

Reynolds could beat you in other ways, too. In five of the six World Series in which he played, he batted .333 or better. In fact, three times he hit .500.

Allie Reynolds has been highly successful in business. But his family life was not going as well when I spoke to him by telephone several summers ago. Four years before, his son Allie and his grandson Michael had been killed in an airplane crash. Earlene, his wife of forty-eight years, had also died. His father had died the year before, and his mother was on a life-support system. He himself was suffering from diabetes and lymphatic cancer. I called him at ten o'clock, and we talked until one o'clock in the morning. By midnight, Allie was into a nostalgic mood and didn't want to end the conversation. So we talked about the "good old days" for the better part of another hour. I thoroughly enjoyed sharing three hours in the life of Allie Reynolds.

I never played baseball till I was at Oklahoma A&M. It's called Oklahoma State now. All baseball in Oklahoma was on Sunday at that time. But my father was a minister, so I didn't do anything on Sunday. Eventually, I went to Oklahoma A&M on a track scholarship. I ran the 100 in 9.8. At that time I weighed 155 pounds. Later, with the Yankees, I weighed 210.

At Oklahoma A&M I also played football and baseball. In football I played tailback two years and full-back my last year. In baseball I played the outfield most of the time. I hit .500 my first year. But we only played about fifteen games a year.

The Indians signed me—for a thousand dollars. That was the most money ever given to a kid down here at that time. But going from college to pro ball was the most disconcerting thing that ever happened to me. The competition in the pros was so tough. And no one took an interest in you. At least with Cleveland. Not with the Yankees, though. The Yankees were a first-class organization. Cleveland played hard to finish fifth or sixth every year. There was no intense desire on the Indians. Lou Boudreau was a young manager. He had problems. It was tough to get veterans on the bus at certain times. He was a very good shortstop, and a pretty good manager. But he had to change his attitude to get players to go along.

The 1946 World Series turned my career around. Bucky Harris, the new Yankee manager, said to Larry McPhail, one of the Yankee owners, "We have a chance to get a young Cleveland pitcher for Joe Gordon." I guess McPhail didn't like Gordon. Why, I don't know. He was one of the best second basemen I ever saw, and he was some hitter, too. Red Embree, whom the Yankees were interested in, was a year younger than the other young pitchers. I was not one of the young pitchers.

McPhail said, "Who do you think we should take?"

Harris said, "I don't know. I haven't been in the league for a while. But there's DiMaggio and Henrich sitting together. Why don't we ask them?"

Both of them said, "Reynolds."

I'm glad. It changed my life. The Yankees had a

burning desire to win, which I liked. They were head and shoulders above the rest.

When I came to the Yankees, Mel Allen, the announcer, gave me the nicknames "Superchief" and "Old Wahoo." That was an immediate improvement. They used to call me "Blanket Ass" and "Copperhead."

I was tickled to death with the trade. Everyone at that time would give their right arms to play with the Yankees. They were a class outfit.

They didn't act that way in 1947, my first year with them, though. I had 19 wins with two-and-a-half weeks to go in the season. But they wouldn't let me go for the twentieth win. They pitched me in relief. I had so many opportunities to win 20, if they had let me. The team scored so many runs. But they told me they were saving me for the World Series. The truth, though, was they didn't want me to win 20.

I didn't finish too many games in my early years with the Yankees. Some people thought I eased up against the easy hitters. That wasn't the case. Some people thought I didn't work well with a lot of runs. I didn't feel that way. I had back problems. I couldn't go nine.

There were times when I could, though, and wasn't given the chance. Frank Shea had arm problems. One day I was winning, 13–0, and they put him in to get some work. We were winning too many games easily, so Joe Page needed work, too. I understood that. I didn't like it, though.

The years 1947 and 1949 were tremendous ones for Page. He had the livest fastball I've ever seen a left-hander have. As long as he didn't think, he was great. He couldn't have two good years in a row, though. You can't relax. He did. That led to his problems. He and Yogi didn't know how tough the game was. They just enjoyed playing it.

Of course, there were some days when you were out there when you didn't want to be. Some days it was your day in the barrel. That's when Casey didn't have any fresh arms. Regardless what happened, you were in for the full nine. Once against Boston, I was out on the mound for three and a half hours. I gave up 17 hits and 17 runs. A reporter said to me after the game, "That killed your ERA this year."

"Hell, it ruined it for my whole career," I said.

But that's the way they operated. If it was your turn to take a beating, you took it.

The first game of the 1949 World Series, they couldn't take me out. I wasn't behind and I wasn't ahead. It was nothing-nothing. When Tommy Henrich hit that home run in the bottom of the ninth, I almost kissed him. Don Newcombe fell behind in the count, 2–0. Then he tried to throw a fastball by Henrich. That was a mistake. I know. I tried it when I was with Cleveland, with the same results. The day Henrich hit that game-winning home run against Newcombe, I could have pitched a no-hitter. Actually, I gave up two hits. The first was a double that the left fielder—it could have been Johnny Lindell [it was]—lost in the sun. Pee Wee Reese in the ninth hit a ball right through my legs. I should have had it.

Henrich was great with men on base. I felt sorry for Newk, tickled for me. Newk was good. But he didn't have the diversification that a great pitcher should have. He didn't have a good curveball, and he didn't change speeds well.

Someone could have helped Newk the same way Spud Chandler helped me. When I came to the Yankees, Chandler was in his last year in the majors.

The year before, he had won 20. But he had a sore arm in 1947. One night Chandler said to me, "You're having a great year, but you're not helping the club the way you ought to be. You're not bearing down."

I was ready to bust him in the nose.

"Don't get mad," he said. "I'm trying to help you."

"Will you help me?" I said.

"Yes, I will." And he did.

The Yankee players had a policy of policing their own players. If a young player wasn't bearing down, a veteran would tell the youngster that he was fooling around with his Series money. The players policed themselves. Not the manager. That was unusual. Charlie Keller was good at that. He was well-respected. But we didn't have many problems like that. We had so many bear-down players who showed through example. You can teach better by showing than telling.

There was very good chemistry on those Yankee teams. We had an awful lot of injuries in 1949. It pulled the guys together. Everyone took turns picking the other players up. It made everyone feel like they were part of the team, knowing they were contributing.

The 1949–53 Yankees were great. There were twelve players who played on all five world title teams. That's amazing. Johnny Mize was one of them. He helped us. He could handle a bat. Of course, he couldn't move too well at first base. Overall, it was a team effort. It was fun to play with those guys. The idea of the game was to give yourself up for the team.

And we had tremendous defense. Take Gerry Coleman, for example. He was the smoothest second baseman I ever saw. I was talking to Bill Dickey in Arkansas the other day, and he said, "You couldn't take Coleman out of a play. He got rid of the ball so quick. You couldn't get a shot at him. First the ball was gone. Then he was gone."

I was the luckiest guy in the world. I had Boudreau and Rizzuto at shortstop and Joe and Mickey in center. How could you beat that? With my type of pitching, I needed that. I threw a riding fastball. You could run for two hours for a ball at Yankee Stadium. I didn't bear down all the time, but I had good location. To my knowledge I hit only six batters in my entire career. I was reading in the newspaper the other day that Don Drysdale hit 154. I don't think that's necessary. I wasn't backwards about coming inside. If a hitter could be intimidated, I'd find out. But I didn't have to hit him.

Once my control wasn't so good, though. I tried to low-bridge a batter, missed him, and got fined $100. That's the only time I was ever fined. Clint Courtney was with us once. He was a fresh youngster when we were training at Phoenix in 1951. We were working on a rundown play. Jerry Snyder slid into him and he needed stitches.

In the clubhouse Courtney said, "When I get stitched, I'm going out to whip him."

I said, "He didn't do it on purpose. You get up after you're stitched, and you'll have to tangle with me first." I guess I talked him out of that fight.

One day I'm pitching at Sportsman's Park in St. Louis. Courtney's with the Browns now. He steps up to the plate and announces to no one in particular, "I'm going to cut the first guy I reach."

I said, "I wouldn't do it, Clint."

I tried to low-bridge him, but I missed, and he hit the ball off the screen. When he slid into second, he cut Rizzuto. I nailed him and someone ended up cold-cocking me. Billy Martin, who didn't do anything, got fined $150, the most that anyone got socked.

The next day he complained in the clubhouse, "What did I do?"

"Nothing, Billy," I said, "but what can you do? You've got a reputation."

That same day, I'm coming out the runway, and I see Courtney standing at the end of it with a bat in his hands. I say to myself, "Uh-oh, am I going to have to take on this guy with a bat in his hands?"

But I don't stop. I keep on walking. I pass him and don't say anything. Finally, he calls from behind, "Heh, Allie, you hit me pretty good yesterday."

How about that! By the way, the club paid my fine.

We had great pitching on the 1949–53 Yankees. Branch Rickey once said, "Allie Reynolds, Vic Raschi, Eddie Lopat, and Whitey Ford are the best balanced pitching staff in the history of baseball."

When you play with successful people, you tend to be successful yourself.

Vic left one year. I left the next. Lopat wrote both of us letters. Kiddingly, he said, "I've been exposed." He used to pitch between us.

The Dodgers had tremendous hitters. Man for man, you had to say they had better teams. We were fortunate to beat them four times in a row. It defies everything. It comes back to pitching.

I roomed with Lopat for six years. He was very helpful. He could tell you what you were doing wrong when you didn't know yourself. He had all the guts in the world. He was egotistical and intelligent. At the plate you couldn't time him. And he never threw a strike.

In 1950 Jim Turner asked me to room with Whitey, who had just come up from the minors.

"Give him some class," Turner said.

I would tell Whitey, "Dinner's at six. Put a shirt and slacks on. And wear a jacket."

"Why do I have to wear a coat?" he'd complain. "Why a tie? I don't have one."

"Take mine."

"I can't wear yours. It makes me look middle-aged."

Bob Feller was my roommate in Cleveland. Some pretty good roomies, heh? DiMag wore him out. Feller used to say Joe hit him so well because he wouldn't pitch the "big fellow" up-and-in. Heck, he gave him too many good balls to hit.

I beat Feller in my first no-hitter, 1–0. In the ninth inning with two outs and Bobby Avila up, Gil McDougald wanted to play up close to take away the bunt. I didn't want Mac there so I moved him back. No, Casey didn't come out to the mound. I didn't want Mac up close because I could field my position. Remember, I went to Oklahoma A&M on a track scholarship. In my whole career, with runners on first and second, I never had a batter push the runners to second and third with a bunt. And it's a tough play to make.

After the eighth inning I came into the dugout and popped off. "Ed, do you think I can pitch a no-hitter?" I said.

Lopat was superstitious. He left the dugout and the ballpark. I went back out to the mound, got the first two hitters out, and ran a two-one count on Avila. I'm thinking to myself, *If I can get one by Avila, I can pitch a no-hitter*. I decided to throw the next pitch harder than I had ever thrown before. But Feller had dug a big hole in front of the mound. I threw over it and fell flat on my face. I began to laugh. Everyone wondered what was going on. Turner came out. I told him, "I didn't know whether I should laugh or cry, so I laughed."

All's well that ends well, though. I struck out Avila and pitched the first no-hitter of my major-league career.

The second no-hitter I pitched that year, the one that clinched a tie for the pennant, came down to the last out of the game, also. We had a big lead over the Red Sox at Yankee Stadium, and Ted Williams was the batter. How would you like to get Ted Williams for the last out of a no-hitter? Well, as it turned out, I had to get him twice. The first time, he hit a towering pop fly, foul, toward the Yankee dugout. Yogi circled and circled under the ball. Finally he lunged for it, and dropped it. I could have caught the ball easily. I could have caught it, also, if it had popped out of Yogi's glove toward me. But it popped the wrong way. It was no easy play, though. The ball was nine miles high. There's a tough wind above the Stadium.

I said to him, "Did I cut you, Yogi?"

He said, "No."

"Okay, let's try it again."

On the next pitch Williams popped the ball in the same direction. Yogi had trouble with the ball again, but this time he dived and caught it. I didn't worry about Williams at the time. I was winning big. All winter long, I worried about that first pop-up, though. As I said, the win clinched a tie for the pennant. Raschi clinched the pennant in the nightcap.

Turner said afterwards, "That was one of the strongest ninth innings I ever saw." I walked Dom DiMaggio, I didn't want to do that, but I was in a groove to the others.

In 1951 I ended up pitching two no-hitters and had a 17–6 record. What would that be worth today? Well, when it came time to talk contract, Weiss said to me, "Well, Allie, it's good to see you. You didn't finish too many games for us, but we're not going to cut your contract."

I said, "Well, I'm going to cut you, right below the belt. I had much better than a fair year."

The most I ever got was $47,500 plus $1,500 expense money for a ballplayers' tournament. It's hard to relate to today's salaries. I don't understand it. I don't begrudge the players what they're getting. I just don't understand how a business can operate the way baseball does now.

In the 1951 World Series I opened against Dave Koslo. The Giants didn't like pitching their best pitchers against ours. That's not the way we worked. It wasn't good for our own personal records, though. Anyway, I never got my feet settled that day. Koslo beat me.

A day of rain helped our pitching staff in that Series. I got an extra day's rest, and I came back to win my second start. I remember I got Mays out the first two times. The third time, I threw two straight pitches by him. Casey came out to the mound. That was strange—he never came out.

"How many curveballs have you thrown him today?" he said.

"None," I said.

"Try one." He started to walk toward the dugout. Then he stopped. "But keep it down."

I didn't like *that*. But Mays hit into a double play. I looked at Casey. He put his fingers up in a zero symbol. That's the only advice he ever gave me. Casey was aware of players' ability. He was better at analyzing players' ability than any manager I ever saw. For example, he would take an outfielder with a lesser arm out, and invariably the substitute would save the game with a big throw.

We were talking about Yogi before. You might be surprised that he didn't call our pitches for us. We called our own pitches. When he came up from the minors, he had been playing professional ball for only a year and a half, and he didn't have an exceptional arm. He was concerned about calling pitches and throwing runners out.

One day I said to him, "Are they calling the pitches from the bench?"

He said, "No."

"I'll call the game," I said. "Do you want me to tell them?"

"Yeah, it would help."

Lopat started to do the same. I don't know if Vic did.

When I came over to the Yankees, I became a better pitcher. You can't tell a pitcher's best years by the stats. You can have a good year, but lose a lot of close games. You can have a mediocre year, but have great stats. Look who I pitched against. Boston, Cleveland, Detroit, I never missed them. St. Louis, Chicago, Washington, I missed them a lot.

In the 1950 World Series, Eddie Sawyer of the Phillies wouldn't say who he was going to start in Game One. Casey told us, "If it's Roberts, Reynolds will start. If it's anyone else, it's Raschi."

I relieved Ford and struck out Stan Lopata on three pitches for the final out of that World Series. Years later, Lopata said, "I'd like to have seen the speed gun that day."

"How fast?" I said.

"At least a hundred."

For two consecutive years I relieved for the Yankees and never lost a game. And I didn't have any soft ones. I went out to the bullpen on my own. I told Casey, "If you need me, I can get a few batters out."

Later, Casey tried to make a reliever out of me. He said, "Why not do it?"

"I can't make any money out there," I said.

He called Dan Topping and Del Webb, the owners. "If we can make him a relief pitcher," Casey said, "it's good for the team. When he climbs over the bullpen fence, one half of the bats will be lying on the bench."

Webb asked me, "How much would it take to convince you?"

I said, "The same salary plus a modest raise."

He said, "You've got it."

But they couldn't find a fourth starter, so it never happened.

The year before I relieved Whitey, in the 1949 World Series, I came in for Lopat in the fourth game and retired the last nine batters in a row. In the ninth inning I struck out Eddie Miksis on a slider. He swung at a pitch out of the strike zone and said, "Dadgummit, he didn't throw like that in spring training."

The only time I could ever fault Casey was in the 1952 World Series. I won the last game of the season. It was my 20th win. Then he started me in the first game of the World Series against the Dodgers. Joe Black beat me, 4–2. Casey thought I was automatic in World Series play.

I said before that the Dodgers had tremendous hitters. But I always had good success against them.

I beat them five of six times. And I saved three games against them. The day I lost, I pitched consecutive starts.

Carl Furillo hit a home run off me, on a 2–2 pitch, in the last inning of the last game of the 1953 World Series. That tied the score, 3–3. Billy Martin's hit scored Hank Bauer with the winning run in the bottom of the ninth. That was the first hit Furillo ever got off me. Oh well, there's always a first time.

I saw Duke Snider recently.

He said, "You know, you struck me out several times."

I didn't say, *"Eight times in a row."*

I had a lead one day, though, and threw him a curveball. He hit it over the screen at Ebbets Field.

Robinson and Campanella didn't give me much trouble, either, but Robinson once hit a home run off me on as good a pitch as I could throw.

Bobby Brown said, "Was it a slider?"

I said, "Yes."

"He's a good breaking-ball hitter."

I didn't see that in the scouting report. Well, in the fourth game of the 1952 World Series, I beat Joe Black, 2–0. I struck out 10 batters. I got Robinson three times; Campanella, twice. Robinson struck out three times looking. I can assure you he didn't see any breaking balls that day.

Campanella was a three-time MVP. I just laugh. I side-wheeled him a lot. His front foot would end up in the third-base dugout. Bobby Brown would put his glove in front of his face and laugh. "I think you've got him," he'd say.

Robinson, Snider, Campanella, and Hodges. They're all in the Hall of Fame. They couldn't credit me for getting them there. Their combined World Series batting average against me was .124.

On the other hand, you don't know why certain batters hit you. Skeeter Webb and Eddie Mayo, who had career averages of .210 (.219) and .260 (.252), hit .400 and .350 against me. I never knew why. Some batters can just read your pitches, I guess.

I retired after the 1954 season. That year I was 13–3. Not too bad for a guy who was 37. But I had recently been in a bus crash. I had hurt my back. It was a difficult injury in a difficult place. Afterwards I had running problems. I could no longer condition myself. I would pitch with back spasms. Then I would have to go to the dugout for cold spray. I couldn't put up with that for too long. In 1954 I didn't want to play anyway. The game didn't appeal to me any more. It took me away from my family too much.

But I appreciate everything the game did for me. I used the game afterwards. I'm still using it.

In 1952 I got into the oil-field service business, with a mud company. In 1980 I merged with another company. Made a sizable deal. But after my wife, Earlene, died, I decided to retire. It was a tough time for me. I've got diabetes and lymphoma. I've been off chemotherapy for three or four months. They say they've got it under control. But the guy who has it is never really sure. Four years ago, my son Allie and my grandson Michael, who was a student at Oklahoma State, were killed in an airplane crash.

My father died last year. Right now my mother is on a life-support system in a nursing home. As soon as you and I finish talking, my brother is coming over, and we're going to decide whether we should tell them to take her off the support system. Even with it, she only has a week or two to live.

So I'm glad you got in touch with me. You've

allowed me to turn back the clock. To take my mind off my problems for a few hours, and think of happier days.

Well, anyway, I got bored with retirement. So I got back into my former business. I found out that the company that bought me out was happy to have me back. New Park Services set up a minority company. With Indian blood, I was able to qualify. The government pushes the oil companies to do a percentage of their business with minority groups.

But I was talking about happier times. Do you remember the night in Cleveland when Bill Veeck placed an automobile in our bullpen to drive our relief pitchers to the mound? Casey wouldn't let our pitchers use it, though.

After the game the reporters asked, "Why?"

He said, "The Yankees drive only in Cadillacs."

Veeck, going along with the line, placed a Cadillac out there the next night.

When I saw it, I laughed. That night was my turn to pitch. I worked hard to keep anyone out of it. That's the night I pitched the 1–0 no-hitter against Feller.

Vic Raschi

Vic Raschi was consistent. *His life-time record was 132–66. With the Yankees he was 120–50. From 1949–51 he won 21 games in each year. In seven years in the Bronx, he averaged more than 30 starts a season, and he never lost more than 10 games in one year.*

Four times in his career with the Yankees, his winning percentage was over .700. In 1950 he posted a league-leading .724. Overall, his winning mark with the Yankees was .710. In World Series play he won five of eight decisions for a .625 mark. Two of his losses were by 1–0 and 3–2 scores. And his ERA was 2.24.

Vic Raschi was competitive. *In his eight years with the Yankees, he never missed a start. And he didn't need many runs. He lost a 1–0 decision to Preacher Roe of the Dodgers in the l949 World Series. In the opening game of the following World Series, he blanked Jim Konstanty of the Phillies, 1–0. He and Don Drysdale have been the only pitchers to both win and lose 1–0 decisions in World Series play.*

On the day of a game, he wouldn't allow any pictures of him to be taken. He wouldn't allow any infielders to visit him on the mound during a game, either. He didn't want anyone or anything to break his concentration. He was a bear-down guy who could get up for a big game. And he won some big ones, including the pennant winner on the final day of the 1949 season and the World Series finales in 1949 and 1951.

Vic Raschi was very candid. *He knew what he could do and what he couldn't do, and he was totally honest about it. In 1947 the Yankees were using him as a batting-practice pitcher before they returned him to the minors. Knowing that he was being misused, he refused to go down to the minors. But his wife talked him out of retirement and into reporting to Oregon. The rest is history.*

In 1955, his last season in the majors, he felt that he "wasn't pulling his weight" with Kansas City, so he retired permanently. He said simply, "I'm retiring because I can no longer pitch like Vic Raschi."

The Yankees won six world championships during Vic Raschi's seven productive seasons in the Bronx. In 1948, the year in which they didn't win, Vic won 19 games, lost eight, and spun six shutouts; but the Yankees were edged out for the pennant in the last weekend of the season. In essence, they came very close to winning seven consecutive world titles. It was the proud Yankees' proudest period—and one of the primary reasons that the Yankees were so successful during that era was Vic Raschi.

One afternoon not long ago, I drove up to Conesus, New York, and spent a few enjoyable hours with Vic. He lives just up the street from the house in which Sally Glenn once lived. Sally Glenn has been Mrs. Vic Raschi for more than forty years. When I spoke with "The Springfield Rifle," he had recently sold his lucrative liquor store in nearby Geneseo, New York, and had a new hip inserted. But he lives adjacent to a golf course and he plays tennis whenever he can get a foursome together

When Vic was in high school, he was an all-around athlete. Ohio State wanted him as a tight end; William and Mary got him as a basketball and baseball player. But once the Yankees signed him, they insisted that he concentrate exclusively on baseball. That was just fine with Vic Raschi. He was always an intense competitor who didn't want anything to interfere with his concentration. Infielders were afraid to visit the mound when he was pitching. "Get back to your position," he would snap. "You have enough trouble doing your job without telling me how to do mine."

I found Vic Raschi much more approachable. He was soft-spoken, amiable, and polite as we sipped coffee at his kitchen table while a team of carpenters renovated a nearby room. Their saws and drills posed no distraction as we talked of bygone years. It was as though Vic were back in the summer of 1951, standing on the mound at Yankee Stadium, ready to face the heart of the Cleveland Indian batting order. The palms of his hands were sweaty as he looked in toward the plate and thought of the first five batters: Bobby Avila, Dale Mitchell, Al Rosen, Larry Doby, and Luke Easter. He still had that phenomenal concentration.

My family was Italian. My father was a carpenter for the New York–New Haven–Hartford railroad. My mother was a good homemaker and family-raiser. We lived in Springfield, Massachusetts, and my father bought the Springfield Army Officers' Home, which was about 150 yards away from the Springfield Armory, where they made the Springfield rifle and the Gatling machine gun. That's why Mel Allen called me "The Springfield Rifle."

I was sixteen years old as a high school freshman when we had a baseball sectional title in the spring. One of the fellows who came in from Boston was a catcher by the name of Jim Hegan. A scout who saw me during that tournament said he wanted to talk to my father and me. So we went home that night and talked. Basically we talked about colleges. In those days the Yankees wanted their players to be educated. There were two colleges that they were sending their kids to. One was Manhattan College in New York City, and the other was William and Mary in Virginia.

Basketball was my best sport—and maybe I shouldn't say this, but at the time I was an end on the football team, and Ohio State was interested in getting me there on a football scholarship. By the time we got through with our conversation in my house that night, the scout, and I can't remember his name, said, "We'll pay Vic's way through school, no matter how long it takes him." So my father and I signed a conditional contract to those terms. Now remember, I was only sixteen years old and a high school freshman at the time. And after I signed the contract, the scout said, "Oh, by the way, no more football." From that day on, the Yankees controlled my life.

I graduated from high school and decided on Manhattan College. But when my dad and I went down there, I forgot my application. They said, "Go home and get your application and come back next week. We'll enroll you then."

But when I came back, they said, "We're sorry, but all our departments are filled up."

I called the Yankees and they said, "Don't worry."

They called back and said, "William and Mary said, 'Come right on down.' "

Of course, I was two weeks late. But in the winter season I made All-State center in basketball. Shortly afterwards, I got a call from the Yankees. They said, "Congratulations on your basketball award, but . . . no more basketball."

My baseball career at William and Mary was interrupted by World War II. When I got out of the service, I married a girl who was a student at William and Mary, and she lived right down the road here, right across the street from where we live, and her name was Sally Glenn.

I returned to William and Mary and graduated in 1949 with a degree in physical education. At that time I wanted to teach physical education in the elementary school system. I was pitching with the Yankees—but they were *still* paying my way through school.

At the end of the 1946 season, I joined the Yankees. My first day up, I pitched. In the clubhouse before the game, the sweat in the palms of my hands was unbelievable. I put my uniform on, sat in the dugout, and looked up at the big ballpark in awe. It was incredible. I didn't want to walk out on the field. I wanted to go back up the runway and hide. But I went out and stood around the batting cage, and talked to DiMaggio and some of the guys, and that loosened me up. Then I went out and pitched and did a fairly good job. In the seventh or eighth inning, the other team got a man on first base. Bill Summers, who was the umpire at first base, had to go past the mound to second when there was a runner on first. I'm taking my position on the mound, and all of a sudden I hear, "He can't hit a high fastball." I couldn't believe what I heard, so I stepped off the rubber. Bill was squatting over, with his hands on his knees, and he looked up at me and said, "You heard it. We Massachusetts boys have to stick together." So I returned to the mound, threw high fastballs, struck the batter out, and went on to win the ball game.

In 1947, when they sent me back down, I came back home, disappointed because they were using me as a batting-practice pitcher, and I thought I was capable of much more than that. So I said to my wife, "I am not going anywhere. I am going to quit baseball."

The club called and said, "You haven't reported."

I said, "No, I'm not going to." The second time they called, I repeated, "I won't go."

Now get this. They said, "If you don't report, we're going to blackball you from baseball." At that time they could do that.

My wife said, "I've never seen Portland, so let's go."

Six weeks later, I was recalled by the Yankees. I was called up with Bobo Newsom, and we both pitched in a doubleheader in Chicago the first day we got there, and it was the hottest day of the year. I pitched the first game and I couldn't believe the heat. We had those flannel uniforms at that time. I must have changed my uniform six times. Bobo pitched the second game. We both won. They were games thirteen and fourteen of that 19-game winning streak, I think. I know I won the last game of the streak in Detroit.

At the end of the 1947 season, Jim Turner told me to put some weight on. I weighed 195 pounds. They didn't think I could go nine innings. So I went home and came back at 224. I averaged about 215 the rest of my career, and from that time on I never had trouble going nine innings.

I was twenty-nine before I pitched my first full season in the majors. The war had something to do with our coming up late. But I think it was more the way the organizations kept the players in the minor-league system. They would move us up one level at a time. Consequently, it took quite a while to get there. But it's hard to say if I would have done well if I had been a starter at twenty-three or twenty-four. Experience is what really makes a player a star.

The 1949 season was a very good one for me. That year we set a record for the number of injuries by a team. Fortunately for me, I remained healthy. But I think that team was spectacular. The players hung together and picked each other up. It was a marvelous example of sticking together. It was unbelievable: the effort, the comradeship, and the belief in each other.

When you think of 1949, you think of Tommy Henrich. "Old Reliable" was a great name for him. Mel Allen came up with that one, too. Henrich always played 100 percent. I remember one game, I think it was in Chicago, he ran into the fence and broke his toe. But he cut a piece out of his shoe, and painted the spot black so that he could continue playing. Now that took a lot of guts.

One of the highlights of my career was the last game of the 1949 season. The Red Sox and the Yankees were tied for first place, and we were playing for the pennant at Yankee Stadium. Casey gave me the start and I was pumped up for the game. I always felt that if you couldn't get up for a big game, you weren't the right guy to pitch that game. The sweat stayed in my palms all game long. I remember in the ninth inning, Joe DiMaggio didn't get to a ball that ordinarily is an automatic out. But he didn't get to it because he was run down physically. Then something that no one could believe happened. DiMag stopped the game and took himself out. He didn't want to contribute any further in a negative manner. Cliff Mapes took his place. That was the thing about Joe D. He always demanded perfection of himself, but he always placed the *team* first.

After Joe didn't catch that ball, we were in trouble. The tying run, Birdie Tebbetts, was at the plate. Henrich, who was playing first base, had the ball, and he was stalling. Finally, he came over to offer me encouragement, but I said, "Give me the goddamn ball and get back to your position."

I didn't want to lose my concentration. On the next pitch Tebbetts popped the ball off the first-base line. Henrich was yelling, "I got it. I got it!" He was swinging his arms to keep everyone else away from it. And when he caught it, it was the most unbelievable moment I ever remember.

That year, in the World Series, Henrich hit a home run in the bottom of the ninth inning to win the first game. He really crushed that Newcombe fastball. In the next game I turned around and lost, 1–0, to Preacher Roe. Jackie Robinson cost me the game. He was on third base and he was a dangerous runner. So I pitched from the stretch instead of the windup to prevent him from stealing home. Consequently, I got a fast ball up to Hodges, and he hit it for a base hit to win the game.

The next year, I won a 1–0 game in the World Series against the Phillies. I was very happy to get the opening-game start, and I was thrilled to win the game, especially because I had a bad knee. I slid into

Jim Hegan one night in a game I beat Bob Feller, 1–0, and tore a tendon in my knee. My teammates were very considerate, though. They never said anything about it, even when they went to other teams. If my opponents knew about my injury, they would have bunted me out of the league.

I won 21 games every year from 1949 to 1951. However, when I dropped to 16 wins in 1952, they thought I was slipping. But I had a 2.78 ERA and I won two games in the Series. I lost a lot of close games that year. Your luck can change at any time on a ball field. I think it's the law of averages. The one thing I did notice was that I wasn't finishing some of the games I won. They were putting someone else in to save them. I was losing some of my stamina.

Yes, I took pride in finishing what I started, and, yes, I took pride in taking the mound every time it was my turn to take the ball. It's true that I never missed a start in my eight years with the Yankees. Even when I was hurt, mainly with my knee. I'm proud of that fact. You never wanted to let Casey know that you were hurt. Other players knew it, but they kept it quiet. Casey knew it, too. But I always wanted to go out there every start.

Funny, I don't remember too much about my two wins in the 1952 World Series. I remember the losses more than the wins. The wins, you feel, are automatic. But I remember vividly my loss in the 1953 World Series when Roy Campanella's home run beat me, 3–2. Casey told me before I walked out to the mound, "Don't throw him a high fastball." Just before I pitched to Campy, Casey yelled from the dugout, "Don't throw him a high fastball." So what do you think I did? I threw him a high fastball. And he hit it out of the ball park. Those are the times you want to dig a hole on the mound and crawl in it so that no one will see you. Casey was disappointed, but he never mentioned it to me.

The 1949–53 Yankees were the best team I ever saw. At that time there were great players in both leagues. But our players were special because they blended together better. We believed in each other. I think belief in each other is the best thing you can have in a professional sport. If a player made an error, we knew it was because he was trying. It was a quiet kind of belief. We never chewed each other out. If a young player was loafing, and he made an error because he wasn't concentrating, the look in the eye of Joe would straighten him out. But Joe wouldn't say anything. Some things don't have to be said.

I said before that you seem to remember the losses more than the wins. There's always one team in the league you can't beat, no matter how low in the standings they finish. Washington was that team for me. They'd beat me, 1–0 or 3–2. I just couldn't beat them. The same thing applies to hitters. Some guys you could hit right between the eyes, and they'd get up and hit the next pitch for a base hit.

The toughest hitter for me to get out—there were two of them, one more than the other—was Hoot Evers. The other was George Kell. They both played for the Tigers. There was no way that I could intimidate Evers. He just kept on hitting me.

Fortunately, the greatest player that I ever saw was on my team. Joe DiMaggio. There just wasn't anything he couldn't do on a ball field. Hitters like

DiMaggio and Williams could pick up the spin of the ball further out toward the mound than other hitters. Consequently, they never strode too soon or made a hitch with the bat. They waited on the ball. They were really great hitters.

Of course, when it came to sheer power, Mickey Mantle was in a class all by himself. Take that ball he hit in Washington. It kept going, going, going. We knew that it was an automatic home run. But the distance that the ball picked up going out of the ballpark was unbelievable. Red Patterson measured it. He was a very efficient traveling secretary. I don't know if he measured it correctly, but we were afraid for the people who lived beyond the park. We thought that they might get hurt.

That reminds me of a Mickey Mantle-Billy Martin story. We were in Cleveland and they were rooming together. Gene Mauch, the trainer, and I were going to church on a Sunday morning. We were standing by our cars when three boiled eggs hit the roof and splattered us. Of course, in those days we had to dress in a suit, shirt, and tie. We raced up the elevator, and when we got to their room, they had the door barricaded with all of the furniture inside. But from that time on, we had them under our thumb. They knew they couldn't say no.

Yes, I set a record for balks in one game. Four. This one game, the umpire called a balk on me and explained that they were cracking down on pitchers who were abusing the balk rule: that is, not coming to a one-second stop, after the ball and glove made contact, before going to first or home. There were certain pitchers, like Reynolds and myself, who liked to get an edge by just coming to a slight hesitation. So the umpires decided to bear down.

This one day, we're playing the White Sox, and the umpire calls a balk on me for not stopping. On the next pitch he calls another balk for the same reason. We were winning, 5–3, but I did it two more times to bring pressure on the umpires to go back to the practice when they let us "cheat a little." After the fourth balk—the game was still in doubt—Casey jumped up on the dugout steps and yelled, "If you do that again, it's going to cost you money."

The next day, Allie, the first time he had a runner on base, held the ball and held the ball and held the ball, and then he stepped off the rubber. Then he got back on the rubber, and he held the ball and held the ball and held the ball. The fans were getting restless. So were the umpires. The plate umpire finally went out and asked Allie what was wrong.

"Why aren't you throwing the ball?" he said.

Allie said, "Why, I'm afraid to release the ball, because I might be called for a balk." That was the end of it. The umpires went back to calling the balk the way they had been.

Reynolds and Lopat were great pitchers. They called us "The Big Three." We believed in each other. No doubt about that. Every time one of us walked out on the mound, the others felt he would give 100 percent, and he would win, regardless of who the opponent was. Every series was a big series, regardless of the opponent. But we had confidence in whoever was pitching. If he didn't win, we had confidence that whoever pitched the next day would.

We never had a fourth starter to go along with us. But when Whitey Ford came up, we could tell he was something special, and we passed along tips to him, and we believed in him, too, and gradually we became "The Big Four."

It seems like I can remember my good hitting days better than my good pitching days. Yes, I set an American League record when I drove home seven runs in one game. It was against the Tigers. Fortunately, Hoot Evers wasn't playing. I came up with the bases loaded and hit a double, I think, and scored three runs. Anyway, I got up to seven RBI's and we were way ahead, so I said to Casey, "Why don't you put someone else in? We're ahead by so many runs."

He said, "No way. You've got seven runs batted in. If I took you out now, I'd get creamed before I left the park." So he made me finish the game.

In the bottom of the eighth, Phil Rizzuto said, "If I get a hit, I'm going to steal second so that you can get another RBI. He got a hit and tried to steal second, but he was thrown out. The only way I could get an RBI then was if I hit a home run, which was impossible, so I made an out.

The 1948 All-Star Game was in St. Louis. I was the second pitcher. It was my time to hit, and we had second and third with two outs in a close game. We had DiMaggio and Williams, who were hurt, sitting on the bench. But they could swing a bat, so I figured Bucky Harris would pinch hit for me. Consequently, I didn't make any motion to get off the bench. But Harris turned to me and said, "Get up there, you're hitting."

I said, "Gee whiz, you got Joe and Ted sitting on the bench and you're going to let me hit?"

He said again, "You're hitting."

Well, I got up there, got a base hit, and won the game. But even afterwards I couldn't believe he let me hit. I wonder what Joe and Ted were thinking.

Casey was a believer, too. He believed in his hitters, his fielders, and his coaches. He would ask a coach how he felt about a certain hitter, and when he was told, he believed. I think that was one of his greatest strengths. He believed in all his personnel.

My top salary was $40,000, plus a bonus. It was tough to get up to $40,000 in those days.

The negotiations with Mr. Weiss were something. We always thought he got a percentage of the savings he made for the owners. Whenever we went in to talk contract, he always had a set of negatives in mind for every positive thing we mentioned. We'd go back and forth, till I'd say, "Listen, Mr. Weiss, am I of value to the club?" That would be the end of it. I would get what I wanted. They had a policy that they would never give anyone a 25 percent raise. But when I went in in 1952, after I'd dropped from 21 to 16 wins, he said, "Listen, if you don't win 20 or 21 games, we're going to cut you 25 percent." Then he warned me, "You better never have a bad season."

The next year he kept his promise and tried to cut me 25 percent. I didn't think it was necessary and wouldn't sign. I guess in the back of their minds they knew they were going to get rid of me. When they sold me to the Cardinals, no one ever said a thing to me. The first time I knew I had been sold was when the reporters surrounded my house in St. Petersburg.

Not one word was said. I never talked to Casey about it later. I never got the opportunity. Casey couldn't bring himself to tell players who were traded away or let loose. I think he took the side of the veteran players with management, and I think that was why he sometimes got mad at management. But those hard feelings were never carried over to the ball club.

I think you should be paid according to how you perform. If you don't perform, you don't deserve it. Some of these players today are being paid too much for what they contribute to themselves, their fellow players, and their teams.

Coming back to Mr. Weiss, though. He never looked you in the eye. He always looked away. It was like he was saying to himself, "How can I get rid of this guy without talking to him?"

When I went over to the Cards in 1954, I wasn't physically sound. I had a slipped disc. But the Cards should have won the pennant in 1954. As I recall, we were in first place about the first of June. When you're that high at that time, you should have a good chance to win. I really don't know how to say it, but our manager [Eddie Stanky] was not a good one. He hated to lose, even if it was 15–1. He was too intense. Then he started to use starters as relievers, and the pitching staff got tired, and the team faded.

I slipped a disc in the spring of 1954. Really, I think I did it earlier, when I was substitute teaching in physical education at Dansville High School. I was doing calisthenics on the floor at the time. I hurt it again in the spring. It got worse and worse and they put me on medication. They told me they didn't operate on that type of injury. It finally came around and I got off to a good start—I won my first five games—but I just didn't have it any more.

The middle of the following year, with Kansas City, I just couldn't finish. We had a good ball club, and I didn't want to create tension by taking up a key role, so I decided to retire because I could no longer pitch like Vic Raschi.

I made a final contribution to the Yankees, though. Jim Turner talked to me about some of our good players—Bobby Shantz, Clete Boyer, and Art Ditmar —and later the Yankees made deals for them.

Baseball has been my whole life since I was nine years old. I put everything into it and I got a lot out of it. If I had to do it all over again, I'd do it the same way. Two years ago, I got a new hip. It made a new person out of me. I feel like a kid again. Ready to go to spring training.

With the Yankees, of course.

Vic Raschi died October 14, 1988.

Eddie Lopat

Some of Eddie Lopat's critics said he was a "junk-ball pitcher." They said he had three speeds: slow, slower, and slowest. Lopat shakes his head in disbelief when he still hears that description of himself. It is as though he's saying to himself, "I still have them in the palm of my hand."

A pitcher can't win with just one pitch in the major leagues, Lopat explains for perhaps the one thousandth time. In reality, he had four basic pitches: a screwball, a fastball, a curveball, and a slider. But he threw the screwball with two speeds and the other three pitches with three speeds. That gave him a total of 11 pitches. His detractors thought he had only one. That's why he was always one step ahead of them.

Actually, Lopat was smarter than many of the batters he faced. If the batter swung at a pitch that was an inch off the plate, Lopat would throw the next serve two inches off the plate. If the batter swung again, Lopat's following offering would be three inches off the plate. That's why Whitey Ford, when he came up to the majors in 1950, was so willing to listen to Lopat's advice. Whitey was intelligent *enough to know that Eddie was the master craftsman on the mound. One of the things Lopat taught Ford was that the team was more important than personal pride. "Every starting pitcher wants to go nine innings," Lopat told Ford. "But if you get tired, let Casey know. No one will hold it against you. You know, the bullpen pitchers have to earn their money, too." Whitey Ford demonstrated in his major-league career that he could go nine innings. But often he voluntarily handed the ball over to relief specialists like Ryne Duren and Luis Arroyo. The precocious student had learned a valuable lesson from the master*

Eddie Lopat was a competitor, too. During the 1951 World Series the newspaper writers said that Lopat, a lefty, could not win at the Polo Grounds. Casey Stengel seemed to be influenced by their thinking. He hedged. But eventually he pitched Lopat at the Polo Grounds in Game Five, and Eddie came away from the game with an easy 13–1 "laugher."

In that victory, however, he strained his arm. The injury put him on the sidelines for a considerable part of the 1952 season. It was finally diagnosed as tendinitis. When his arm responded to treatment, he pitched even better than before. From the point at which he returned to the starting rotation through the 1954 season, he won 33 games and lost just eight.

Quite a few of those victories came over the Indians, against whom the Yankees played some classic contests during their 1949–53 world title streak. His career mark against Cleveland was 40–12. In fact, when the Indians won an American League record 111 games in 1954, Lopat defeated them five of five times. His success against Cleveland was truly phenomenal; one has to remember that his wins came at the expense of pitchers such as Bob Feller, Bob Lemon, Early Wynn, and Mike Garcia.

Lopat also showed his competitive nature in World Series play. Overall he was 4–1 in the Fall Classic. One win that stands out in his mind is a 4–2 complete-game victory over the Dodgers at Yankee Stadium. Before Lopat defeated the Dodgers in Game Two, Brooklyn had beaten 18 consecutive left-handed pitchers. In fact, the Dodger lineup was so menacing against left-handed pitching that the Braves for years rarely pitched the great Warren Spahn against it. Very few "experts" thought Lopat would be the exception to the rule. Lopat privately disagreed with them. He decided before the game that he was going to win and he was going to go nine innings. That's exactly what he did.

They called Lopat "Steady Eddie." From 1944–54 he won games in double figures every year. The first four years were spent with the White Sox. In 1947 he was 16–13 with Chicago. But the White Sox traded him to the Yankees. Lopat still doesn't know why they traded him. But he and the Yankees are happy they did. From 1949–53 Lopat averaged 16 wins a season with New York. His best seasons with the Yankees were 1951 when he was 21–9 with two wins in the World Series and 1953 when he was 16–4 with one win in the Fall Classic. In 1953 he led the American League in winning percentage (.800) and ERA (2.42).

Eddie Lopat was consistent with the bat, too. In regular-season play during his career, he batted .211. In World Series play he batted .211, too.

"Steady Eddie" almost turned out to be unsteady for me. When I contacted him by phone to set up the interview, he said, "Let's make it early next Monday, so we don't tie up the whole day. I'd like to get a little golf in." Well, it's a good thing that I got to his house in Hillsdale, New Jersey, a little early, because he and his wife Elizabeth were coming out the front door, headed for shopping. He had completely forgotten about our interview. But he didn't get flustered. Instead he smoothly shifted gears, and for an hour-and-a-half, while Elizabeth waited patiently in another room, "Steady Eddie" helped me turn back the clock.

The Dodgers signed me originally. As a first baseman. In those days I was a pretty good hitter. In fact, in my years with the White Sox I hit pretty well, too. They let me take batting practice every day, and they used me to pinch hit, also.

Jimmy Dykes was the manager of the White Sox when I reported there in '44. In the middle of '46, he was replaced by Ted Lyons, who was very instrumental in putting the finishing touches on my pitching in the major leagues. He taught me how to operate. He taught me a slow curve, and he taught me a short-arm and a long-arm release. In short, he really revolutionized my pitching. When I left Chicago and came to New York, it was just a matter of "Give me the ball and let me pitch."

Why did the White Sox trade me? Well, I don't know. I had some pretty good years over there. Maybe it was the $6,000 raise I was holding out for. That was a lot of money in those days. Also, there had been a change in the front-office personnel. They might have wanted to bring up some minor leaguers. And they needed some catching at the time. They got Aaron Robinson from the Yankees. But really I don't know why they traded me. I'm just happy they did.

The Yankees were my club growing up. Babe Ruth and Lou Gehrig were my heroes. The trade was a dream come true. When I got to the majors, my first visit to the Stadium made a great impression on me. I remember standing on the field and saying to myself, "What a thrill! I remember, as a kid, coming out to root for these guys. Now I'm pitching against them!"

In '48, though, I had a little trouble getting started. I was trying so hard, I wasn't being myself. I was trying to pitch beyond my means, figuring every game was so important, until finally on the first of June I was 2–5, which was no great shakes. I said to myself, "The heck with this. I'm going to pitch the way I did when I was with the White Sox." After that I was all right. I went on to win nine in a row, and I finished at 17–11. So I came on like gangbusters.

Everything revolved around my screwball. That set up all my other pitches. They said I pitched slow, slower, and slowest. But you can't do that all the time. I changed speeds. I threw my fastball, curve, and slider at three different speeds. And I had two speeds for my screwball.

In '48 we got knocked out of the pennant race by the Red Sox on the next-to-last day of the season. In '49 we got even. There were some memorable events in '49. Like Joe's comeback in Boston. He had a fantastic series for someone who hadn't played the first half of the season. It was just like coming to spring training and starting all over. He played like gangbusters. He did everything well. He was just phenomenal.

Tommy Henrich had a great year, too. He hit 24 home runs and, I think, 18 of them either tied or won the game for us. We got Johnny Mize in the middle of the season, and he did a great job for us, too. They got him for only one or two years, and he stayed five, and he really contributed, and we won five straight world titles.

We had to win the last two games of the season, against the Red Sox, to win the pennant. We knew that we had a tough road in front of us, but when

Johnny Lindell hit that game-winning home run on Saturday, we knew we had them on Sunday. Of course, we didn't run them out of the park, but we won.

Joe McCarthy of the Red Sox had a tough decision to make in the top of the eighth. His club was down 1–0 so he pinch hit for Ellis Kinder. He did the right thing. They were down one run and Mel Parnell was in the bullpen. Kinder and Parnell between them had won 52 games that year. You were splitting hairs with those two guys. But the move backfired. Henrich greeted Parnell with a home run and Gerry Coleman tripled with the bases loaded.

In the top of the ninth we got a scare. With a couple of guys on, Bobby Doerr hit a ball to right center, and Joe's legs went out from under him when he started to run. Joe took himself out and Cliff Mapes took his place. If Joe's legs hadn't collapsed, he would have caught the ball easily, and the game would have been over, and it would have been a shutout. But eventually Birdie Tebbetts popped up to Henrich, and I was walking on clouds. It was a big thrill for me and players like Joe Collins and Gerry Coleman who had never been in a World Series before.

Joe Page had a great season. He was a Jack Armstrong-type guy. In '49, if he came in with second and third or first and third, with one or no outs, I knew that he would strike the first batter out and get the next one to pop up. I didn't care who the hitters were. That's the way he pitched. When he came in, the other team was dead. He was used to relieving for two or three innings. If any starting pitcher looked like he tripped over a blade of grass, he was out and Page was in. (Today short men go for only one inning or four or five outs.) Then in the '49 World Series, after not pitching more than three innings in a game all year long, he came into the final game, and pitched six-and-one-third innings, and allowed only one run.

The first game of that year's World Series picked up where the last game of the regular season left off. It was a well-pitched game on both sides. Don Newcombe struck out 11; Allie Reynolds, I think, struck out 10. Going into the bottom of the ninth, there was no score. When Newk got behind 2–0 on Henrich, we sat there and said, "If he gets the ball a little down and over the plate, this game will end right here." Sure enough Newk came back with a fastball about six inches above the knees. He didn't even turn around to look at the hit. You could tell from the crack of the bat it was gone.

I got my first World Series win that year. I was going well until the seventh inning, when they knocked me out of the box. I was winning 6–0, and they hit five or six clunkers in a row. Just out of someone's reach. Casey brought Reynolds in, and Allie struck out five of the seven batters he faced. That was some performance, because Brooklyn's lineup was much like Cleveland's.

Do I remember the night Cleveland broke my winning streak? I sure do. Lifetime, I was 40–12 against the Indians. That night Bill Veeck sold rabbits' feet. You know, those little gimmick chain things. But the black cat stunt wasn't Veeck's idea. A fellow took it upon himself to come out on the mound. I don't even know how he got there. When I turned around and saw him, it kind of startled me. "How the hell did he get here?" I said to myself. He had a little black cat in his hands. He sort of threw it at me, so I threw my arms up so that the cat didn't scratch me in the face or hit my pitching arm. But their strategy worked. I got beat that night.

We beat the Indians out from '49 to '53. But they put it all together in '54. We felt bad because we won 103 games, more than we ever had. But we weren't upset because we knew we couldn't keep winning year after year. It had to come to an end sooner or later. The reason the Indians won it was because they beat the second-division clubs to death. They beat Boston, I think, 22 out of 22. The same with Philadelphia. And they lost only one to Baltimore. If I'm not mistaken, we won 15 of 22 against them. That year I beat them five times myself. But it wasn't enough. They would always swamp the second-division clubs, and we couldn't do it. You have to give them credit for that.

Wins-and-losses-wise, I guess I would say '51 was my best year. I was 21–9 during the regular season, and I won two games in the World Series. Two years later, I won 16, lost 4, and won the ERA title. At that time I was nursing a little tendinitis, which made it even more special to me. I was pitching only once a week. I couldn't come back every fifth day. But over-all '51 was my banner year, you might say.

I remember my two World Series wins that year. The first one was tough because the game was close. We were winning 2–0. In the seventh or the eighth the Giants loaded the bases. Then Bill Rigney hit a sacrifice fly, and I got the next guy out. In the bottom of the inning, I got a bouncing-ball single through the middle to score Billy Martin. That made it 3–1 and that was it.

Before my next start, Game Five, Casey made a statement to the press that sort of irritated me. He said he was concerned about me pitching in the Polo Grounds because of the short fences. I have a heck of a year for him, and he's worried about the park I'm pitching in. So I just decided to do the best I could, and, the way it turned out, we got eight or nine runs in the first two or three innings, and it wound up 13–1. It was a laugher. But it could have been otherwise. The next day I walked up to Casey and said, "Well, Casey, it looks like the Giants didn't tear the walls down afterwards, like you said they would." He sort of grinned and winked and walked off.

I came up with tendinitis in 1952. I got the injury in the second game I pitched against the Giants. That laugher. It was a cool day and the arm started tightening up in the seventh inning. Had it been any other game but a World Series one, I would have gotten right out of there. But I said to Jim Turner, "If I get in any trouble, get me out." As it turned out, I retired the last nine men in a row. But 30 minutes after the game, I couldn't raise my arm.

In the spring I tried to pitch it out, but it didn't work. When the season started, I didn't know what was wrong with me. My doctor told me, "Heat and rest." But after four weeks there was no improvement. Then they sent me to an orthopedic specialist in Baltimore, and he said, "Look at how long you've been pitching. Just do the best you can."

I said, "What kind of a deal is that? Here I come all the way to Baltimore to see you, and you say, 'Just do the best you can.'"

He said, "Wel-l-l-l. . . ."

I finally got in touch with an orthopedic specialist in Chicago who was there when I pitched with the White Sox, and he told me what I had—tendinitis—and prescribed a treatment. Ten days later, I started in Boston. Where do you think Casey started me? Fenway Park. I thanked him for that.

After three months on the shelf, I started eight games down the stretch, and I won five of them. Someone else picked up the other three decisions. That wasn't such a bad comeback, especially in the stretch run.

I never realized that I was 33–8 from the time I came back through the '54 season. I was in a groove, and it's an easy job when you pitch just once a week. Don't lose, though. If you lose three or four in a row, you lose an entire month. But it gives you plenty of time to prepare yourself and get ready for your next assignment.

In '55 I was sent to Baltimore on a waiver deal. I felt terrible, awful. After '55 I said I didn't want to play anymore, I didn't have anything more to prove. Then the Yankees offered me the job of managing Richmond in the International League. I decided to take it and start a new career.

How was I told about the waiver deal? Casey called me into his office in the clubhouse. He said, "We made a deal for you. You're going to Baltimore. I enjoyed being with you and your playing for me. But you realize that these things happen."

I said, "Yes, Casey, I realize that things have to come to an end somewhere along the line."

Casey was a great psychologist. We didn't find that out until he was with us for a while. He had a great memory, too. Nowadays they have all these computer stat sheets: who did what against what and who plays well against who and so forth. But he had all that at his fingertips. He showed his generalship in '49, the first year he was with us. We had some 70-odd injuries that year, but he did a great job of manipulating players, and even though we won the pennant on the last day of the season, we still won it. That's the bottom line.

In those days we did all of our traveling on the train. Once in a while, if you caught him in the right mood, you might ask him, "Why'd you do that a month ago?" He'd remember it and tell you precisely why he did it. One day we're in Detroit for a double-header. In the first game we played terrible and we got beat. But he didn't say a word. In the second game we were winning 16–2, but he was ranting and raving like we had never seen him. We're saying to ourselves, "What's wrong with the Old Man? Is he losing his marbles? Why didn't he get on us in the first game when we played so bad?"

A month later, we asked him about it. "Well, I'll tell you," he said. "I've got some good players on this team, and they know when they play bad or good. So I don't have to tell them too much. But every so often you have to get to certain individuals. When they're going bad, it's no time to jump on someone's back, because you might get punched in the nose. But when they're winning and they're not going well, they'll listen to you, and they'll absorb more."

We used to call McDougald "Redneck," because he would get so angry. He was a great player and a wonderful guy, but he dropped one year to about .240. The following year, we were in spring training, and we were coming out of the clubhouse the first day, and Casey said to Gil, "Young man, I don't want to see you hit a ball to left field in spring training—in batting practice or otherwise. And you better learn to hit to right field, and if you don't, you won't be playing."

Well, Gil was a dead pull-hitter. He huffed and he puffed at Casey's criticism, and he came over to us very upset. But we said, "Don't worry about it. It's for your own good. Learn to do what he said, and you'll be a better player." And he found it was so. He became a much tougher hitter.

Another time, Casey benched Joe for about 10 days. He said, "Get some rest." It took a lot of courage on Casey's part.

The news guys came around and said, "What, are you guys feuding?" You know, trying to create something.

So he said to them, "Where'd you get your information?"

They'd say, "Well, so-and-so said. . . ."

"There's no such thing," Casey replied. "The man's tired. And if the manager deems it best to rest him, he's going to rest him. That's all there is to it."

During that span Mize was inserted into the lineup, and that week he hit eight home runs. Seven of them either tied or won the game for us. Then Joe came back and he got hot, and both of them stayed hot for the next two weeks. We couldn't wait for our turn to come around to pitch. We knew with them in the lineup we were going to get some runs out there.

The Big Three? We got along great, just great. In fact, I roomed with Allie for seven years. We weren't egotistical, but we were proud of what we accomplished, and we were proud that we were able to do the job that was expected of us.

We saw Whitey in the spring of '50. He looked like he could get the ball over the plate, and he looked like he was not too far away. He did pretty good, but they decided to send him back to the minors, and I guess it was the best thing for him. They brought him back in the middle of the year. Turner and Casey did a great job with him. They pitched him against second-division teams his first seven or eight games. He pitched great. Finally Turner said to me, "Well, we're going to see what this young man's made of in this next series."

"What do you mean?" I said.

"Well, we're one arm short for the series in Detroit. We're going to pitch him against the Tigers." That's when Detroit was battling us for the pennant and when they had won eight in a row. He pitched against Dizzy Trout. For eight innings the game was scoreless or 1–0, but we scored seven runs in the top of the ninth and won it. The next day we said to Turner, "Well, what do you think of him?"

He said, "I think we've got a Big Four now."

He was a cocky sort of guy, which was good. But he had a good pitching sense when you sat down and talked to him. At that point Turner said to me, "I want you to take him over and put him under your wing."

I said, "Okay, if he listens and works at it, I'll do it."

He did. I'd go over the lineup with him, and he very seldom forgot anything I told him. If he did forget anything—remember, he was only twenty years old—he'd look in the dugout, and I'd give him a sign, and we'd take it from there.

The 1949–53 Yankees? We were pretty good. The big thing was that we didn't make too many mistakes day-in and day-out. We didn't beat ourselves. That's what pays off. The pitching was solid and the defense was great. Everyone thought we had so much power. That just wasn't so. We had the ability to win a lot of one-run games.

It was a happy-go-lucky bunch of guys. They all rooted for each other. The fellows who weren't playing would root for the ones who were, and it was just one big happy family. We'd try to instill that togetherness in young pitchers who were coming up.

"Listen," we'd say, "when you get tired, let Casey know. Don't try to be a martyr. No one's going to reprimand you. This is the way we operate. Other guys get paid to do a job, too." You wanted to go nine innings if you could. That's what you got paid the big bucks for. But if you couldn't go nine, you put the team above yourself.

Not too many lefties besides me ever pitched a complete-game win over the Brooklyn Dodgers in the World Series. [Marius Russo of the 1941 Yankees was one, Tommy Byrne of the 1955 Yankees was another.] Well, that's the game I'm proudest of: my 4–2 win over the Dogers at Yankee Stadium in '53. They were known to kill left-handed pitchers. Duke Snider was the only lefty in their lineup. So, no southpaws were going nine innings against them. I said to myself, "Well, I got a score to settle with these guys. I'm going to beat them and I'm going nine innings."

In those days the newspaper guys would spend a half-year with us and a half-year with the National League teams in New York. They'd tell me, "You don't have a chance, Eddie."

I'd say, "What do you mean I don't have a chance?"

"Well, in the home stretch, they beat 18 lefties in a row. The Braves haven't pitched Warren Spahn against them for years."

"We'll just have to find out, I guess," I said.

I guess we did.

One final note on the "Big Three." During Charlie Silvera's interview, he said, "Every year Raschi, Reynolds, and Lopat get three or four votes for the Hall of Fame. Isn't that ridiculous!" I agree. In my mind the players enshrined at Cooperstown are like those who win the Most Valuable Player Award—but over longer periods. They are players who, given the chance to make the difference, did so. Vic Raschi, Allie Reynolds, and Eddie Lopat were three such players. (As were Tinker, Evers, and Chance, who were inducted into the Hall of Fame at the same time and for similar reasons—they were winners, without the individual career accomplishments that would merit election.)

Consider their records for a moment. During the 1949–53 championship streak Raschi won 92 games and lost 40; Reynolds, 83 and 41; and Lopat, 80 and 36. They had a combined record of 255 wins and 117 losses for a winning percentage of .685. In their respective careers with the Yankees, Raschi won 120 games and lost 50; Reynolds, 131 and 60; and Lopat, 120 and 59. Combined, they won 371 games and lost 169 for a winning percentage of .687. Whitey Ford has the highest all-time winning percentage— .690—for pitchers with 200 or more career wins. Raschi, Reynolds, and Lopat won well over 300 career games, and their combined winning record during their Yankee years is just three points lower than Ford's. As a unit, they would rank in second place, winning-percentage-wise, for pitchers with 200 or more wins. For pitchers with 300 or more wins, they would rank first.

One further note. Their combined win-loss record in 1949–53 World Series play was 14–6. That's a winning percentage of .700. Their combined win-loss record in overall World Series play was 16–6. That's a winning percentage of .727. How many other pitching staffs in the history of baseball can match those numbers over an extended period? None. If it were up to me, I would enshrine Raschi, Reynolds, and Lopat as a unit at Cooperstown—as the "Big Three."

Bobby Brown

From an early age, Bobby Brown had wanted to pursue a major-league career and a professional career at the same time. While he was in the major leagues, he spent half of each year studying medicine and the other half playing baseball with the Yankees. In two of those years, on the first day of the season he reported directly to the Yankees from medical school.

When he returned from the Korean War, which served as a bridge between his two careers, he had to make a difficult decision. The Yankees had just reeled off a record five consecutive world championships. And, by Bobby's assessment, the 1950s were the peak period in baseball history. But it was time to concentrate on medicine. So he quit baseball at the youthful age of twenty-nine.

Bobby Brown wonders what kinds of seasons he might have had if he had been able to concentrate completely on baseball. He sometimes thinks of the peak seasons that he lost because of Korea. And he is tempted once in a while to speculate about what might have happened had he not retired from the game at such a young age.

Dr. Bobby Brown's baseball career was far from over,

though. In 1974, after many years as a cardiologist, he returned to baseball as the interim president of the Texas Rangers. After spending six months in that position, he returned to private medical practice. Then, in 1984, he came back to New York to assume the presidency of the American League.

Bobby Brown truly is a "man for all seasons." And some of the seasons that he remembers best took place when he was young and wearing the pin-striped uniform of the Yankees of the late 1940s and early 1950s.

I talked to Dr. Brown recently in his office on Park Avenue in New York City. He met me at the door with a handshake and a smile, took my jacket, offered me coffee, and invited me to sit down and talk. The extension wire from my tape recorder didn't reach the outlet plug on his side of the desk. I thought we had a problem. But he quickly said, "We can easily correct that, Dom. You sit on my side of the desk, and I'll sit on yours."

From the seat behind the desk of the president of the American League, I interviewed the president of the American League—a man who, in the words of Robert Frost, has truly "traveled both roads and been one traveler."

Joe Devine, Bill Essex, and Johnny Dee all scouted me. Although Colonel Larry McPhail actually signed me, Devine had a very big influence on me. But the biggest influence, by far, was my father. He started me playing before I can remember. He worked with me constantly, not only up until I got to the big leagues, but also afterwards.

My father was in a position that he could retire if he wanted to, and when I got to the big leagues, he really did. He came back from the West Coast with my mother, brother, and sister, and they saw almost every game I played.

One game that he saw that he never forgot occurred in the 1951 World Series against the Giants. I was actually robbed of a hit when Willie Mays dropped my fly ball, but got credit for a catch. I hit the ball over his head, and he dropped the ball with two men on base. None of the six umpires saw the ball hit the ground, because Mays was trying to catch the ball straight over his head, and his body was right between them and the ball, which bounced straight up to him. But all of the people in the center-field bleachers at the Polo Grounds saw Mays drop the ball. The reason that I know Willie dropped the ball is because my dad was out there. He saw it.

Yes, I sometimes think about the fact that I hit .439 in four World Series, and hardly anyone knows about it. In fact, I think about it all the time. [Here, Dr. Robert Brown, the president of the American League, leaned back in his chair and laughed heartily.] But, no, I don't feel slighted. It doesn't bother me too much. I know that I hit the ball well in those Series. I'm grateful for that. I'm also pleased that almost half my hits in the World Series were for extra bases. [He had a total of 18 hits, eight of which were for more than one base.] If I had gotten credit for a hit on the ball that Mays dropped, half of my hits *would* have been for extra bases.

The ball Mays didn't catch reminds me of a fly ball that got away from Gene Woodling the year before. If Gene had caught it, Whitey Ford would have sewn up the four-game sweep of the Phillies with a 5–0 shutout. As it turned out, Allie Reynolds came in and struck out Stan Lopata to save the 5–2 win.

Reynolds wasn't really a reliever. In September,

though, we would have some off days, so every once in a while he would go down to the bullpen and pitch an inning or two if he had to. Joe Page was our number-one relief man in 1947 and 1949. When he came into a game in the seventh or eighth inning, you knew the game was yours. When you had him and Reynolds out in the bullpen during a World Series, well, it was a very secure feeling. Reynolds had super stuff.

But I want to come back to Woodling. First, he didn't drop the ball. He was blinded by the sun and the ball hit him in the chest. I'm sure he never saw it. There's no way he would have dropped it if he had seen it. He was a great left fielder.

The Phillies had an excellent relief pitcher in that World Series, too. Jim Konstanty pitched great ball for them. He was a surprise starter in Game One and lost a heartbreaker to Vic Raschi, 1–0. He also relieved in the third and fourth games, as I remember.

All our scouting reports said, "You have to wait on him. He throws a lot of off-speed pitches." I made the mistake of thinking about the scouting reports too much. Consequently, I was behind the ball the first game. I got lucky, though. In the fourth inning of the first game, I hit a double down the third-base line. It went between third base and the third baseman, Willie Jones. I then scored the only run of the game on long flies by Hank Bauer and Gerry Coleman.

In Game Three Konstanty came in with the bases loaded, and Casey sent me up to bat. I hit seven or eight foul fly balls before I hit a ground ball to Granny Hamner, who booted it, allowing us to tie the game. That was in the eighth inning. In the ninth Coleman singled home Woodling with the winning run.

After the game I realized that I was waiting too long on Konstanty. In the fourth game I finally felt that I had him figured out, and I tripled off the wall in a three-run fifth inning.

How did I combine a baseball career with a medical career? Well, it happened by accident, I think. From an early age I had wanted to pursue a professional career and a major-league career at the same time. I always did well in school and liked to study, so it was never any problem for me to continue with my medical studies after the baseball season was over. I knew that ultimately that's what I wanted to do.

I actually switched to pre-med my first year at Stanford. Initially I wanted to be a chemical engineer, but I found out that I didn't like chemistry, so I made the switch midway through the year.

I left medical school in 1946 when I'd almost completed my second year. That year I played for the Newark Bears and the Yankees. I went back to medical school that year the first week of October. Each year thereafter, I went back to school on approximately October 15 and stayed in school till somewhere between March 15 and April 15, and I was able to complete my last two years in four years. I reported to spring training either late or not at all. With the exception of the 1947 season, when I reported the first day, I was always late. A couple of years, I didn't get to spring training at all. I showed up the first day of the season.

There wasn't much the Yankees could do about it. They realized how important medical school was to me; and they knew if they forced me to make a choice what that choice would be.

Once, by the way, when I was in medical school and was playing for Newark, Yogi Berra, my roommate, saw me studying a medical book, and said, "Let me know how the book comes out." I don't have any more Yogi stories. He just generally delights me. He's one of my all-time favorite people.

Overall, though, it worked out well about both careers. I quit baseball when I was twenty-nine. The only reason that I did so was that it was time to begin my residency, and I thought it would be a detriment if I continued with my baseball career.

In retrospect, the Korean conflict had a profound effect on my baseball career. I knew that I was coming back to the Yankees at the age of twenty-nine, and I knew that I had missed those years which should have been my most productive ones. So I decided that when I finally did get back, I should get into my medical career.

I started my residency on July 1, 1954. I had completed my internship in the spring of 1952, gone into the Army, and been an Army doctor in Korea and Japan. I served my internal residency at the San Francisco County Hospital in San Francisco from 1954–57. From 1957 until 1958 I was in the Stanford program there. On August 1, 1958, I took a cardiology fellowship at Tulane University. After the fellowship I started private practice in cardiology in Fort Worth, Texas.

In 1974 a friend of mine, Brad Corbett, bought the Texas Rangers. I never had any financial interest in the Rangers. He didn't know anything about the running of a team, though, so I took a leave of absence for six months and served as interim president during that time. I remained in practice until

February 1, 1984, at which time I came to New York and became president of the American League.

Yes, my major-league career was shorter than it could have been. In fact, my minor-league career was very limited, too. In 1946 I was sent to the Bears in the International League. I played the entire season with Newark, came up to the Bronx at the end of the season, and never left the Yankees.

Anytime you made the trip from Newark to New York, it was supposed to be the longest twelve miles in America. We—Vic Raschi, Frank Coleman, Berra and I—were all very excited to be joining the Yankees. But as a teenager in California, I'd had the experience of trying out in different major-league parks. I had spent an entire week in New York, so when I came to the Yankees, it didn't awe me the way it did Vic Raschi.

In 1947, with the Yankees, I alternated with Billy Johnson at third base. I didn't think that I played that well, however. When I started to hit well, Mel Parnell of the Red Sox hit me with a pitch. I broke a finger and was out for three weeks. By the time I was ready to play again, the team was rolling in high gear, and I specialized in pinch-hitting the rest of the year. I would fill in if someone got hurt, but basically I was a pinch-hitter and platoon player. The other infielders were all very good, and basically they all hit right-handed. If I got in at all, it was basically against right-handed pitching. I hit .300, though. I hit .300 in 1948, too. But, going into the 1949 season, I still hadn't won a starting position.

In the 1947 World Series I pinch hit four times and got three hits and a walk. I got two doubles and a single. I hit a ball against Ralph Branca, I think it was in Game Three, that cleared the fence by twenty-five feet and hit the little screen that went along the foul pole. The ball bounced back on the field, and I ended up with a double. In those days the ball was in play. Today it would be a home run.

Yes, they called me "The Golden Boy." I was never overjoyed about that type of name, though. I think that it was given to me when I came out of medical school, and they gave me a sizable bonus. A sizable bonus then, not now.

I was very pleased with my rookie year, though. My first year in the majors we won the pennant and World Series. It was incredible. I couldn't believe what was happening to me. I was most pleased about doing most of the important pinch hitting for a world championship team at the age of 22.

My first World Series was an exciting one. There were many dramatic happenings. Bill Bevens was involved in one of them. He pitched an unusual game. There were a lot of bases on balls and base runners. In a key situation the Dodgers put Al Gionfriddo in to run, and he stole second base, leaving first base open with Pete Reiser at the plate. Reiser, who was pinch hitting, had a sprained ankle, so it became a big decision for manager Bucky Harris: should he pitch to Reiser or should he walk him, even though he represented the winning run? Of course, Harris walked Reiser, and Cookie Lavagetto hit the ball off the wall, and it decided the game.

Looking back, you wonder what would have happened if Gionfriddo had been thrown out. You also wonder what would have happened if we had pitched to Reiser. You just don't know, though.

I said that I didn't have a starting position going into the 1949 season. Joe DiMaggio was out with a heel injury the first three months of the season.

When he was hurt, I was hitting very well. But I ruptured some ligaments in my ankle, and I was out for six weeks, which hurt me terribly, as far as I was concerned. I was having the best year I had ever had when I got hurt.

I once hit a "foul homer" that won a game. It was against the Browns. I think it was the bottom of the eighth. I hit a ball that turned out to be the game-winning home run. The next day a New York newspaper ran a headline banner saying, "Yanks Win on Foul Homer." Zack Taylor, the Browns' manager, thought that the ball was foul, too. But I don't know. The plate umpire called the ball "Fair," and I very well thought the ball could have been fair, too. But, that's right, instead of saying, "Yanks Win on Brown's Home Run," the newspaper said, "Yanks Win on Foul Homer."

I was lucky to have had two good managers with the Yankees. Bucky Harris was a nice man. Everyone got along well with Bucky. His relationship with the team was excellent. And he managed well. If we had won in 1948, he might have managed through 1953. Who knows?

Casey Stengel's main strength, in my opinion, was that he could utilize his talent very well. He had excellent talent, and he could interchange his players because they had comparable skills. I do think he took great advantage of that situation, though.

He did get hunches every once in a while. I remember that in the 1949 World Series against the Dodgers, it came to a pivotal point in the fourth game, and they walked Joe DiMaggio intentionally to load the bases. We had a 2–1 lead in games at the time, and I was batting fifth. But they brought in a left-handed pitcher, and I thought Casey might take me out for a right-handed batter. But he left me in, and I tripled off the wall to score all three runners, and to this day I don't know why he let me hit.

We won a lot of World Series in those days. That's because we had a tremendous pitching staff. The writers called them "The Big Three": Reynolds, Raschi, and Eddie Lopat. You have to add Whitey Ford, though. Johnny Sain pitched well at the end of his career, too. Tom Morgan and others did well, also. "The Big Three" or "The Big Four" didn't go into a prolonged slump, because they pitched so well. It was difficult for all three or four of them to lose consecutively. You always got a good game pitched if you played behind those guys. They were able, if you had a good pitcher going against you, like Bob Lemon, Early Wynn, or Hal Newhouser, to make three runs stand up, or two, or even one. They were just great pitchers.

They were all competitors. Raschi was especially intense. He didn't want anyone coming in to the mound to talk to him. When the ball went around the infield, after an out, he always held out his glove, and he expected the third baseman to hit it with the throw. If you didn't, he would get mad. I can remember one game—and I was reminding him about it at the last Old Timers' Day Game—that was into the eighth inning, and he was getting tired. So I ran in to the mound. Usually I didn't say anything. I'd just stand there. This day I said, "I'm just here to give you a rest."

He surprised me when he said, "For God's sake, where have you been? I'm dying out here. I've been looking for you for two innings." After thirty seconds, he said, "Okay, I'm all right." So, you never know.

The 1949–53 Yankees were great teams. We had great pitching and we had great defense. Compared to today's teams, we probably didn't have as much speed. But we had teams that gave away very little, and once we got an opportunity or a break, we capitalized upon it. And the greatest thing about those teams was their ability to play well in big games. Everyone could come through in the clutch.

The camaraderie on the clubs was great, too. Everyone got along with everyone else. There were no cliques. People ate with whoever came down to the dining room at the same time. We all liked each other. Obviously, some preferred some to others. But, as far as I knew, there were no feuds or rifts. We didn't have bad guys. We had good guys. We enjoyed each other then and we enjoy each other now.

It was an unforgettable and a great experience, not only because the team was extremely successful, but because they were great guys. And I think that we played during the peak period of baseball. We traveled on trains. That made us closer. We had 16 teams that were very competitive. It was just a delightful time to play baseball.

What kind of a hitter was I? Well, I always thought I was a good hitter. I was a line-drive hitter. I didn't hit with much power, but I could handle the bat, and hit to all fields. I always thought that against right-handed pitching, I had as good a chance as anyone to get a hit, and I felt I was good at hitting with men on base. I thought that I could score men from third base, with less than two out, as well as anyone, too. Basically, I thought that if we needed a hit in a tough spot, I could get it.

No, I didn't get paid much. My highest salary was

$19,500. That was my last year. I would have gotten paid that in 1952, too, had I not gone into the service. The contract carried over. Negotiations were tough but they were no problem. One year I held out until Opening Day, because I couldn't get out of medical school until that time.

I'm just proud of the times in which I played. There was nothing that the players of my generation could do about the salary structure. We played under the existing conditions. Had the present conditions existed when I played, I wonder whether I would have had the ambition and drive to go through medical school and become a doctor. I think that the pressures not to do it would have been great. For that reason I'm rather relieved that I wasn't forced to make the choice, because the way my life has evolved has been very satisfying. But I'm not sure that if the money had been that great that I would have been able to withstand the temptation.

The thing I do regret is that I was not able to play two or three years when I could have concentrated completely on baseball—when I could have done whatever I wanted to do in the wintertime, gone to spring training on time, and devoted my entire efforts to baseball. I would have liked to see how well I could have played. I regret having to quit so early in my career. I think I could have played a lot better under normal circumstances. Of course, you just don't know. But, then again, you didn't know about Korea, either.

My biggest thrill? The seventh game of the 1947 World Series against the Dodgers. Bevens and Shea had sore arms, so everyone had to contribute. That was the reason they sent me in to pinch-hit so early in the game. Hal Gregg was pitching, and he had either a 2–0 or 3–1 count on me, and he threw a ball on the outside part of the plate. We were down 2–1 at the time. I thought it might have been a little outside, but I said to myself, "The ball's good enough to hit," and I hit it to left field for a double that tied the game. Tommy Henrich then singled to drive me home with the run that put us ahead for good in the Series. When I was standing on second base, after my double, I took time out, for the first time in my career, to listen to the crowd for a second or two.

And I looked at my parents and I saw my father throw his hat into the air. I guess that was the biggest thrill—and the happiest moment I ever had in baseball.

Phil Rizzuto

Phil Rizzuto has reached every baseball goal he never thought he would—except the Baseball Hall of Fame. But the year-by-year snub of the Hall of Fame's Veterans' Committee doesn't seem to bother him. He feels that he has been fortunate in handling the things in his baseball life that have been within his control. The Baseball Hall of Fame is not one of those things.

When he first started his professional baseball career, Casey Stengel of the Dodgers and Bill Terry of the Giants told him that he was too small to be a baseball player. Stengel and Terry, of course, are both in the Hall of Fame. But Rizzuto wasn't discouraged. He believed in himself. So he persevered. And he was lucky.

He was in the right place at the right time. When he came up to the Yankees in 1941, Frankie Crosetti was winding down as a shortstop, so Phil moved into the starting lineup and played beside men who had been his heroes. That year he was a firsthand witness to Joe DiMaggio's 56-game hitting streak during the regular season and Mickey Owen's passed ball in the World Series. At the age of twenty-three, in his first major-league season, he played on a *world championship team. And he played no small part in the team's success. He batted .307.*

But that was just the beginning. Over the next fifteen years he played on nine pennant winners and seven world title teams. During his big-league career he was a perennial All-Star Game choice, and he won the Babe Ruth and MVP awards. He also led the league in double plays by a shortstop three times and fielding percentage by a shortstop twice. In the World Series he set a record by playing errorless ball in 25 consecutive games. Ted Williams has said many times that Phil Rizzuto was the difference in many of the Yankee-Red Sox pennant races. If Rizzuto had been with Boston instead of New York, Ted says, the Red Sox, not the Yankees, would have won many of those pennants. Gil McDougald concurs. He says that Phil was the meal ticket of the Yankees' infield.

Rizzuto, who was once considered too small to be a major leaguer became one of the best shortstops of his time by perfecting the little things. He mastered the art of bunting and the science of hitting behind the runner. He didn't have the strongest arm of the shortstops of his time, but he developed the quickest release. In addition, he was without a peer in going to the outfield on short fly balls. And not of least importance, he believed in Yankee tradition. Many of today's Bronx Bombers, Rizzuto readily admits, do not believe in the Yankee tradition and the mystique of the Yankee uniform. "Maybe that's why they haven't played on many pennant winners and world championship teams," Rizzuto concludes.

For three years I tried unsuccessfully to catch up with Phil; all of my letters went unanswered. In desperation I wrote to his wife, Cora, outlining my reason for attempting to contact her husband and my frustrations to date. That weekend my youngest son, Ted, and I traveled to New England to look at prospective colleges. Ted, who was a *good high school basketball player wanted to talk to some of the coaches who had contacted him. When we got home, we learned that I had missed phone calls from Phil Rizzuto and Jill Guiver, Billy Martin's fiancée. Phil had been a friend of my wife, Nancy's, father, Johnny Kinder, who had been the golf pro at the Plainfield, New Jersey, Country Club for twenty years, and Nancy and Phil had reminisced for ten minutes over the phone. He told her that he rarely received his mail from the Stadium, and suggested that I call him for a telephone interview date. I interviewed him while we both watched a Monday Night Football game in which William "The Refrigerator" Perry was stopped short of the goal line on a fourth-and-inches call. Phil was just as relaxed, nonchalant, and candid as he is when he broadcasts Yankee games. "Look at that," he laughed. "[Mike] Ditka's going crazy. I bet that's the last time that 'The Refrigerator' carries the ball down there this year." He was right.*

The Hall of Fame? No, I'm not upset. I don't think I belong. I've told people that. Actually I'm sorry to see them lower the standards. It used to be harder. That's the way it should be. My family and friends feel worse about it than I do. But I've got no regrets. I've been very lucky.

Look at the way I started out. I had a tryout with the Dodgers in 1936. Casey Stengel, who was Brooklyn's manager at the time, said, "You'll never make it. You're too small." In the same year I had a tryout with the Giants. Bill Terry, their manager, said, "You should get a shoeshine kit." They were *very* encouraging.

Yet in 1941, five years later, I was playing on a team on which all of my teammates were my heroes.

I was in awe of them. At first they wouldn't let me get near them. I was too small. The clubhouse guy thought I was trying to break in to get autographs. Fortunately Lefty Gomez came by, laughing. We had played some exhibition games together. Lefty pointed to a nearby lake with ducks and said, "You better let him in or the ducks will walk over him."

In the dressing room they put me in between Ruffing and Rolfe. It was tough. Crosetti was idolized by the players. They didn't want to see him lose his job. In fact, I had a tough time getting in the batting cage. But McCarthy was shrewd. He let it happen. He wanted to see if I could take it.

The whole season was like a fairy tale. On Opening Day, in Washington, President Roosevelt threw out the first ball. I stood ten feet away. I couldn't believe it. Everything about my rookie year made a deep impression on me. I can remember it all: my first hit, my first error, my first everything.

That was the year of DiMaggio's 56-game hitting streak. Joe never showed any emotion. That was why the reporters made a big thing of him kicking the dirt at second base after Al Gionfriddo made that catch in the 1947 World Series. But one time during the streak he got mad. Johnny Babich of the Athletics came out in the papers and said he was going to walk Joe every time up. Joe was closing in on George Sisler's record of 41 consecutive games at the time. Joe got very upset when he read Babich's comments in the paper. And Babich meant it. He wouldn't throw Joe a strike. Joe had to reach out and swing at a bad pitch to get a hit. Then someone stole his bat after he broke Sisler's mark. Broadcasters pleaded over the radio for the guy to return the bat. He did the next day.

I remember the night the streak ended. Kenny Keltner was playing so deep at third base that Joe could have bunted and *walked* to first base before the throw. But Joe wouldn't do that. And Keltner made two sensational stops to break the streak. Joe and I were the last players in the clubhouse after the game. Then we walked to the hotel up the street. There was a bar between the hotel and the park.

Joe said, "I'm going to stop."

I said, "I'll go with you."

"No, you go back." He wanted to be alone. He went in but he came right back out. He had left his wallet in the clubhouse safe. He knew that the clubhouse was closed, so he asked me to loan him some money. I had eighteen dollars for the whole road trip, but I gave it to him anyway. I was just a rookie making $5,000 a year. I never got the money back. He never returned it. But I wouldn't accept it if he did. It would ruin a great story.

I pinch-hit for Joe once. That's how I met my wife, Cora. It was right after the 1941 World Series. Joe was the scheduled speaker at a fireman's banquet. Cora's dad was a fireman. But that was the night Joe's son was born. It was a breach birth. Joe called me at the last moment to fill in. I was just a rookie, so I was nervous. But I showed up and Cora's dad took me home afterwards and that's how I met Cora. We've been married forty-four years.

At the banquet, people were still talking about Mickey Owen's passed ball in the World Series. We were so close to the stands at Ebbets Field. When Henrich swung and missed Casey's last pitch, the fans jumped out on the field. They thought the game was over. But Tommy, who saw Owen miss the pitch, ran to first base; however, he had to dodge the fans to get there. I wasn't due to bat so I had gathered up all the gloves. We didn't leave them on the field at the time, because the fans would grab them. The guys started going up the runway. But then they came back. Everyone was saying, "That's what we needed. Now we'll get them." That was the secret of our success. We took advantage of opportunities. DiMag, Keller, Dickey, and Gordon all hit the wall, and we turned defeat into victory. But the biggest blow to the Dodgers was a swinging third strike.

We went on to win the World Series. There was a big celebration in New York. I lived there, so all my buddies came out, and we talked about the games until the early hours of the morning. They wouldn't do that today.

Al Kunitz, my high school coach, was the reason I made it. He was the biggest influence on my career. He had caught Johnny Murphy in college and had played minor-league ball. For some reason he thought I was going to make it. He was small, too. He prepared me for the pitfalls, telling me what would happen. He taught me how to bunt and he sharpened my defense. Every good team, he said, needed someone who was fundamentally sound. Someone who could do the *little* things. He's also the reason I say, "Holy cow!" He told me I should never get thrown out of a game. It doesn't help your team, he said. I never was. Not in the majors, nor in the minors.

"You need an expression you can use when you get mad," he said.

I said, "A lot of times I say, 'Holy cow.' "

"Good," he said, "keep on saying it."

In 1942 I had a better year than I'd had in 1941, even though I batted .307 in my rookie year. I knew the pitchers better, and I knew how to play the hitters better. Consequently I had more confidence in myself. "Crow" was great. He showed me a lot of things. And McCarthy was great at breaking rookies in. Even if you were playing well, he would take you out and explain things to you. Very helpful! In 1941 he tried an experiment. He switched Gordon from second to first, he put me at short, and Gerry Priddy at second. But Gerry and I started to go bad, and he sat us down. He almost broke my heart when he called me in and told me he was going to bench me. I got back in there, though. Gerry never did.

We couldn't believe it when the Cardinals beat us in five games in the 1942 World Series. We were used to winning. We expected to win. Losing hit us like a sudden shock. But we didn't lose because we were overconfident. McCarthy wouldn't let that happen. Before the World Series started, he told us he didn't want us to read the papers. The Cardinals had a great outfield. Terry Moore, Stan Musial, Enos Slaughter. But the way the writers were reporting it, you would think they had ten guys on motorcycles out there. We won the first game but then we lost four straight. Here's something that's never been written before. Whether we won or we lost the last game, I had to report to the Navy at Norfolk, Virginia, the next morning. If the World Series had gone seven games, I would have had to miss the last two games.

I was in the Navy from 1942 till 1945. My first year I spent at Norfolk. That was like a picnic. We had great teams. But the parents protested—they said the athletes were coddled. I couldn't blame them. Their sons were in the middle of the fighting. So all of the athletes were shipped overseas. But we weren't trained for fighting, we were trained to raise money for War Bonds. I was in the first landing at New Guinea. Later, as the invasion moved north from Australia, we moved to the Philippines. But they still managed to hold a World Series baseball tournament in Hawaii every year between the Army and the Navy. They pulled players from all over the world. For example, Dom DiMaggio and I came from Australia, and Johnny Mize came from the Great Lakes. We won seven of the nine games. The admirals won a lot of money from the generals in that series. Bill Dickey, who was a lieutenant commander, was our manager. He put Reese at short and me at third. Pee Wee and I are the best of friends, but I couldn't believe that Dickey would do that to me.

Speaking of managers, Joe McCarthy was my favorite. He had great power. He could do things then that you couldn't do now. He never played in the majors. But the players—great players—were in awe of him. I loved him because he was a smart manager who would never embarrass you, like other managers. If he had something to say to you, he would say it in his office. He was a percentage manager who didn't platoon. You knew you were in the lineup everyday, unless you were hurt. But you had to eat, drink, and sleep baseball, twenty-four hours a day. There was no messing around. Once we lost a doubleheader in Philadelphia. We had a card game on the train afterwards. Mac walked by and said, "Funny, you know every card in the deck, but you can't read a sign when you see one." He kept walking but we didn't keep playing. One of the players in the game had missed a sign that afternoon.

Bucky Harris was a great manager, too. He was

my second favorite. He and Mac were the same. They knew you were big leaguers. They weren't after you all the time. They knew you were entitled to a bad play. Not a *dumb* one. Then they'd get on you. If Bucky hadn't had a falling out with Weiss, he would have been the manager of the great teams Stengel inherited. He just missed winning in 1948. If we had won, he probably would have stuck around. Then he would have won *seven* World Series in a row. Wouldn't that have been something!

The year after Bucky left, Joe Page and Tommy Henrich had super seasons, and we beat out the Red Sox by one game. Page was unbelievable, but he was a little weird to play behind. It wasn't easy, like it was with Whitey and Lopat. Page was 3–2 on everyone. You were always back on your heels. Ford and Lopat were always around the plate. It was a different feeling with Page. You were waiting for the strike-out. The others would throw ground balls. They'd say the day before, "Get a good night's sleep, I'm pitching tomorrow."

Tommy was "Old Reliable." He was underrated, except by the players and managers. He never got the recognition he should have. He was a brainy, outstanding player who could do the little things. When there were runners on first and second, he used to let the ball hit his glove and drop at his feet. He would get the double play every time. They had to change the rules because of him. In the final game of the 1949 season, when we beat the Red Sox for the pennant, I led off the bottom of the first with a triple. Henrich grounded me home. He saw the second baseman playing deep, so he took a half-swing. He gave himself up for the run. And he told me he was going to do that. Things like that didn't show up in the box score. But he did it many times. And they won games—and pennants!

When Tommy hit that home run against Newcombe in the first game of that year's World Series, he was very happy. We didn't get big salaries in those days. So they offered incentives, like trips to Bermuda and back for two, if you did something important to win a big game. Tommy was excited to win the trip. But he earned it. He was a thinking man's ballplayer. He let Newcombe throw him fastballs for strikes all day. He was setting him up for the right moment. When Newcombe threw that fastball in the ninth, the ball was in the seats before Newk finished his delivery.

Yes, 1950 was my big year. I hit .324 and won the MVP Award. It's funny, I started the season 0–11. I was very superstitious, as many people know. I would worry till I got my first hit. Then Johnny Mize said, "Do me a favor. Use this bat." It was a big bat. I choked up six inches. But it had good balance, with a big handle and a big barrel. The first time I used it, I tried to check my swing and lined a drive over the infield. After that the pitchers couldn't get me out. I got over 200 hits. I had done it in the minors, but I had never done it before in the majors. I could hit the ball wherever it was pitched. But you never get smart enough. That year I did everything I could to help myself. For example, I went to the eye doctor and worked on exercises to strengthen my eye muscles. But I never went again. When you get on a roll, you think it's automatic. I could have kicked myself later.

But I was talking about little things we used to do to win games. Take that 2–1 win over Lemon late in September in 1951. In those days we didn't need a sign from the manager. I had a signal with anyone who was on third base. We worked on hit-and-run plays and squeeze bunts. I would take a pitch and hope the umpire would call it a strike. Then I'd argue. While I was complaining, I would hold the bat at both ends. That was the signal. Against the Indians, I looked at Joe, who was on third base. He tipped his cap so I knew he had the sign. Joe started late, the way you should. But somehow Lemon knew anyway. He threw at my head. I could bunt any pitch, though. I worked so hard at it. I put the ball down the first-base line, and Joe scored the winning run. Lemon was so mad, he threw the ball up on the screen. I ran to first base, though. I wanted the base hit. Bunting is one of the few arts of baseball that can be taught. You can't teach power or speed.

Stanky? He was easy to dislike. I played against him in the minors from 1938 till 1940. I also played against him in two World Series, when he was with the Dodgers and the Giants. Of course, he did succeed in kicking the ball out of my glove in the 1951 World Series. I felt terrible. It cost us the game. I don't feel bad about it now. Ironically, it turned out to be the turning point of the Series. The guys got mad. Sometimes you need something like that to turn you around. I remember the next day, I'm on second base after I hit a double, and Stanky's calling me a string of bad words. But he did it for a reason. I yelled back at him. So he succeeded in distracting me. That was his plan. He had a sign on with catcher Wes Westrum, who proceeded to pick me off. They got me in a rundown. But I was pretty good at getting out of them. Stanky's throw hit me in the head, and I ended up scoring on his error. How about *that* for poetic justice!

Winning five in a row means more today than it

did then. We took it for granted. It was like Joe's streak of 56 games. After he broke George Sisler's mark, he had no further record to shoot for. We were used to winning. Now it means more. I've got that World Series ring that has a string of diamond chips in it. It makes a nice "5." The kids and grandkids like to look at it.

That group of players was so much better than any other group I've ever seen. Where else could you find such a combination of pitching, defense, speed, hitting, and power? We were strong up the middle. Yogi was behind the plate; the "Big Three" was on the mound; Gerry, Billy, and I were the double-play combination; and Joe and Mickey were in center. Our staff and Cleveland's were comparable. They had the "Big Four." Feller, Lemon, Wynn, and Garcia. They had harder throwers. We had more finesse. But put it all together and we were hard to beat.

No, I don't think Brooklyn was a better team, man for man, than we were. In their park maybe. Ebbets Field was a picnic for them. The Stadium was different. We had better pitching, too. And pitching is ninety percent of the game.

Casey? No, I'm not big on him. He fell into it. In the National League, with the Braves and the Dodgers, he was considered a clown. He inherited a great team, and he started the two-platoon system with it. The reporters loved his stories. He was a funny man. Public relations-wise, he was good for baseball. But he didn't get along with his veterans. He wanted a bunch of young players he could control.

Old Timers' Day? I knew you were going to bring that up. That day every year I would take my camera to the park and take motion pictures of the old players. It was great to see the players from the past. When I was taking pictures on the field, the bat boy came up to me and said, "Casey and Weiss want to see you." I didn't think anything of it.

They were sitting in the office with a sheet of players for the World Series in front of them. They said, "Help us out. Who should we let go?"

"How about Silvera?" I said. He could have gone to the beach for a month and he wouldn't have been missed.

"Nah, Yogi might get hurt," they said.

Then I pointed out two pitchers who hadn't pitched in a month.

"Nah, a pitcher might get hurt."

We went through the whole list again. Suddenly I thought to myself, *Uh-oh!* "Let's go through that list again," I said.

Finally Casey said, "We want to give you your release. We have a chance to get Slaughter from Kansas City." That made me madder still. He was older than I was. "You'll get a World Series share. We'll reactivate you after September 1." They had to release me by the last day of August for Enos to be eligible for the World Series. "You can come back next year in the spring again and try out."

I dressed for the game in a state of shock. But in the fourth inning I took the uniform off and walked out. As I did, I saw George Stirnweiss. "What happened?" Snuffy said. I told him. "Wow!" he said. It had happened to him, too. "Look," he said, "leave your car here. I'll drive you home. Take Cora and the kids and get out of the house. The writers will call you and you'll say something you'll regret." It was the best advice I ever got. I went up to Grossinger's for a week. If I hadn't, I probably would have ripped everyone. As it turned out, I got a lot of television offers. Everything, it seemed, came my way. In fact, I turned out to be the first guest on *What's My Line?*

Al Lopez and other managers wanted to know if I was interested in playing another year. But I got some broadcasting offers, including one from Baltimore. But it had to be a twelve-month contract. I didn't want that. Instead I did some Giant games at the end of 1957. They wanted me to go to San Francisco with them, but I wasn't interested. Finally John Farrell of Ballantine called and said, "Would you be interested in doing the Yankee games with Mel Allen?"

I couldn't believe it. "Are you kidding!" I said. "Yes." I've been doing them ever since. *Thirty-one years.*

Yes, I can identify with the Yankee mystique. Today players pooh-pooh it. That may have something to do with the way they're playing. It used to be that the Yankee uniform made you a .300 hitter or a great pitcher. They used to promote Yankee tradition and convert it into winning. Mac was good at building Yankee image. Everyone had to wear a shirt and tie. No one wore jeans and sneakers. They were *smart* that way.

I've been pretty lucky to be part of that Yankee mystique. In fact, I was very lucky. I came along at the right time. They needed a shortstop. I've got no regrets. No, not even the Hall of Fame.

The one time I thought I might make it was when Pee Wee got in. All the reporters told me I would go in with Pee Wee. We were in spring training at the time. The Yanks were playing Baltimore, and I had the day off. But the reporters wanted me at the game. As it turned out, John Gordon, my colleague, called in sick. I was upset. I had to take his place. Just before the game, he walked in, and I left—mad! Leaving the park in my car, I was listening to the game on the radio. Frank Messer was saying to Bill White, "The Hall of Fame names are coming in. Pee Wee Reese—"

I said to myself, *I got a chance.* Then he said, "Rick Ferrell." I almost drove off the road. I hit as many home runs as he did. The reporters had seen me leave the park. They knew I was mad. But I was mad because I had to come to the park on my day off. They said in their stories that I was upset. I was. But they didn't report it the way it was. They made me look bad.

Up in the broadcast booth today I still look out at shortstop and see the "Scooter" with #10 on his back. I see a guy they said was too small. A guy they said would never make it. A guy who played in nine World Series. A guy who started in many All-Star Games. A guy who won the Babe Ruth Award and the Most Valuable Player Award.

And every goal I've reached, I never thought I would. The Hall of Fame would be great. But I've been blessed. I'd do it all over—the same way!

Frank Shea

Frank Shea had a super rookie season in 1947. He won 14 games and lost five during the regular season. Three of those wins, including a 1–0 decision, came against Hal Newhouser of the Tigers. In the World Series he won both of his decisions, including a first-game starting assignment. Pitching the middle innings, he picked up the win in the All-Star Game. In order to find a rookie who won more big games in his rookie year one would have to go back to the 1909 World Series when Babe Adams won all three of his decisions.

Yet his season could have been much better. He was shelved for seven weeks in mid-season by a neck injury. In his absence the Yankees won a record-tying 19 consecutive games. If he had been in the rotation during that streak, he might have challenged Jackie Robinson for baseball's first official Rookie of the Year Award.

It seemed that Frank Shea had a bright future. But ironically, his rookie year turned out to be his best. The neck injury that put him on the sidelines for seven weeks in 1947 sidetracked him for the better part of the next four seasons. Diagnosed incorrectly, it led to four wasted seasons.

By the time he regained his health, the "Big Three" of Allie Reynolds, Vic Raschi, and Eddie Lopat had established themselves as the bellwethers of the starting rotation. Without any bitterness, he departed for Washington, where he would find new friends and better fortune.

When he got to Washington, he joined a seventh-place club. But owner Clark Griffith and manager Bucky Harris treated him well and gave him the chance to pitch. Shea reciprocated. His arm got well. In 1952 and 1953 he turned in seasons of 11–7 and 12–7, helping the Senators to fifth-place finishes in each year. It was his "last hurrah." Overall his major-league record was 56–46.

Frank Shea is an affable Irishman and a good storyteller. Blessed with a sense of humor and a positive outlook, he sees the cup as half full rather than half empty. He is thankful for the "great" managers that he had: Eddie Sawyer in the minors, Casey Stengel and Bucky Harris in the majors. He is grateful for the friends he made in New York and Washington.

Still, once in a while he wonders how many games he would have won if he had stayed in the rotation in 1947; how many games he would have won in 1952 and 1953, if he had been pitching for the Yankees; and how many career games he would have won if he had stayed healthy. He doesn't begrudge the money that he missed, but he regrets the wins that he lost. Still, he is as comfortable with the bat boy of the local Little League team as he was kibitzing with Ted Williams in Yankee Stadium.

To talk with Frank Shea, I traveled to Naugatuck, Connecticut. He's the Director of Recreation in his hometown. We started the conversation in his outer office because there were a few matters that he had to take care of. About a dozen people were lined up to see him. Most of them were men and women dressed in the uniforms of the town's softball league teams. One wanted to file a protest, a second wanted

a rule interpretation, a third wanted a permit for a field.
Frank Shea handled their queries as deftly as he had the
middle of the Red Sox lineup in the late 1940s. Soon we
retreated to his inner office, with Frank's specific instruc-
tions to his secretary that we were not to be distracted for a
couple of hours. His wall was lined with pictures of former
teammates. "There's Joe DiMaggio," he would say "What a
great guy!" Then he'd give me three reasons why he thought
so. He repeated that pattern with every player he singled
out.

My original name was Frank J. O'Shea.
That's the way I was baptized and confirmed. When
I got into school, however, I started writing Frank
Shea instead of Frank O'Shea. For no reason. My
father carried his name through all his life, and it was
no big problem.

How'd I get the nickname "Spec?" Well, my father
was fair-skinned and had a lot of freckles, so they
called him *Speckle*. Later on, when he was playing
semi-pro ball, they cropped it to *Speck*. I got tagged
with the same name. But when I was pitching against
Hal Newhouser one day, Ben Epstein, the writer
with the New York *Daily Mirror,* called the story in,
and when it appeared, the headline read, "Newhouser
Bested by Spec." They didn't have room for the "k,"
so it's been Spec ever since.

It was funny how I attracted the attention of the
Yankees, too. Midway through 1942, I was called
into the service, and I missed the 1943–46 seasons.
When I got out, a fellow from Waterbury, Connecticut, asked me if I'd like to pitch against one of the
major-league clubs that would be traveling through

the area. In those days the local teams played against the Braves, the Red Sox, the Dodgers, and the Yankees. I pitched against the Yankees and beat them, 1–0. That got me the chance to go to spring training with them.

In the minors I was fortunate to play for Eddie Sawyer, who later managed the Philadelphia Phillies' "Whiz Kids," and Joe Kuhel. Then I played for Casey Stengel out on the Coast, and he was a dream. Another guy I was fortunate enough to play under was Bucky Harris with the Yankees and the Senators. He and Casey were two of the best guys I ever knew. Bucky was an easygoing guy. He reminded me of Connie Mack. He'd sit back, nice and quiet, not get excited, but when it was time to make a move, he was right on top of the situation.

In 1947, with the Yankees, I had a 14–5 season, an All-Star Game win, and two wins in the World Series. You would think, as a rookie, I'd be happy with those numbers. But, you know, it was all coming so fast. The thing that I regretted the most about that season, during our 19-game winning streak (the American League record), I didn't get a chance to pitch. I had pulled a muscle in my neck, in the upper shoulder. In all, I missed seven weeks. If I had pitched during that time, I could have had a really good year.

The year 1947 saw a big comeback for the Yankees. The year before, we finished 17 games behind the Red Sox. If you remember, Spud Chandler developed bone chips in his elbow, and Bill Bevens had tough luck. He was always losing, 1–0, 2–1, or 3–2. There was just no pitching on the 1946 club.

Then, in 1947, Allie Reynolds came over from Cleveland, and I had a good year. Vic Raschi and

Bobo Newsom came up in mid-season, and we were solid up the middle. George McQuinn came over from St. Louis and had a banner year. Tommy Henrich, Charlie Keller, Joe DiMaggio, and Billy Johnson also had great years.

That year I beat Newhouser three times. In one of those games I pitched a one-hitter. I used to like to pitch against Detroit. Boston, too. I didn't have good luck against the Red Sox, but I did pitch well against them. I especially liked to pitch against Ted Williams, and he was the greatest hitter I ever saw. I had good luck against him early, but he caught up to me later, like he caught up to everyone else.

I enjoyed getting on him from the bench, too. If I wasn't pitching that day, I thought that I should make some type of contribution. So occasionally I'd give the opposition a blast.

Ted would say to Yogi, "Who's that popping off over there? Is that Shea?"

"Yeah, that's him," Yogi would say.

"Tell him to get out on the mound."

My first assignment in New York, I beat Boston, 1–0. I gave up three hits. Tex Hughson gave up two. I went up to Boston the next time and struck him out with two men on base. Then I struck him out with the bases loaded. He got pretty put out about it. We both came out to the park early the next day. He wanted to know what pitch I was getting him out with. I said, "It'll take a while, but you'll figure it out." He did.

I used to throw him a slider, up-and-in. Eventually he caught up with it. He went into the service [the Korean War] with Gerry Coleman, and he came back, and I met up with him in Washington. I was pitching and he wasn't in the lineup.

"How come you're not playing?" I said. "Put a lamb in there. I want to get someone out."

"Are you pitching today?" he said.

"Yeah."

"Well, I'm going to make sure I'm playing then."

So he went in, had his name penciled into the lineup, and the numbers in the lineup changed on the scoreboard. Well, he got three hits off me, all line-drive singles. We went back to Washington. I opened the Series down there. And he got three more hits off me. The next time that he got up, I walked halfway down from the mound and told him, "The next one's going to be in your rear." And I hit him. When he trotted to first, I thought he'd be put out, and he mumbled something.

"Did you say anything?" I yelled.

He said, "Yeah, I just wanted you to know that if I had someone rough me up the way I've roughed you up, I would have hit him a long time ago."

The next day I met him and said, "I aimed low. I didn't want to hurt you."

He said, "Listen, if I were pitching and someone had two hits against me, he'd be hit in the rear, too. He'd have to go down."

He was really a great guy and a really great hitter. You couldn't intimidate him.

We used to get on Rizzuto, too. When we had a home game on a Sunday, and the following day off, I used to go home to Naugatuck and look for garden snakes and worms. I'd come back the next night and give them to Johnny Lindell, who used to put them in Phil's glove. In those days the fielders used to leave their gloves in the field. Lindell would come in from left field, drop his glove, pick up Phil's, and put the worms in it. Phil used to raise hell, saying he wouldn't play unless he had a different glove. And he meant it. He was afraid of everything.

Keller and I got him one time. You know those big trunks they have for shipping bats? Well, this one day we threw him down, and I flipped the top down, and the damn lock snapped. Well, we had a team meeting, and after it, we had to get Pete Sheehey, the clubhouse man, to open the lock. You should have seen Phil when he got out of there: soaking wet and *white as a ghost!*

Phil's afraid of lightning, too. When he started out in Class D—Easton, Maryland, I think it was—one of the players got hit by lightning. I think he got killed. Since that time, Phil's been deathly afraid of it.

Opposing batters were afraid of Joe Page. Boy, could he smoke the ball. We were good friends. They had a lot of stories about him that weren't true. Joe Page was a great guy. He never made a lot of money. But he was generous. He'd be walking down the street in New York and see a kid who seemed like he needed help and he'd slip him a bill. That's the kind of guy he was.

As a pitcher, he used to say, "Anytime you need me, I'm ready." Boy, he showed it, too. He had a real banner year in 1947. The next year he came back and he was just missing. Pitching's a game of inches. In 1948, not too many people knew it, he had a sore arm. But he didn't let people know it. It healed up over the winter, though, and in 1949 he had another great year. Then he hurt his foot, and he hurt his elbow from compensating, and he never did much after that.

There were two guys on those clubs that were real princes. Keller and Henrich. Both played the outfield well. Charlie ran into trouble with his back. Tommy was "Old Reliable." I'll tell you, when you needed a hit, he got it. He consistently came through in the clutch. In 1949, in the first game of the World Series, against Don Newcombe, he came over to me in the ninth inning and said, "He's been fastballing me all day on the first pitch, and I've been taking it. If he does it this time, I'm going to park it."

And that's what he did.

Joe D was a prince, too. Whenever you mention the name *Joe D* to me, I remember my rookie year in 1947. We stayed at the Edison Hotel. He always bought my breakfast. He'd say, "You don't make the money I do. This is my treat."

You always remember something like that. Not because he was buying my breakfast, but because he knew I wasn't making the money he was.

Of course, I'd drive him, Hank Bauer, Cliff Mapes, or whoever was around to the ballpark every day. I got real friendly with Joe. See, I've got pictures with him all over the office.

I remember when he came back from his injury in 1949 and had that great series in Boston. He had a gimpy heel, but they put him in the lineup, and he had a real DiMag series. The biggest thing I remember about his performance, though, was after the series, we were sitting around and he came down and said, "My greatest thrill is that I could come back and help my team." He was really a team player.

Yogi was another great guy. I broke in with him. You can say whatever you want about Yogi. But a lot of guys you just have to like. He's one of them. He was a good hitter, a good bad-ball hitter. He did everything according to Hoyle. He obeyed all the rules and regulations. I went with him over to New

Jersey when he picked out his first house. He roomed with me at the time.

He said to me, "Should I buy it?"

I said, "Yeah."

We came back to the Stadium, and he was telling everyone about the house. He said, "It's a big house. All it's got in it is rooms."

Yogi reminds me of World Series. It was a great thrill to pitch in the Series. But there was a lot of pressure, too. Not only was I worried about pitching in the World Series, but I was also worried about pitching at Ebbets Field, which was a small park.

My teammates were saying, "We got to win this. We can make the big bucks."

You're thinking that you can't put the ball up to the batter, or he's going to put it out of the park. You're telling yourself that you got to keep the ball down for the double play. You're reminding yourself that you can't let the batter hit behind the runner. I had all those things going through my mind. Of course, you thought about all those things during the regular season, too. But the regular season didn't compare with the World Series.

I had a fastball that moved, a change, a slider, a curve that wasn't that good, and I poked around with a knuckleball that I didn't get over the plate. But I used it as a change. I had good stuff. If I didn't have arm problems, I would have had some pretty good years in baseball.

But we were talking about the World Series. I went to school the day Bill Bevens lost both his no-hitter and the game on one pitch. Cookie Lavagetto's pinch-hit double cost Bill both.

When Cookie got up to the plate, the coaching staff said, "We should pitch this guy outside."

The pitchers on the bench were saying, "Why would you pitch him outside when you have a sinker-ball pitcher who can throw you on the fists?"

Chuck Dressen, our coach, went out to the mound and said, "I know this guy and I think we should pitch him outside."

But Bevens was wild that day, and if you're wild, you'd rather be up-and-in rather than away, and Lavagetto hit it off the right-field wall to win the game.

Bevens walked a record ten batters that day. We said to each other, "He's going to come out without giving up a hit." If he didn't walk a batter, he had him 3–2. It was one of those games. When it was over, he was exhausted.

After Bill got beat in that World Series game, he was sitting in front of his locker with his head down. I came up to him and said, "You know, Bill, you're snake-bit."

He said, "You're damn right I am."

"I got an idea. Why don't you let me wear your jockstrap tomorrow, and we'll get all of those snakes out of there."

"It's worth a try. Go to it."

So we got Pete Sheehey to wash it and clean it up. I went out the next day and beat Rex Barney, 2–1. Joe D had trouble with Barney early. First, he hit into a double play. Then he struck out with the bases loaded. Joe came back to the bench and said, "Well, I'll tell you right now, I've never seen anyone throw as hard as this guy's throwing."

But Joe went to school, too. In the fifth inning he hit the game-winning home run—off a fastball.

I got out of a couple of jams that day. When we got into the ninth, we were all referring to what had happened the day before, when Bevens lost the game and the no-hitter. The same situation came up. They came out and said, "You know what you have to do?"

I said, "Yeah."

Aaron Robinson was catching, for the Dodgers were stealing at will off Yogi. He went to management and said, "They're stealing on me. Why don't you put in a catcher who can throw someone out?" That took a lot of guts on Yogi's part. Later on, of course, he became a great catcher, and not too many runners ran on him.

Well, at any rate, I got the last hitter, and wound up the game with a four-hit win.

In that same game I got an RBI double off Hugh Casey. The pitch was a spitter. I hit it on the dry side. To left center. Funny thing, I thought it was a home run, and went into my trot, but I ended up sliding into second to avoid the tag.

After the game I said to Bevens, "All the snakes and curses are gone now, Bill. You're going to be all right."

Well, it didn't work out that way. He pitched shutout ball in a seventh-game relief outing. But it turned out that his one-hit loss was the last start he made in the major leagues.

Al Gionfriddo, another World Series star that year, never played another major-league game, either. The catch he made against DiMaggio wasn't one of his better ones, though. But with the press, it was the World Series, and DiMaggio was the batter. Joe hit it really good, no doubt about that, but Gionfriddo turned too soon, and had to backtrack before he hit the fence. So he looked clumsy. If he had continued to run the way he started, and turned at the right moment, he would have caught the ball easily.

We were hoping to wrap up the World Series in Game Six. But after Gionfriddo made that catch, we knew we would have to go to Game Seven. And our pitching staff was in bad shape. Reynolds had a tired arm. Raschi had a tired arm. Everyone was aching.

The coaches said, "Who's going to pitch?"

I'd had only one day's rest, but I said, "Heck, I'll pitch."

They said, "You've had only one day's rest."

I said, "What difference does that make? Someone's got to pitch. Just warm someone up in the bullpen with me, and if I get in trouble, get me out of there."

They said, "Who do you think we should warm up?"

"How about Bevens? He went the day before me. He could probably go an inning or two."

After I warmed up, I came in and told Bucky, "I don't have anything. Better get Bevens hot and me out of there."

I lasted one and one-third innings. But Bevens pitched two and two-thirds innings of shutout ball, and Page finished up with five scoreless innings to wrap up the championship. Those were clutch innings by Bevens. Overall, it was an amazing series for him. But he never pitched again in the majors. Isn't that remarkable!

Bobby Brown got three clutch hits in that World Series. One of them set up the seventh-game win. He drove home the tying run and scored what proved to be the winning run. Of course, he's the president of the American League now. I met him at a recent Old Timers' Day game, and I said to him, "Are you the same old Bobby Brown, or are you a big shot now?"

He laughed and said, "I'm the same old Bobby Brown."

He was, and is, a great guy. One of the best in baseball. He was a good ballplayer, too. A great pinch hitter. As time went on, he became a better infielder. I think he'll agree, if he didn't have it on his mind to become a doctor, he would have been an even better ballplayer than he was.

I said before that I missed seven weeks in 1947. They thought I hurt my arm. But it was actually my neck. The Yankees sent me to Boston, Johns Hopkins, and Minnesota to have it checked out. Three years went down the drain that way.

They'd say, "There's nothing wrong with your arm." The implication was that something was wrong with my head.

I'd tell them, "I know there's nothing wrong with my arm. But it's not in my head, either. I can't make any money in this game unless I pitch, and I want to pitch because I love baseball. I agree there's nothing wrong with my arm. But if you're saying there's nothing wrong with me physically, there's something wrong with the doctors in this world."

In 1951 I had a gas station in Waterbury. In the winter, this one night, the snow was really coming down, and everyone wanted chains put on their tires. My neck started to bother me. I called my wife. She said, "Why don't you go to see Dr. Anderson [the chiropractor in town]? You're always saying that you're going to see him."

I went to him, and he said, "Who said the problem's in your arm?"

I said, "I don't know. But I know the problem's somewhere else."

"You're right. It's in your neck."

He told me to go home, lie on the floor, and put my feet up on the couch. I felt foolish, because my wife had company. But after fifteen minutes, I said, "I don't have any more pain."

My wife said, "Get out, you're kidding." But, fortunately, I wasn't.

The chiropractor gave me a list of doctors in the towns in which I played. In Cleveland on a Friday night, warming up before a Saturday start, I was throwing in the rain. I slipped on the clay and I felt that thing come out.

"Oh, no," I said.

That night I called a doctor. He was a German. The next morning he fixed me up, and that day I pitched a two-hit shutout against the Indians.

I said before that Casey was a dream. He'd come out to the mound and say, "You look like you're tired. I'm going to get you out of here."

I'd say, "Hell, no, I'm not tired."

He'd leave me in. But he'd holler over his shoulder, "If you don't pitch better, you're gone."

He tried to get you all souped up, and he did a good job of it. We had some hotheads on the club. Bauer was one, Woodling was another, and McDougald was a third. Casey liked to stir them up, because he knew they played better when they were juiced up.

One day in Detroit, Bauer was batting against a right-hander. He had three hits: two doubles and a single. In the seventh or eighth inning he came up against a left-hander. Casey told Woodling to go up to hit for him.

Gene said, "You want me to bat against a left-hander?"

Casey said, "Yeah, I want you to go up there."

Hank came back to the bench steaming. He yelled,

"What the hell are you doing? I'm three-for-three, and there's a left-hander out there."

Casey said, "Go in the clubhouse. I'll talk to you later."

By God, Gene doubled off the lower screen in right.

After the game, Casey called Hank into his office. Five minutes later, Casey came out and yelled, "The beer's on the house. I'm buying."

Hank came over, and I asked him, "What went on in there?"

He said, "I don't know why I get mad at the Old Man. I never win."

Casey's justification of his move went like this: "Logically, you were three-for-three, and you probably wouldn't go four-for-four. So I helped your average. You're always feuding with Woodling. So I figured I'd put Woodling up against a left-hander, and he'd make out. That would help your average more."

Hank didn't have any comeback for that one.

Those Yankees had everything you'd want. They had a good starting lineup, but they could also platoon. They had a good pitching staff, too. Great starters. Raschi, Reynolds, and Lopat won so many big games. And they had a deep bullpen. They were a bunch of guys who loved to play baseball. Every year they won, they'd say, "Let's do it again next year." It became a habit.

In the midst of that streak, in 1950, my arm was still bothering me, so they sent me out to Kansas City to work it out, and that's when I first met young Ed Ford. We became pretty friendly. He had poise and great stuff. I could tell right away he was going to win games. The only question was how many.

One night in St. Paul, we got knocked around pretty good. I think it was 8–1. After the game we were walking down the right-field line, and we came to a little opening in the fence, where their clubhouse was, and they were hollering pretty good, because they won big. Whitey went up, opened the door, and yelled, "This is young Ed Ford, and you'd better celebrate good tonight, because I'm going to stick those bats into you tomorrow."

You know, he goes out the next night and shuts them out. *True story.*

Mickey Mantle was a great kid, too. He remained a kid throughout his entire career, because he had all those problems. Cancer ran in his family. His dad had it, and his kid had it, and he was sure he was going to get it, too. He didn't mature until two or three years after he retired, when he realized he could have been a lot better, and he could have made a lot more money. But life goes on. He was one hell of a player. He could run and hit and do everything one would want to do. But he'd be the first to admit he could have been much better. He was always certain he was going to die young, though, and why worry about it.

The year Mickey came up to the Yankees, they traded me to Washington. It was a funny thing about that. The Yankees weren't using me, but I was feeling good. One day it was raining and I was warming up under the stands. Bucky Harris, who was then managing Washington, came by. Yogi said to him, "Look, he's not pitching here. Why don't you make a deal for him? He's gone to the doctor, and he's throwing as well as I've ever caught him."

Bucky got interested. He asked me to throw a curveball and a slider. He couldn't believe my ball was so live.

The Yankees wanted Irv Noren, a left-handed-hitting outfielder. The Senators wanted me included in the deal. Casey didn't want to let me go. He was like a father to me.

But finally he said, "Look, you're starting to look good. I hate to see you go, but you have a chance to pitch every four or five days down there. That's not the case here."

The Senators didn't have a very good ball club, but I had two pretty good years with them. I won 11 and 12. With the Yankees I probably would have won 18 games both years. But I have no complaints about the trade. Actually the Yankees stayed with me longer than they should have.

Playing in New York, you live first class, you eat first class, and you room first class. When I went to Washington, it was different. But Clark Griffith, the owner, was a prince, too. When I got to Washington, he came up to me and said, "Spec, you're not going to get extra money down here."

I said, "Yes, I know, but I appreciate the chance to pitch."

He said, "I don't want you to feel slighted, but here's a check for $2,500 to ease the difference."

I thought that was really great. He did the same for other players who came down from New York.

Bucky Harris was the same type of man. He would say, "I know the club can't pay you what you want. But the club needs money. Have a couple of good years, and they'll sell you to a contender." It happened to Jackie Jensen and Pete Runnels, and they had really good years in Boston.

My top salary was $28,000 in 1948. I don't blame the players for today's salaries. I blame it on the owners. They brought it on themselves. The people

I feel sorry for, though, are the fans. If you live a distance and travel to the ballpark, it can be an expensive item. It's $9.75 for a box seat. You've got the gas, the tolls, the parking, and the use of the car. You have to get programs and souvenirs for the kids. Then you have to eat and have a few drinks. On the way home you have to stop to eat. It's going to cost you an easy $100. So maybe the next time you don't take the family as soon as you would.

Do you know, when I was playing, how many busloads would leave Naugatuck for Yankee Stadium on weekends? Six to ten. You know how many leave today? None!

I also feel sorry for the old-time ballplayers. Today's players want to retire at forty-five with $100,000 a year. I was talking to Enos Slaughter at a recent Old Timers' Day game. He played nineteen years in the big leagues, and finished with a .300 career average. You know what he gets? Six hundred dollars a month!

It was brought up at one of the recent pension meetings that today's players should take care of yesterday's players. Someone—and I don't know who it was—said, "Let the old-time ballplayers take care of themselves."

I think that's a lousy attitude.

But I don't regret that I missed out on the big salaries. The only regret I have is that my arm went bad. I said before I could have had a big year in 1947. I could have had a big career. I'd like to know how many wins I could have put on the board if I had stayed healthy.

Hank Bauer

Mel Allen coined a catchy phrase about Hank Bauer, "Hank Bauer the Man of the Hour."

The first five full seasons that Bauer spent in the majors, he played on world championship teams. Overall, he played on nine pennant winners and seven world title teams. In addition, he managed the 1966 Orioles to a four-game sweep over the Dodgers in the World Series.

In Game Six of the 1951 World Series, he tripled home three runs to provide the margin of victory in the championship-clinching contest. In the ninth inning he thwarted a Giant rally when he made a sensational sliding catch of Sal Yvars' line-drive bid for a game-tying hit.

Two years later, he scored the winning run of the 1953 World Series when Billy Martin tallied him from second base with a single to center field.

In the 1955 World Series he hit the ball at a .429 clip. From the first game of the 1956 World Series through the third contest of the 1958 Fall Classic, he hit safely in a record 17 consecutive post-season games. He hit seven home runs in those three World Series. Four of them came in the 1958 Fall Classic, and tied a record for home runs in one

Series. The mark was shared by Lou Gehrig, Babe Ruth, Duke Snider (twice), and Gene Tenace. Reggie Jackson broke the record when he hit five home runs in the 1977 World Series.

Some of his safeties in his 17-game hitting streak were "Man-of-the-Hour" blows. In Game Six of the 1957 World Series, he homered in the seventh inning to give the Yankees a 3–2 win over the Braves. In Game Three of the 1958 Fall Classic, he drove home all four runs in a 4–0 victory over the Braves. The runs were provided by a two-run single and a two-run homer. In the 1958 World Series he hit a home run in each of the first three games to tie the record for home runs in consecutive games. It had been set by Johnny Mize of the 1952 Yankees.

Eight years later, as a manager, Hank Bauer led the 1966 Orioles to a four-game sweep over the Dodgers in the World Series. Gene Woodling was his first-base coach. Bauer and Woodling were still playing two-platoon baseball. Hank did the managing. Gene took care of the distractions to the manager.

In that 1966 Fall Classic Hank Bauer bowed out of baseball, World Series style, the way he broke in—a winner. He was still "Hank Bauer, the Man of the Hour."

I had been trying without success for three summers to get in touch with Hank. He has an unlisted telephone number at his home in Overland Park, Kansas. But one day I saw in the local newspaper that Hank Bauer and Bill Skowron would be signing autographed pictures of themselves for diners at the Clinton House in Clinton, New Jersey. It turned out that Al Rosenberg, the manager of the Clinton House, had been at a Yankee Fantasy Baseball Camp, where he had met both Bauer and Skowron. I called the Clinton House, spoke to Rosenberg, and got the promise of an introduction that night.

Hank Bauer retired as a Yankee scout midway through

the 1987 season. He and Charlene, his wife of more than forty years, are enjoying retirement. They have four children, two daughters and two sons. Hank was influenced most by his older brother Herm, who was killed in France during World War II. Herm, a catcher, was a good ballplayer, much better than he, says Hank. One of Hank's sons is named after Herm. Hank himself had been hit twice and had contracted malaria in the war. He almost didn't continue his baseball career after he was discharged. But Danny Menendez, the scout who signed him, and his brother Joe persuaded him to change his mind. Otherwise he would have continued as an iron worker—making three dollars an hour, a lot of money then. The most that Hank made in one baseball season was $34,500. That was a lot of money then. "But it's not now," Hank quipped. "Hell, the bat boy makes that much today!"

My brother Herm influenced me the most. He was a few years older than me. A catcher. And much better than me. Unfortunately, he was killed in France in 1944, in World War II. But he left me with my love of baseball. One of my four children is named after him.

I served in World War II, also. From 1942 till 1946, with the United States Marines. I didn't know whether I was going to return to baseball after the war. I was hit twice and I had malaria. Before the war I was making three dollars an hour as an iron worker. That was big money at the time. But my brother Joe and Danny Menendez, who signed me to a contract at Oshkosh, Wisconsin, in 1941, talked me into it.

When I came up to the Yankees in 1948, they had

Keller, DiMag, and Henrich in the outfield. I thought I'd never break in. But Charlie came up with a disc problem in his back, and the Old Man moved Tommy to first base. Mapes and I split time in right, and Woodling and Lindell swapped in left. That was the beginning of platoon baseball.

In my first three at bats in the majors, I got three singles. "Hell," I thought, "this is going to be easy." Well, I found out. I ended up the season batting .180.

In 1949 I got 301 at bats, hit 10 home runs, and batted .272. What do I remember about Joe's comeback in Boston? Well, I remember in his first game back he hit a big home run against Mickey McDermott. I also remember that I hit two home runs in that game. But Joe got the headline. In a footnote to the story, it said, "By the way, Bauer hit two home runs."

I guess I was still feeling a little insecure. By 1950 I was beginning to feel more comfortable. But Casey was still using the platoon. I didn't care for it too much at the time. Later I gave him credit. It probably allowed me to play a couple of more years. But it didn't help me make any money. Gene and I were "red-asses," bear-down players, and we had hit both ways in the minors. We were convinced we could do the same in the majors. So we questioned the Old Man. Privately. Not the way they do in the papers today. He was the boss. And I respected him for that.

I remember Allie Reynolds' two no-hitters in 1951. In one of them, the 1–0 victory over Bob Feller and the Indians, a guy by the name of Sam Chapman hit a ball into the right-field seats. But the wind brought it back and I caught it over the fence.

Allie said, "Thanks."

I said, "Don't thank me. Thank the wind."

Game Six of the 1951 World Series was a big one for me. I hit a three-run triple. I remember that Dave Koslo was pitching for the Giants and Wes Westrum was catching. Wes had played with my brother Herm. The count was 2–2 and Koslo threw me a knuckleball. I didn't know he had one. So I took it. I thought it was strike three. But the National League umpire, I don't remember who it was, called it a ball. The next pitch I hit off the 402-foot sign for a bases-clearing triple.

In the same game I made the Series-ending catch on Sal Yvars. He was the only guy we didn't review in the team meeting before the Series. I didn't know where to play him. I motioned to the bench. They signaled back that they didn't know where I should play, either. Fortunately, Bob Kuzava knew something about Sal. He told me which way to shade. Toward the line. First I saw the sinking liner, then I didn't see it, then I saw it again. I ended up the hero. But I just as easily could have been the goat.

In 1952 my production stats started to go up. Henrich and DiMag were gone, Mickey moved to center, and I started to play more against right-handed pitching.

Those two plays in the last game of the 1953 World Series stand out in my mind, too. Reynolds came on for Whitey Ford in the ninth inning and gave up a two-run homer to Carl Furillo. That tied the game. I tried everything human to climb that wall, but I just couldn't reach the ball. That's the way I played the game. I wasn't afraid of that concrete wall. The worst injury it ever gave me was a sore hip. And I often think what might have happened if

Duke Snider had been able to make a play at the plate on Billy Martin's game-winning and Series-winning hit in the bottom of the ninth inning. I was on second and scored the winning run. If there had been a play, Campy and I would have had a hell of a collision.

That run I scored made it five consecutive world championships. That's a record. And we're all very proud of it. It was my fifth full season in the big leagues and my fifth winning check in the World Series. But speaking of money, I said before that you can't make money in the majors unless you play every day. That's the way it used to be anyway. I never negotiated with George Weiss until the end of my career. I always talked money with Roy Hamey. My top salary was $34,500. Hell, the bat boy makes that much money today. Hamey would say, "Well, you didn't play every day."

I'd say, "Hell, I was the first one at the park every day, and I was ready to play. You can't blame me if the Old Man doesn't pencil my name in the lineup."

But Bobby Brown was right. We were close-knit. It helped a lot that we traveled by train. We played cards together and we talked baseball together. My first four years I didn't say too much. I just listened. We had ballplayers who ran the club. Stengel didn't say anything. The veterans did. You could make a physical mistake. But you couldn't make a mental one. They'd chew you out. We got up for games. Somebody in Kansas City would be ready to take your job. It's not that way anymore. The competition just isn't the same.

Yeah, we were disappointed in 1954 when we didn't win again. But, hey, we won 103 games. And we had won five years in a row, and Cleveland had a great club. If you got rid of Bob Lemon, which was rare, you didn't get any favors. Ray Narleski, the righty in the bullpen, could bring the ball up to the plate around one hundred miles an hour, and Don Mossi, the lefty, wasn't any slouch, either. You didn't get any favors with that pitching staff.

Around 1955 my home run production started to go up and my batting average started to slide. But I don't think I was sacrificing average for power. The home runs just started to come. I could have had a lot more, though. I hit a lot of long outs in left center. DiMag, too. He would have hit a lot more somewhere else. He hit a lot of 450-foot outs. But he never bitched. That wasn't his style. He never showed his emotions outwardly. But I'm sure it bothered him. He'd hit a 450-foot out and Yogi'd hit a 320-foot homer in the corner. You just had to make comparisons to yourself. The ballpark just wasn't suited to me, or Joe, but the team was. The bottom line was we walked to the bank.

One game in 1955 stands out in my mind. Ellis Kinder was pitching for the Red Sox at Yankee Stadium. It was a big game in late September, and the Red Sox were winning by one run with two outs in the ninth. I hit a homer to tie the game, and Yogi followed with a homer to win it. After the game the reporters flocked around Yogi, and he said, "Heh, Hank hit the homer to tie it up." We had players like that.

I can't say why I hit 26 home runs in 1956. I was thirty-four years old. I remember in spring training the following year I said to Casey, "I'm having trouble playing day games after night games."

He said, "Of course, you're not as young as you used to be."

Speaking of Casey, he'd outmanage Paul Richards all the time. We'd go into Baltimore and Paul would try to outmaneuver Casey. But by the seventh inning Paul would be out of players, and Casey would be laughing at him.

How could I forget the day Don Larsen pitched the perfect game? It was in the fifth game of the 1956 World Series. We won 2–0. Mickey hit a homer for the first run. I drove in the second run with a single. We knew what was going on out there. After the eighth inning Don sat next to Mickey on the bench and said, "Wouldn't it be something if I pitched a no-hitter."

Well, in those days, ballplayers were superstitious. Mickey said, "Get the hell away from me."

Me? I was saying to myself, "Dale Mitchell, don't you hit me a low line drive." Don struck him out. Dale, I think, was looking for a fastball inside. Larsen had a good fastball that day. Instead, Dale got an offspeed curve outside.

Was the pitch a ball? It can happen. One day in a World Series game I took a borderline two-strike pitch, and Cal Hubbard, who was umpiring, said, "Don't take that pitch again. I might miss it next time."

The 1958 World Series was my best personal one. I batted .323 and hit four home runs. That was the record before Reggie hit five in 1977. I had a chance to set a new record in Game Seven. Lew Burdette was pitching for the Braves. He and I were good buddies with the Yankees in spring training in 1951. We were working out in Arizona—the only year we were out there—and he came down with a cold. I was in the trainer's room when the trainer gave him a shot. Lew turned out to be allergic to the medicine.

That's the reason the Yankees traded him for Johnny Sain. If he hadn't reacted adversely to that shot, he might have won three games for us, rather than against us, in the 1957 World Series. Well, anyway, he hung a slider to me in 1958, and I fouled it off. He walked halfway down to home plate and said, "You know you're not going to get that one again." That's the type of competitor he was.

I took a lot of pride in my 17-game hitting streak in the World Series. That's where your competitive nature comes out. But, hey, I played in 53 World Series games. When you play in that many games, you're bound to do something. Warren Spahn stopped me. Usually I hit him pretty well. But he had outstanding control that day. Getting stopped that day didn't bother me. But another day he picked me off in a World Series game. That was tough. One of those mental mistakes I was talking about. It was tough to run back to the dugout that day.

Overall I hit seven home runs in World Series play. In my first six World Series I didn't hit any. Then in my last three I hit seven. My most important one was probably against Don McMahon in Game Three of 1958. We were down two games to none at the time. That two-run homer gave us a 2–0 lead. We wound up winning the game, 4–0. I drove home all four runs. Another day I hit the foul pole off Ernie Johnson, who's now a broadcaster for Atlanta. My first one was off Don Drysdale of the Dodgers. He was a rookie, I think. The Old Man flashed a hit-and-run sign, and I hit the ball into the left-field seats.

I played in nine World Series, and we lost only twice. Both times in seven games. In 1955 the substitution of Sandy Amoros for Jim Gilliam made the difference. There was no way that a right-handed fielder would have made that play. In 1957 we just couldn't do anything with Burdette.

The Copacabana? The guy was looking for a cheap dollar. Dan Topping, Del Webb, and Casey asked me if I had clobbered the guy. I replied truthfully, "I wanted to but I didn't." What bothered me was that the case went to the grand jury, and I didn't get a chance to testify. Everyone else did.

Finally the district attorney said to the plaintiff, "You and your party can go. Bauer, you and your party stay." Then he said, "Hank, we've thrown the case out of court. Here, will you autograph this ball for my grandson?" I was ready to sign anything at that point.

Then I wanted to sue for defamation of character. I felt that I had been portrayed as John Dillinger. But Topping and Webb said, "No, it ends here."

So what could I do? I said, "All right, it ends here."

Before the case went to the grand jury, I was on a train going to Washington, and I came out of the dining room. A handsome young gentleman who was seated said, "Hi, Hank, how are things at the Copa?" Then he added, "Don't worry. Things will turn out all right." I didn't know who the guy was. All I knew was I wanted to hit him. But I didn't. Good thing. He was John F. Kennedy, the next president of the United States.

Clint Courtney in St. Louis? I didn't get there fast enough to be in on that fight. What I remember is Clint crawling out from under the pile looking for his glasses. But he couldn't find them. That's because Bob Cerv ground them into the grass with his cleats.

No, I wasn't upset when the Yankees traded me to

Kansas City after the 1959 season. I lived in Kansas City. And remember, I played with the Blues in 1947 and 1948, before I came up to the Yankees. So you might say my career began and ended in my hometown. I never moved to New York or New Jersey when I played with the Yankees. And I was thirty-seven. I was finished. It was a downhill slide from 35. I felt all right. I was coming home. The only upsetting thing was that I didn't learn about the trade from the Yankees. I heard about it elsewhere. That was George Weiss's style.

For a while I was the player-manager in Kansas City. I was 39 at the time. Charlie Finley and Frank Lane asked me, "How would you like to manage in the minors?"

I said, "No way."

Charlie responded, "How would you like to manage this team?"

I said, " Sure."

I remember my last game as a player. We beat Frank Lary of Detroit, 3–2. I hit a home run and threw out Rocky Colavito going from first to third. Rocky said later, "Heh, Hank, you can still throw."

I said, "Don't give me any credit. You still can't run."

Well, I got in the dugout and I received this message from Lane. It said, "You've played your last game."

Charlie Finley was a good guy. A player's man. But I said to him one day, "Charlie, you've got a problem. You hire the right guy for the job. You pay him well. But you won't let him manage. You want to do the job." He was once a bat boy in Birmingham. He ended up a frustrated player. Just like the guy in New York.

I managed in between two dynasties. One in Baltimore and one in Oakland. But I don't feel cheated. I feel I laid the groundwork for Earl Weaver and Dick Williams. There's only one other guy who's 4–0 in games in World Series play: George Stallings of the 1914 Braves. The "Miracle Braves," they called them. In 1966 we were on our way in Baltimore. But we came up with some tender arms. We also came up with a case of complacency. We won in 1966. We figured it would be easy in 1967. But you still have to play the game between the white lines.

By the way, Gene Woodling was my first-base coach in Baltimore. He was my first lieutenant. A manager's job is a tough one. There are a lot of distractions. Like the media. I told Gene, "If you see anything you don't like, take care of it." He did.

That reminds me of a story about Gene and me. One day in Detroit I hit two homers and a double. They had a lefty on the mound, so I thought I was going to add to my day's production. But the Old Man sent Gene up to hit for me. I threw the bat and it almost hit Gene. Case gave me some daffy reason for his move. But it made sense at the time. But what you have to remember is he had so many good players on the bench. They'd make anyone look good.

I resigned as a scout for the Yankees on July 9, 1987. I'm retired. But I have no regrets. I had a good career. If I hadn't played baseball, I would have been an ironman carrying a lunch bucket for three dollars an hour. Nothing wrong with that.

Instead I ended up wearing the insignia of the New York Yankees on my chest for twelve years. Proudly. There wasn't anything wrong with that, either.

Billy Johnson

   Billy Johnson played on world championship teams for three very successful managers: Joe McCarthy, Bucky Harris, and Casey Stengel.

 McCarthy's teams won nine pennants and seven world championships. Harris' clubs copped three pennants and two world titles. Harris, like McCarthy, endured. He won Fall Classics with two different teams (the 1924 Senators and the 1947 Yankees) twenty-three years apart. Stengel's units clinched ten pennants and seven world titles.

 All of the men in this book who played for McCarthy and Harris liked them. Most of the men in this book who played for Stengel liked him. Some of them didn't. Billy Johnson was one of them.

 Billy preferred McCarthy's approach to the game. McCarthy used a set lineup every day—and he got results. Stengel used the two-platoon system. He batted lefties against righties and righties against lefties—and he got results, too. But Johnson didn't like the two-platoon format. He preferred the continuity of McCarthy's game. He had his best seasons when he was an everyday player. "If you're a good hitter who's going good, you can hit any pitching, lefty or righty," he says. Johnson was a solid .271 lifetime hitter.

But when Billy recalls his days with the Yankees, the good times come readily to mind. He has many reasons to be thankful. First, he didn't expect to be scouted. Second, he didn't expect to get out of the minors. He spent six years there. Third, he didn't expect to crack the starting lineup when he did reach the majors. And fourth, he never expected to play on the same team with his teenage idol, Joe DiMaggio. But he did all of the above.

As a rookie in 1943, he cracked a lineup that had contributed to six pennants and five world titles in the previous seven years, and he took over the starting thirdbase job from Red Roff, who was synonymous with Yankee success. Billy had a good year. He batted .280 and drove home 94 runs with just five round-trippers. It's very rare to see a player with 10 or less home runs drive home close to 100 runs. But Billy was a good RBI man. In 1947 he had 95 runs batted in with just 10 home runs.

Billy was good in World Series play too. He played on four world title teams; he never played on a loser. In Game Three of 1943, his triple with the bases loaded against Al Brazle of the Cardinals gave the Yankees the lead, which they never lost, in the series.

In the 1947 World Series he hit a torrid three triples in one series. In total Series play he hit a record four three-baggers, and displayed a good glove and a strong arm.

Billy Johnson still shakes his head in awe when he recalls how good the 1943 Yankees were. They had so much depth, he points out. Billy Johnson was a pivotal part of that team. Billy lives in Augusta, Georgia, these days. He played there in the minor leagues in 1939 and 1940. That's where he met his wife, Louise, to whom he has been married since 1941. They have two children, a daughter and a son.

Billy, who retired after 29 years of overseeing the

Graniteville Construction Company considers himself lucky. He never played on a loser in the Fall Classic.

"Hey, I know a lot of players who were better than I was, and played in the majors for fifteen to twenty years, and never played in a World Series," he said. "I was one of the lucky ones."

Casey Stengel wasn't the best kind of manager for me. He believed in the two-platoon system. I didn't. He didn't think that a right-handed batter could hit a right-handed pitcher or a left-handed batter could hit a left-handed pitcher. I disagree. I believe if you're hitting good, it doesn't matter who's pitching.

My favorite manager was Joe McCarthy. He really understood all of his players. He had a high temper for some of his players and a low one for others. He could adjust to the occasion and to his personnel. And he played a set lineup. He really made you want to play for him.

There was a time, though, when I didn't think he knew I was around. After six years in the minors, I went to spring training at Asbury Park with the Yankees in 1943. We trained up north because of the war. Every morning I checked the bulletin board to see if my name was on any of the drill sheets. But it never was. After two weeks of the same routine, I asked Frankie Crosetti to hit me some grounders one day. It was snowing. But I was making the throws to first anyway. Finally McCarthy came up to me and said, "Do you think you can play third base in the majors?"

I said, "Give me a chance."

He said, "You're getting one. Make the most of it. Starting today, you're my third baseman."

It was a big thrill to me to make the Yankees in 1943. When I was a youngster, I admired Joe DiMaggio so much. I thought he had incredible ability. And he handled himself so well. Suddenly I had the opportunity to play with him. He was the greatest player I ever saw. He could run, he could catch, he could throw. He made every play look easy. Nothing was spectacular with him. He was always under the ball, waiting for it. And, of course, he was a great hitter. In essence, he was a great inspiration to the rest of us. Take that series in Boston in 1949, when he came back from that bad heel. It bothered him a lot. But he had an extraordinary series. He hit four home runs and drove home nine runs in three games. And we went on to win the pennant and World Series that put the other four in sequence.

But the 1943 Yankees were the best team that I played on. They had a lot of better players at different positions than any other club I was associated with. They were so good. I didn't think that I would be able to stay with them. I didn't think that I had the ability that the rest of the players had. But Crow helped me out till I got to know the hitters. And at the plate things gradually worked out, too.

That first year I batted .280 and drove home 94 runs. That was with just five home runs. In 1947 I hit 10 home runs and drove home a personal-high 95 runs. The following year, I hit 12 home runs and batted .294, two all-time highs for me with the Yankees. One year I hit 14 homers with the Cardinals.

I spent the next two years after 1943 in the Army during World War II. I was in Germany in 1944 and 1945. After the war I was discharged in Augusta,

Georgia. I had played two years there in the minors, in 1939 and 1940. That's where I met my wife, Louise. We got married in 1941. I still live in Augusta. I grew up in Montclair, New Jersey, but I prefer the warmer climate down south. In fact, I got my nickname, "The Bull," in Augusta, too. I used to play center field here, and a lot of balls hit the outfield fence. I guess I ran into that fence a lot one year. The radio announcer down here at the time gave me the name. Later Mel Allen refined it. He called me "El Toro, the Bull."

In 1946, our first year back from the war, we had a bad year. A lot of us had off years. Joe Gordon . . . Phil Rizzuto . . . George Stirnweiss . . . Tommy Henrich . . . Joe DiMaggio . . . myself. And Bill Dickey and Red Ruffing were gone. In the meantime, the Red Sox had one great year. They beat the Tigers out by 12 games. We finished 17 games back. Red Sox owner Tom Yawkey had bought a lot of players, and for that one year it paid off. By way of contrast, we had brought most of our players up through the farm system. George McQuinn and Johnny Mize were two exceptions. McQuinn helped us win in 1947, and Mize played an important part in the five consecutive world championships.

The following year, in 1947, we won the pennant and defeated the Dodgers in the World Series. I had a good Series. I hit three triples, two to right center and one to left center. Overall, I hit four. That's a record for career World Series triples. The first one I hit was against Al Brazle of the Cardinals in 1943. It was with the bases loaded. We were down 2–1 at the time, but we went on to win 6–2. That was my biggest thrill. That and a day the Yankees gave me at the Stadium in 1948. All my friends from Montclair were there.

No, I wouldn't want to say how much I made in my best year, but George Weiss was a very hard man to bargain with. You either agreed with him or you lost. Like Vic Raschi. Vic had one bad year and ended up with the Cardinals. So did I. In 1951 Weiss called me into the office and said, "The Cards need a third baseman. We're going to let you go. We hope when your career's over, you'll come back and coach for us."

The Yankees got first baseman Don Bollweg and $15,000 for me. I didn't like leaving the Yankees, but I enjoyed my two years with the Cardinals. They had a good team. They didn't have the number of good players at different positions that the Yankees did, but they were good. I played for Marty Marion and Eddie Stanky. Their organization treated me well. When I retired, they offered me a coaching job, but the pay in coaching wasn't good at the time, so I didn't take it. Instead I returned to Georgia and took a job overseeing the Graniteville Construction Company for twenty-nine years. Then I retired for good.

I had a good career. The only regret I had was getting caught up in Casey Stengel's platoon baseball. It was pretty hard for me to adjust to his system. You would sit one day, play two games, and then sit again. In later years, when Bobby Brown was having some fielding problems, I would sit for six innings and then go in for three. I guess that's what I was getting paid to do. But it was very hard for me.

Yogi Berra was the best argument against platoon baseball. Shortly after he came up to the Yankees, we went into St. Louis. The manager asked Yogi to hit some balls in practice. "Let's see what you have," he said.

"Where do you want me to hit the balls?" Yogi asked.

"You see that lower screen out there in right?"

"Yeah."

"That's where I want you to hit the balls."

Yogi hit four or five balls off the screen. The last pitch he hit was about six inches off the ground.

"Where was that last pitch?" the manager asked.

"Right down the middle," Yogi said.

Yogi was just a good bad-ball hitter. As I said before, if you're a good hitter, you can hit any pitching, lefty or righty.

But, looking back, I've got just fond memories. In 1937, when I was eighteen, I was playing semi-pro baseball in New Jersey, just dying to be scouted. But none of the scouts ever came around. One evening I was playing center field in a twilight game in Belleville, and I had a good game. Afterwards I was walking with a friend to his car when I felt a tap on my shoulder. It was Paul Kritchell, the scout who signed Lou Gehrig.

"Would you like to sign a contract with the Yankees?" he said.

I couldn't believe it. But I managed to mumble, "Sure."

"We'll need your parents' permission. You'll be going away from home. To Butler."

Mom and Dad said okay and I started my professional career that year. Six years later, in my rookie year, I played in the World Series and batted .300, and we won the world championship. I feel good about that. A lot of guys who were better than I was played fifteen to twenty years in the big leagues and never got to the World Series. I played in four World Series and we won all four times.

It was an honor and a privilege to play for those Yankee teams. It was such a thrill to realize that I was good enough to wear the Yankee uniform and be a Yankee.

They don't have that talent around today. You can't believe how good they were.

Johnny Sain

Johnny Sain's name is synonymous with 20-game winners. Four times he won 20 or more games with the Braves. More than ten of his protégés have won 20 or more games in a season. That's because he has been able to impart to them the many valuable lessons that he has learned along the way.

When he was just starting out as a pitcher he realized he didn't have the power to challenge hitters. He knew he would have to rely on delivery motion, and change of speed. That knowledge—and determined execution—helped make him a great pitcher and a great pitching coach.

When Sain was with the 1946 Braves, he won 20 games. The reporters thought his season was a fluke. They said he wouldn't do it again. Johnny resolved that he would. In a five-year stretch with the Braves he won 20 or more games four times.

In 1951 Johnny hurt his shoulder and his record dropped to 7–14. Before the season ended the Braves gave up on him and traded him to the Yankees for Lew Burdette. But Johnny Sain didn't quit on himself. He won two of his three decisions with the Yankees. Sain didn't think he did so well.

But the Yankees thought he might have made the difference in their stretch drive for the pennant. They awarded him a full World Series share.

When Sain went to the Yankees, he rejoined Casey Stengel, who had been Johnny's manager when he first came up to the majors with the 1942 Braves. The two of them had always liked each other. But of course Casey's bottom line was performance. In the spring of 1952, Sain knew that his lame shoulder was going to hold him back. He was told by doctors that the only type of treatment that would help him was X-ray therapy. There were some risks, but Johnny had always been a believer in the advances in scientific technology, so he agreed to undergo the series of treatments. They worked. Johnny Sain went on to have three outstanding years with the Yankees. During his tenure in the Bronx, the Bombers won three pennants and three World Series.

Indirectly, he was probably responsible for additional Yankee pennant and World Series wins. He later convinced other ailing Yankee pitchers to undergo the same treatment, and they subsequently responded with banner years.

When Johnny Sain played with the Yankees, he was a different type of pitcher than when he hurled with the Braves. He was no longer a complete-game pitcher who could average 273 innings a year. Instead he became a combination spot starter and relief pitcher. He made the adjustment smoothly and completely. In 1946 and 1948 with the Braves, he led the National League in complete games. In 1954, his last full season with the Yankees, he led the American League with 22 saves.

When Sain retired in 1955, Stengel let it be known that he thought Johnny would be a good pitching coach. Johnny asked his old pitching mentor Jim Turner for his opinion. Turner told him, "You'll be an excellent pitching coach.

*What's more important, though, is the game needs people
like you."*

Johnny Sain did become an excellent pitching coach.
Almost everywhere he's worked, he's turned out 20-game
winners. With the Yankees his three prize pupils were Whitey
Ford, Ralph Terry, and Jim Bouton. He's had just as much
success coaching for the Twins, the Tigers, and the White
Sox.

These days, at the age of 71, Johnny Sain is in the
sunset of his baseball career. In the summer of 1987 he was
still working for the Atlanta Braves as an evaluation scout
in the Chicago area. I contacted him at his home in Oakbrook,
Illinois, and found him gentle, charitable, and lavish in his
praise of virtually every one of his former teammates, managers, students, and administrators.

I wonder how much today's Yankees would pay a pitching
coach who could produce three 20-game winners at the
same time?

I had four children by my first wife. Two
girls and two boys. But I got one of *those* divorces in
1970. Lost everything. I had a Chevy dealership, 354
acres, an auto part store, an interest in a warehouse
in Memphis, and an airplane. But I lost it all. About
$400,000. Then in 1972 I remarried. And I started
all over again.

My dad gave me my baseball start. He was the
greatest influence on me. He was a left-handed pitcher
in amateur ball. Later he owned a garage in Havana,
Arkansas, a small community of about five hundred
people. I grew up in that garage by the Rock Island
Railroad. My glove and ball were always with me.
Kids would come in from the country, and we'd play
catch. One day when I was ten, I went to my dad

after lunch and I said, "How do you throw a curve?" Well, he gave me his idea. I remember it like it was yesterday. He showed me how to throw it with the thumb sticking out. It was an old schoolhouse curve. But I learned to spin the ball.

Sam Ferguson, who ran the grocery store, came out one lunchtime and said, "Why don't you put your thumb under the ball?" He never pitched but he could throw a curve. And he gave me his idea. On my own I learned to throw it through trial and error.

I wasn't blessed with power. But I learned motion, delivery, and how to make the ball sink, slide, and curve. The most difficult thing to learn was how to throw the screwball. Management discouraged me. It took me three years to learn it. At first I couldn't spin it. In fact, I couldn't do anything with it. Then I got it to break on the sideline but not in the game. Then I got it to break in the game, but I couldn't control it. It looks so easy when you see someone throw a pitch. That's what makes baseball so interesting. It doesn't matter where you sit. You're always within earshot of an authority. Up in the press box it always looks so easy. I once told Chuck Tanner, "When one of your pitchers gets in trouble, put him up in the press box. Then he'll know how to get out of it."

Rube Thomas signed me for five dollars. But in my second year of pro ball I hurt my elbow, and Osceola, Arkansas, released me. That was Class D. But Thomas knew Bill Dickey and talked to him. Dickey tried his best to discourage me. He wanted me to know how difficult it was to make it to the big leagues. He was the best driving force I could have had. He let me know what I was up against. It would have been easy to walk away from it. But I always thrived on challenges. It became my incentive. It's funny, in the 1952 World Series I was batting in the bottom of the ninth inning with two outs and the score tied. I hit a ground ball to the second baseman, and he bobbled the ball. Gil Hodges stretched for the throw, but I beat it by ten feet. There was a famous photo of the play. At a writers' dinner the picture was blown up to life-size. They pulled the curtain and ran through the play. I don't remember who the umpire was. But I do remember that he didn't umpire afterwards. There was no way that I was out on that play. I do remember that Dickey's in the picture. He was the first-base coach with the Yankees at the time. Isn't that ironic?

Well, when I resumed my minor-league career, I played for Larry Gilbert, an independent owner, in Sanford, Florida, for two years. Starting and relieving. He made a lot of money developing and selling players. He told me I couldn't make the majors as a pitcher. Maybe as a first baseman, he said. I could hit but I didn't have any power. But over the winter a lot of guys went into the service. It was during World War II. I got a year's deferment because I was providing for my parents. So Gilbert needed me to pitch. He offered me $225 a month but I turned him down. Then he made me an offer I couldn't refuse. He asked me if I wanted to go to spring training with the Braves. I did and I made the club. Casey managed the Braves at that time. I remember in my first appearance in the spring, I faced nine Washington Senators, and I retired all nine batters. That was 1942. I got into 40 games and I got paid $600 a month. One day I started against Paul Derringer. I was so in awe of him. He made it look so easy. I got knocked out of the box in the seventh inning. Casey said to me after the game, "You're not a nine-inning pitcher." At the time he was right. He was right about a lot of things. And, it's funny, over the years he became one of my best buddies.

The next year I went into the service. I was stationed at Amherst College in Massachusetts. Ted Williams, Joe Coleman, and Johnny Pesky were there, too. Then we were sent to Chapel Hill, North Carolina, for pre-flight training. The academics were difficult for Ted and me. But President Frank B. Graham of the University of North Carolina gave us special help at night. Ultimately Ted chose the Marines and I chose the Navy. When the war was over, I got my release because the Navy had so many flyers. The Marines didn't. That's why Ted went to Korea.

In the service we faced each other in a playoff series. Athletics were an important part of the program. We played when the cadets were off. But we did the job we were trained for. And learning to fly a plane trained me to concentrate under pressure. Also to be unorthodox. Without the three years in the service, I might not have made it. I was twenty-five when I went in, twenty-eight when I came out. You'd think my career would be over. But it was just beginning.

After the service Williams helped me tremendously. He said so many complimentary things about me. They influenced other people. It made me feel great. Well, in spring training we had a big right-hander who was throwing hard. The writers were impressed with him. But eventually manager Billy Southworth held a meeting with the writers and told them, "He won't be here on Opening Day. But Johnny Sain will pitch on Opening Day, and he'll win 20 games."

That gave me the confidence I needed. Well, I did pitch on Opening Day and I did win 20 games. After the season I didn't know what I was worth, so I asked Mort Cooper, Cy Johnson, and Bill Lee, who were veterans, what I should ask for. They told me to ask for $18,000. And the Braves gave it to me. The next year I won 21 games, and once again I didn't know what I was worth, so I asked the veterans to give me a figure again. They said to ask for $30,000. But this time the Braves balked. They offered me $21,000.

During spring training, management alternately blasted me and buttered me up. I knew I could hold out until March 15. When that date came, I said, "I'll sign but it's not what I want." Then I went on to win 11 games before the All-Star break. Around that time I saw Southworth and said, "I'm asking for what I asked for in spring training. If you don't give it to me, I'll walk away, and you won't be able to give me enough money to come back." I had made up my mind. My future didn't matter. That's how I felt. The next morning I was supposed to have an appointment with owner Lou Perini at 8:30, but I forgot completely about it. They paged me and I said I would be up in a minute. But I didn't hurry. I just didn't care at that point.

"Well, John, what do you want?" Perini said when I sat down.

"I want what I asked for in the spring," I said.

"Next year?"

"I won't hold you up. Make it a two-year deal."

"Okay. And every game over 20 you win, I'll give you an extra thousand." Well, I won 24 games and one in the World Series, so I made an extra five thousand.

Billy Sullivan, who went on to own the New England Patriots, was the Braves' publicist at the time, and he told me later, "I told Mr. Perini, 'John's a man of integrity. I believe if he doesn't do the job, he'll give you the money back.'" That made me feel good.

After I beat Bob Feller in the 1948 World Series, Perini said up in the press box, "Maybe he's as good as he thinks he is." But I had to struggle to win 20. The reporters kept saying I wouldn't do it again. But that just gave me the incentive I needed to do it. And I did. Then they'd say once more that I couldn't do it again. But I would. I was constantly trying to prove myself.

Those 1948 Braves were outstanding. The Cardinals and the Dodgers were the pre-season favorites, but they tailed off, and we exceeded everyone's expectations. Earl Torgeson and Frank McCormick did a great job alternating at first base. Eddie Stanky had a great year with the bat and helped Al Dark, a rookie, at short. Bob Elliott was just an outstanding third baseman. Phil Masi was a good catcher and Bill Salkeld was another catcher I liked to pitch to. In the first game of the 1948 World Series, Bill walked and Phil ran for him. I bunted Phil to second and Tommy Holmes singled home Masi with the run that beat Feller, 1–0. Looking back, I'd have to say that was a very solid infield.

The outfield was solid, too. Jeff Heath came over from the American League and did an outstanding job. Unfortunately he broke his ankle in a slide at home in the last week of the season. Holmes was a year-in, year-out .300 hitter. He was just as stable as he could be. If Heath had played in the World Series, we might have won it.

The media had a saying at that time: "Spahn and Sain and then we pray for rain." Warren won 17 games that year. But Vern Bickford won 18 and Bill Voiselle had a good year, too. Bickford used to make me feel good. He'd say, "You look so smooth out there. I see you do it and I think I can do it, too." And Nelson Potter was just outstanding in relief.

Spahn and I really had a good relationship. I know he was good for me. I believe I was good for him, too. In 1946 I got out of the service earlier than he did. He joined us in Pittsburgh after the season got underway, but he really didn't get going. However, the next year he won 21. Spahn and I were as different as night and day. I couldn't get batters out with the same stuff he used. But we never competed with each other. Actually we were pretty close. We had the utmost respect for each other. I used to tease him, "You know, Warren, it's easier for a left-hander than it is for a right-hander." But you have to give him his due. I often ask baseball people, "Who would you take if you had your choice: Koufax or Spahn?" Koufax dominated two teams I coached in the World Series. The 1963 Yankees and the 1965 Twins. Most anyone would take Koufax. But I say, "Would it be smart?" Spahn won 20 games 13 times, you know.

My three favorite managers were Gilbert, Southworth, and Stengel. You could second-guess all three of them. But in the end they'd be right most of the times. Southworth was a really good man. After his son got killed, on takeoff or landing at LaGuardia Airport in 1945, he used to go out where it happened and just sit there. He was so sad. Then after we won the pennant, he started drinking. But he treated me great. One day we were coming into

Grand Central Station in New York City. It was a good walk to the Commodore Hotel, where we stayed. He picked up my bags and carried them for me. I was embarrassed. But he wouldn't put them down.

The Braves traded me to the Yankees for Lew Burdette in August of 1951. It was a great thing for me and a great thing for Lew, too. He and Spahn got pretty close. That didn't hurt Lew any. And I got a new lease on my baseball life. I won two games in a month. I thought I did pretty poorly. But the Yankees thought I did great. They told me that the pennant race might have ended differently if I didn't come. They awarded me a full World Series share. They were a class outfit.

I'm grateful to Boston, too. They gave me an opportunity. If they had traded me to a non-contender, I probably would have pitched one year and that would have been it. But they traded me to the Yankees, and I had three productive years in New York.

When I came to the Yankees, my shoulder was bothering me, and it continued to hurt me. The next spring I mentioned my problem to a doctor in Dallas whom my first wife knew. He set up some X-rays for me at the Medical Arts Building. They showed an inflammation of the tendon that goes over the top of the shoulder and down the neck and arm. They suggested X-ray therapy. I was the first of many ballplayers to have it done there. The next two treatments I had done at one-week intervals in Little Rock. They relieved the soreness in my shoulder. The pain went away. In spring training I threw free and easy. Of course, I didn't have the stuff I had with the Braves, though.

But I was elated. My arm felt so good. I passed the word along. Eddie Lopat took the treatment. Whitey

Ford took it five times. Mel Stottlemyre took it six times. In 1961 Ford, Bill Stafford, and Ralph Terry all took it. All three of them were back in the lineup within ten days. So I guess it helped win a few pennants. Don't get me wrong, though. I'm not advocating radiation. They say it can make you sterile and give you cancer. I'm just saying it worked for me. And I'd do it all over again.

I was a pretty good hitter. In 1954 I batted .353. Also, I'm one of only 29 pitchers to hit .300 and win 20 games in the same season. I did that in 1947. Once in a World Series game I hit a double with the bases loaded. You know, I struck out only 20 times in eleven years. One year my aim was to get through the entire season without striking out. But I didn't do it. I struck out once. In 1948 I led the National League with 16 sacrifice bunts. I was the first pitcher to lead a league in that category. Denny McLain had 16 sacrifice bunts the year he won 31 games. But he didn't lead the league.

One day Billy Pierce was pitching for the White Sox, and Casey sent me up to pinch hit for Joe Collins. He threw me a breaking pitch that broke in, and I hit it over Minnie Minoso's head in left field for a game-winning double. I usually hit to right but that day I pulled an inside pitch. I dressed next to Allie Reynolds. After the game Allie was mad. He said, "How about the Old Man pinch hitting a pitcher for Collins!"

I said, "What are you mad about? We won, didn't we?" But that day I felt bad for Joe, too.

The 1951–53 Yankees were just great. Just to rub elbows with Joe DiMaggio in his last year was a big thrill. He had superstar aura. Just like Ted Williams. It was great to see him operate. And Mickey was just coming up with the Yankees. The Braves barnstormed north with them that year. They were just unreal. Not only as players, but as people. I couldn't say enough about people like Yogi, McDougald, and Mize. Johnny, by the way, was the first hitter I pitched to in the big leagues. I struck him out. One of the few times. One day he hit three home runs against me. But we beat the Giants, 5–4.

Ernie Lombardi was behind the plate when I pitched to Mize for the first time. Overall I had twenty catchers. Someone once asked me, "Did you let your catchers call the game for you?"

I said, "No, it wouldn't have been very smart of me to turn my bread-and-butter over to twenty different catchers." The pitcher has to have an overall method and plan. Usually the catcher learns the system. Eventually you get to think together.

A smart catcher can bail you out, though. Take Yogi Berra. One day in a World Series game he threw out two consecutive runners at third base. The Dodgers had first and second with no one out. The batter bunted. There was no way the pitcher could have fielded the ball and made the throw. The second batter bunted, also. It would have been a base hit, too. But Yogi threw both runners out at third. He could get out from behind the plate quicker than any other catcher I saw. And he threw well. He had an unorthodox throw to second. But he helped his pitcher a lot. The son of a gun did it all.

The "Big Three" will tell you that. And they were the best. Each of them was different, too. Reynolds had a fastball and a big curve. Now there's a pitcher who should be in the Hall of Fame. Vic Raschi had a good fastball and a slider. He was just as steady as you could be. And he was a competitor from here to there. Eddie Lopat threw a variation of pitches. He and Nelson Potter helped me with my screwball. They say he threw junk. But he could throw his fastball by hitters. I couldn't do that.

Me, I had a big roundhouse curveball. I threw a variation of breaking pitches. I could throw over-hand, three-quarters, sidearm. I had to do those things. One day in Brooklyn Pete Reiser beat me when I threw him the same pitch two times in a row. Southworth said, "Don't make that mistake again." He was right. Reiser was looking for the pitch. I grew up a little that day. A few games later Walt Judnick was the batter with two outs in the ninth inning. My best pitch that day was a three-quarters curveball. Well, I got two quick strikes on him. Then I said to myself, *He's looking for it now.* So I dropped down and threw a sidearm curve. It broke over the plate for a called strike three. Southworth said after-wards, "What was that last pitch? A sidearmed fastball?"

"No," I said, "a sidearm curve." You've just got to call your own game and do the best you can.

When I came over to the Yankees, I told Casey, "I'll do anything you want: spot start, relieve, pinch hit." In the 1951 World Series I was scheduled to start the fourth game against the Giants. But there was a rain-out and Reynolds came back to win. I didn't feel bad about it, though. I felt we were stronger with him starting and me relieving. And my arm wasn't one hundred percent at the time anyway.

In 1952 I started and relieved. It wasn't any prob-lem. Casey always made me feel good. He always told the reporters I could adapt to either. I can't say enough about him. The last time I saw him, in 1975 maybe, he was sitting behind the screen at spring training when I went by. He stood up and carried on about me, trying to convince everyone within hearing distance that I had carried the Yankee pitching staff when I was there.

One day when I pitched for him with the Braves, I relieved with the bases loaded and no outs in the bottom of the ninth. The score was tied. He met me at the mound, walked off, and then came back. "The runner's going to steal home," he said. "Start him off with a curve. But if he tries to squeeze, throw a fastball. But don't hit the batter." The only thing he didn't say was, "Don't balk in a run." And that's what I did. But it was the best thing that happened to me. I always pitched from the set position afterwards. Casey said after the game, "You've got a one-track mind." But I didn't mind. I screwed up.

Another day in Boston I was warming up in the armory across from Braves Field. It was raining and I was experimenting. Casey saw me. He said, "Don't step so far sideways. You lose too much power. Step only a little. That way you can throw overhand rather than sidearm." He was right. It helped me.

Southworth used to tell me to show the batter my hip pocket. "Show the batter three-quarters of your back," he used to say. "It helps to keep you back." I liked that. It kept me closed. That was very important to me. That and learning the screwball.

No, Casey didn't tell me in 1954 I wasn't starting anymore. He never had to come to me with anything. Anything he said, I did. It's funny, though. I got into 45 games that year. That was my most in any one season. And none of them were starts. But I had a good year in the bullpen. Twenty-two saves. I didn't realize until just now that I led the league in that department. That was a pretty impressive number in those days, though. Things were different then. They wanted the starters to go nine innings. So you came in against only the best teams. But I was always ready. I would throw before each game. The second time I threw, in the bullpen, I always felt better. Then I would sit and wait with Silvera and Houk. That's where Ralph and I became pretty close. Out in the bullpen.

The trade to Kansas City in 1955 didn't bother me. I didn't get off right. It was just personnel. Casey knew that I wanted to retire anyway. He talked me out of it in 1952. But this time I was traded to a noncontender, and it turned out to be my last year.

At the time I never thought of becoming a pitching coach. But one day George Kell came by my dealership and said, "Casey asked about you. He said, 'If he doesn't get too fat, he'll make a good pitching coach.'" Shortly after that I got a call from Kansas City. They wanted to know if I was interested in coaching. I didn't make up my mind right away. But a little later I saw Jim Turner when he was inducted into the Arkansas Hall of Fame, and I asked him, "Jim, do you think I'd like coaching?"

"Yes," he said, "and you'd be a good one. Furthermore, baseball needs people like you." That made me feel good. So I accepted Kansas City's offer.

I said that Houk and I were close. Then he got the Yankee job in 1961, he wanted me as his pitching coach. I got the job after a talk with co-owner Del Webb, who made me feel ten feet high. Ralph was walking up and down out in the hall while we talked in Webb's office. Primarily we talked about a four-man rotation. I was in favor of it. So was Webb. He said that he had wanted to see it for quite some time. So I got the job. And Whitey Ford, by the way, who had never won 20 games in a season while in a five-man rotation, won 25 and 24 in 1961 and 1963.

We had three great years from 1961 to 1963. Ralph built a great organization. His coaching staff, for example, was fabulous. You couldn't ask for better coaches than Wally Moses and Jim Hegan. In those three years we won three pennants and two world titles. But in 1964 there were administrative changes. Ralph became the general manager and Yogi became the manager. I would have liked to work with Yogi, but I sensed he would have problems rising up through the ranks. And I asked for a $2,500 raise. We had been successful and I wanted to feel appreciated. The Yankees had treated me great, but everyone wants a pat on the back. But it turned out that there weren't enough pats to go around. Dan Topping, the other owner, said he couldn't go for the $2,500. That was okay with me. The timing for a clean break was there. I asked for my release. After I left, Webb sent me a nice note. He pointed to the change of command and said, "These things happen." But for those three years no one could have been closer than Houk and me. When he became the general manager, however, he had to look at things differently. That's all right. I understood.

Ralph Terry was bitter when they let Moses and me go. Jim Bouton, too. He called me and said with disbelief, "It was over $2,500? I would have paid the difference."

Comments like that kept me going at the time. That's the type of relationships that I tried to build with my pitchers. Maybe that's why I had success with so many of them. It's true that I had a number of 20-game winners. Terry, Bouton, and Ford [twice] with the Yankees. Jim Kaat and Jim Grant with the

Twins. Denny McLain and Earl Wilson with the Tigers. Wilbur Wood, Stan Bahnsen, and Kaat [twice] with the White Sox. And there were others.

Those were highlights. There were some disappointments, too. The biggest one was not seeing the system in Atlanta develop. I would like to see Ted Turner with a winner. I know what he's done for the game and the players. I know he helped me recover from my divorce. He's treated me super.

You know, I never wore any of my World Series rings. I never thought about them at the time. Until my first wife reported that every one of them, a silver tray, and a silver pitcher were stolen. It's like the Hall of Fame. The Hall of Fame wasn't important to me then. It is now. The World Series rings weren't important to me then, either. They are now.

I said that I was worth $400,000 in 1970. That was a lot of money then. But I stood up in court, knowing that I was going to lose everything that I had saved in a lifetime, and said I would sign everything over to my wife so that the kids would get everything at her death. I walked out of court with nothing, except a little piece of property down in Arkansas that had belonged to my parents. She even destroyed my scrapbooks. But all of that just made me a better person. You can take a man's physical possessions away. But you can't take his memories away.

I started all over again. And I'm in good enough shape. I've got my pension and a job with Atlanta that could end this year. And my wife, Mary Ann, works for Metropolitan Life Insurance. My health is good, too. A little while back, I had some chest pain. I found out that I had a ninety percent blockage in two blood vessels. The following week, they inserted a small balloon into them and expanded it. The first time I walked into that hospital I experienced some pain walking up the stairs. Eight days later I returned to the hospital for a stress test. I ran up the stairs and I felt good. I was back to normal. They called me 100 percent. And in that type of procedure, I'm told, that kind of recovery usually doesn't happen.

I've got my memories and I've got my health. So I guess I am in pretty good shape. And, you know, there's something to be said about starting all over again!

Joe Ostrowski

Joe Ostrowski's life has been a series of paradoxes.

He started in professional baseball three years after he began teaching high school in West Wyoming, Pennsylvania. The Board of Education held his job for him. Until he was twenty-four years old, he was a first baseman, but he made it to the major leagues as a pitcher. At first his best pitch was a fastball, but he stayed in the big leagues with a good curve and good control. Career-wise, he would have been satisfied to make it to Class A ball, but he made it all the way to the major leagues instead. Pushing thirty-two at the time, he got called up by the St. Louis Browns on Independence Day, 1948.

He came up with the sixth-place Browns, but he ended up with the first-place Yankees, his childhood idols. While he was with New York, he thought that Casey Stengel made some questionable moves, but he always came out "smelling like a rose," Ostrowski says. In the most important game Joe ever pitched with the Yankees, he was warming up in the bullpen. He didn't think Casey would call for him, but the Old Man did. In the same game he didn't think Casey

135

would let him bat in a scoreless tie, but the Old Man did, and he singled to set up a two-run homer that won the game.

Though he was an integral part of the 1952 World Champions, two years later Joe was out of baseball and soon thereafter he was virtually forgotten by followers of the sport. Twenty-five years after he had hung up his spikes, he returned to Yankee Stadium for an Old Timers' Day game and learned that some of his former teammates didn't even remember him. It was somewhat understandable, though. In 1954, when he left professional baseball, Joe slipped quietly away from the big-city limelight and returned to Pennsylvania. His teaching superiors, who had promised to hold his position, were true to their word. He picked right up in 1954 where he had left off in 1938. It was as though he had never been away; he continued to teach mathematics until he retired in 1978.

Joe Ostrowski was waiting for me patiently when I drove up to West Wyoming, Pennsylvania, to see him in the summer of 1985. He told me I was the first reporter to look him up in the thirty-three years he had been out of the game. The balls he autographed for my three sons were the first he had signed since he had finished up in the Pacific Coast League in 1953.

A humble, soft-spoken, self-effacing man, Joe has always done his job well. He played on three world championship teams in four and one-half years in the major leagues, he devoted his life to professional education, and he fathered three sons who became professionals. Two of them are engineers and one is a chemist. There's something to be said, I guess, for sleepy countrysides.

I'm surprised you found me up in West Wyoming. Life's very quiet up here. Just a small, quiet town. Always has been. Always will be. I was born here, in 1916. I came from a family of ten children. I was number five. Where I am presently living was the garden of our homestead.

The way I got started in professional baseball reflects the town from which I come. After I graduated from West Wyoming High School, I went to Scranton University. After I got my degree, I started teaching here, in 1938. Three years later, in 1941, I broke into professional baseball. By that time I was twenty-five years old. But I wanted to try my luck in baseball and see how far I could go.

One of my school directors encouraged me, too. He told me that he and other school-board members would save my teaching position, just in case I didn't make it in professional ball. They also let me come back in the winter months to teach until spring training.

The Wilkes-Barre Barons first scouted me. They were affiliated with the Indians at the time. But I didn't make it with them. I started 1941 with Centerville, Maryland, in Class D ball. It was a farm team of the Boston Red Sox. On August 9, I was promoted to Canton, Ohio, in Class C ball. The following year, I played for Greenville, North Carolina, where I won 21 games, lost eight, and had an ERA of 1.65. I was supposed to go to Louisville, Kentucky, in 1943 to play in Triple-A, but Uncle Sam called me up for *his* team, and I stayed with him until the end of the 1945 season.

In 1946 and 1947 I played for Louisville. During the winter of 1947, I was sold to the St. Louis Browns. They sent me to Toledo, where I experienced my first losing season. Ironically, though, I was called up to the Browns on July 4, 1948. Independence Day!

I was pushing thirty-two when I got to the major leagues. What kept me going? My love of baseball. I've been a baseball fan since I was eight years old. That was in 1924, when I began to follow the career of Babe Ruth. I've been a Yankee fan ever since. Actually, I would have been satisfied if I had gotten into Class A ball. As it turned out, though, I made it all the way to the majors.

It's funny, I didn't start out as a pitcher. I played first base in sandlot ball. I didn't start pitching until I was twenty-four years old. At the beginning I depended mainly upon a fastball. The man who taught me how to throw a curveball was Herb Pennock, who was the head of the Red Sox farm teams at the time. As I progressed, I let up a little on my fastball and concentrated on control. That was my forte.

With the Browns I was 4–6 in 1948 and 8–8 in 1949. In 1950, the day of the trading deadline, I was sent to the Yankees in a mass transaction. Eight players and cash were involved in the deal. The Yankees gave up Snuffy Stirnweiss, Jim Delsing, Don Johnson, Duane Pillette, and $50,000 in cash for Tom Ferrick, Leo Thomas, Sid Schacht, and myself.

The transition from the Browns to the Yankees was from relaxation—trying your best—to pressure. The Browns were perennial losers; the Yankees, perennial winners. You were expected to lose with the Browns. You were expected to win with the Yankees.

Nevertheless, it was a dream come true. The Yankees were my favorite team. When I stood on the mound for them, I knew that I could depend on the players behind me. They could field and they could hit. And I felt pretty sure I could make some extra money in the fall.

That wasn't the case with the Browns. With them,

if I saw a one-half hop go to the shortstop, I knew there was a good chance the ball would be misplayed. But with the Yankees, Rizzuto would play it and throw the runner out. Phil was a sure glove man. He was an outstanding fielder with a quick release.

Professional-wise, all of the Yankees were good. They were all gentlemen. At that time it was expected that all Yankees be gentlemen. Both on and off the field. Take Joe DiMaggio, for example. I looked up to him as an outstanding ballplayer. But he was also a gentleman all the way. He was easy to get along with. He respected me the way I respected him.

As far as I'm concerned, all of the Yankees were easy to get along with. The Yankees were just one happy family. Joe Collins was everyone's friend. I thought he was a terrific ballplayer. Casey sometimes frowned on him, though. I never quite understood that. Gerry Coleman was the same type of man as Collins. He was an outstanding second baseman. The best double-play man in the business.

Billy Martin was Casey's favorite. He was a fighter. He still is. He was a good instigator. He wasn't, and isn't, the biggest in size, but he wouldn't, and he still doesn't, back away. And Rizzuto was a lot of fun. He was teased and tormented a lot, especially by Tommy Byrne.

Bobby Brown and Gil McDougald were great competitors. They were their own worst enemies if they didn't do well. Yogi Berra was "as dumb as a fox." When I pitched, I never shook him off. I don't think he has an enemy in the world. He didn't speak much with anyone. But he didn't speak against anyone, either. The "Big Three" were bear-down guys. Vic

Raschi was a great competitor. He hated to lose, more so than most people do. Allie Reynolds was a stubborn Indian. He would fight anyone. Argue, too. Casey included. He accepted challenges. For example, in the bullpen. He did well, too. Especially in the big games. Eddie Lopat was, and is, one happy, congenial fellow. He talked to everyone and he still does. He was a little cocky, but that was good for a pitcher. Hank Bauer was a battler. I could understand why he was a tough sergeant in the service. Like Reynolds, he would accept any challenge. And I wouldn't be the one to challenge him.

Casey was something else. He made some decisions which, when he made them, were questionable; but he always ended up holding a bouquet of roses. People build him up as a psychologist, but he never used psychology on me. Charlie Silvera once said to me, "We have a bunch of guys on the bench that would be first-string players in any other city." He had the personnel.

With the Browns I was a starter and a reliever. When I joined the Yankees, I was assigned to the bullpen. Occasionally, I got a spot start.

There wasn't much instruction down in the bullpen. Jim Turner, the pitching coach, was always in the dugout. They might ask Allie how to pitch certain hitters. But if I got in the game, I would pitch the hitters differently. I had a different style than he did. He depended mainly on his fastball. I relied on my curve. The pitching coach would keep track of how many pitches you threw in the bullpen. But it was pretty difficult to count them from the dugout. So he would talk to the bullpen catcher. He would tell the truth. The pitcher would sometimes alibi.

The bullpen is the worst place in the world to

watch a game. You're better off watching it on television. It's hard to see a play clearly, and quite often you're distracted by the guy sitting beside you. It's the bullpen, so you spend most of the time throwing the bull. Once in a while you second-guess a play, but mainly you relax and wonder if and when you're going to get in.

My best year was 1951, when I won six, lost four, and had five saves. In fact, before the World Series, one of the players came up to me and said, "You're going to start against the Giants." But it never came to be. I pitched two innings in that World Series, and I gave up just one hit. I can't remember the game. You're taking me back too many years. I'm like the absent-minded professor. I do remember it was in the Polo Grounds, though. [It was in Game Three, a 6–2 loss to the host Giants.]

The Yankee game that most stands out in my mind took place in 1951, I think. I remember when we were headed from New York to Cleveland, the entire bullpen staff was instructed to get rest because one of us was going to start against the Indians. The starter was to be notified in the clubhouse before the second game of the doubleheader. Stubby Overmire was selected and he pitched a beautiful game. Against Early Wynn. Going into the seventh inning, the game was scoreless. But the Indians got a runner on third with one out. Casey wanted to make a change. I figured he wouldn't use a second left-hander in a row. But they signaled for me. The first batter popped out to third, and the second hitter flied out to right. I thought that that would be the end of my appearance since I was the first man to come up to bat in the eighth. But I grabbed a bat and got into the on-deck circle, thinking I would be called back. So I was putting on the dog and squeezing out the sawdust, waiting for voices behind me. But I never heard any. So I got into the batter's box. Here I am batting probably minus-zero at the time, and Casey permitted me to bat. Why? I never found out.

Early pitched to me and, to my surprise, I singled between first and second. Phil sacrificed me to second, and Gene Woodling, the old Indian killer, hit a home run, and we won, 2–0. It was an important win, because it was late in the year, and the pennant was on the line.

I stayed with the Yankees through the 1952 season. Then I was sold to the Los Angeles Angels in the Pacific Coast League, where I played for one year before I hung up my spikes.

It was time to resume my teaching career fulltime. I taught for 25 more years, until 1978, when I retired. I coached the baseball team for five years at Wyoming Area High. I had one pennant winner. My toughest experience was coaching my youngest son, Joe, Jr. If I played him, I didn't know whether I'd be accused of favoring him. If I didn't play him, I didn't know whether my son might think I didn't like him.

He turned out all right, though. He's a civil engineer. My other two sons turned out well, too. Paul, my oldest, is a chemist. Billy, who went to Penn on a football scholarship, is a mechanical engineer.

Would you believe $8,500 was my top salary in baseball? In 1951 and 1952. All my negotiating was done by mail. I never got to see the big guys. I dealt with the little guys. If I sent an offer back, which I usually did, the usual excuse which I received from one of the front office workers was, "The stars got all the money, and there's nothing left for you."

Today's salaries? Well, I envy them. But if they're getting them, whether they deserve them or not, more power to them. It's up to the owners to decide, not me.

When I retired, I only had four-and-one-half years in. You needed five at that time to be eligible for a pension. But in 1978, when I went back to Yankee Stadium for Old Timers' Day, I talked to Charlie Silvera.

"Do you get a pension?" he said.

"No, I'm not eligible," I said. "I only have four-and-a-half years."

"Do you know that four years is the present requirement?" he asked me.

"Yes, but when I retired, it was five, so I thought I wasn't eligible."

"I know two players who have four years, and they're getting it."

So I wrote a letter to Al Rosen, who was the president of the Yankees at the time, and he started the ball rolling. In 1979 I started receiving my pension.

I love retirement. I'm still a crossword puzzle addict, I read the papers, and I like to walk. I used to have a garden, but I can't anymore. In 1985 I was in the hospital twice—once to have an arterial bypass in my right leg, because of poor circulation, and the other time to have a large toe amputated, because of gangrene. And I've been a diabetic since 1969.

But I'm enjoying the quiet life. As I said, life's very quiet up here. It's just a small, quiet town. You're the first writer who's ever tracked me down. The three autographed balls I signed for your sons are the first balls I've signed since I left the Yankees.

I don't see any of my former teammates. Once I saw Lopat at a game at the Stadium. He hasn't changed. The only other time that I saw any of them was at that Old Timers' Day game in 1978.

Funny thing, not all of them remembered me. I saw Phil Rizzuto standing near me and I said, "Hello, Phil, how are you?"

He said, "I don't remember you."

"I'm Joe Ostrowski," I said.

He replied, "I still don't remember you."

Well, I played with him for two-and-one-half years. But I wasn't hurt. It was no big deal, I guess.

But the *Big Fellow* remembered me. DiMag knew who I was. *That* was a big deal.

Bob Kuzava

Bob Kuzava spent eight years in the minor leagues. But when he finally got to the major leagues, he became an impact pitcher with the Washington Senators. He was happy. He liked manager Bucky Harris, he liked the city, and he liked the low-key atmosphere surrounding the team.

But suddenly, before the trading deadline in 1951, he was dealt to the Yankees. Before the trade, he was injured. He was physically hurt. After the trade, he was emotionally hurt. He didn't want to leave the Senators. He didn't want to go to the Yankees. In Washington he had been loose; in New York there would be pressure to produce.

It didn't take him long to absorb that Yankee pride, though. First, he had played with many of his new Yankee teammates in the minors. Second, he quickly became accustomed to the competition. Every opponent played hard against the Yankees. The Bombers always faced the other team's best trio of pitchers, like Bob Lemon, Early Wynn, and Mike Garcia of the Indians. In the World Series the Giants and the Dodgers were just as formidable. That kind of competition builds team camaraderie—and success breeds success.

Kuzava recorded a 5–1 mark in relief, a 3–3 log in spot starts, and a save in the final game of the 1951 World Series. He was happy again. He felt he had contributed.

The following year he was pitching in the wrong place (Ebbets Field) at the wrong time (with the bases loaded in the seventh game of the World Series). With one out in the seventh, Casey Stengel went against the book. He signaled to the bullpen for left-hander Kuzava to come in to face Duke Snider and Jackie Robinson with the bases loaded. The Dodgers were notoriously deadly against left-handed pitching especially at Ebbets Field. If the move backfired, Stengel would have been second-guessed from Flatbush to Gerard avenues. But Kuzava pitched out of the jam, retired each of the eight batters he faced, and saved the final game of the World Series for a record second year in a row. Casey's hunch and Bob's performance defied all baseball logic.

Bob Kuzava pitched with the Yankees until the second half of the 1954 season, when he was dealt to the White Sox. He was physically and emotionally hurt again. He didn't want to leave the Yankees. Bob Kuzava pitched for eight major-league teams in 10 seasons, but in his three years with the Yankees, he had gone full circle.

Bob has been happily married for more than forty years, and has five children—two boys and three girls—and six grandchilden. After he hung up his spikes, he scouted for a decade. Then he went into the beer business and became a driver and salesman for Molson Black Label for a dozen years. Now retired, he lives in Wyandotte, Michigan.

I played my first year of professional ball with Mansville, Ohio, in 1941. Class D ball. It took me eight seasons to put in a full year in the majors. There were so many ballplayers in the minor leagues in those days. The competition was so intense. You could hit .300 every year and not move. Murry Dickson won 27 and 25 games in back-to-back years and didn't move.

Of course, I spent three years with the Army in World War II. Military police. My tours of duty were India, Burma, and China. That's where I got the name " Sarge."

I came up through the Cleveland chain, but I wasn't happy with the organization. So I told Bill Veeck to trade me if he got the opportunity. He got the chance late in 1948 and sent me to the White Sox on December 2. We had a pretty good club, but we finished sixth. Cass Michaels, Luke Appling, and Gus Zernial each hit over .300. Bill Wight won 15 games; Randy Gumpert, 13. Billy Pierce was just breaking in. He struggled with a 7–15 record. I ended up with 10 wins and six losses.

I got off slow in 1950, though. I was 1–3 at the trading deadline. So they dealt me to Washington for Eddie Robinson. I enjoyed myself in Washington. Bucky Harris was a great guy to play for. And we had some pretty good players: Mickey Vernon, Michaels (who had come over from Chicago, too), Eddie Yost, Irv Noren, and Gil Coan. The pitching wasn't deep, though. Sid Hudson was the only pitcher in double-figure wins. He ended up 14–14. I was 8–7. We finished fifth.

At the trading deadline in 1951, the Yankees gave up Bob Porterfield, Fred Sanford, Tom Ferrick, a minor leaguer, and $100,000 for me. I never could understand that trade. I was on crutches at the time. In a contact play with Nellie Fox, I cut my Achilles tendon. The news of my injury came as a shock to George Weiss. But I joined the club and Jim Turner put me in the bullpen. That's how I became a relief pitcher. That year I was 5–1 as a short reliever and 3–3 as a spot starter for the Yankees.

Actually I wasn't too elated with the trade. Washington was one big happy family. Bucky Harris was a great guy. I was king of the hill. I pitched every three or four days. The money was good. I loved the city. There wasn't too much press. And you didn't have to win. In New York you had to win. You couldn't finish second in those days. There was too much media pressure. The Giants and Dodgers were fighting the Yankees for the fan's dollar. But Washington needed bodies and money. So I was sold to New York. It wasn't so bad, though. I had played with Gene Woodling, Gerry Coleman, Allie Reynolds, and Cliff Mapes in the minors. It took me only a couple of weeks to blend in.

The year turned out to be a great one for me. I was 8–4 with the Yankees. Being on the best team in the world and contributing to it made me feel pretty good. Being connected with the Yankees made me feel pretty good, too. They were class people. One by one, they cared.

Meeting Joe DiMaggio was such a great experience. He was a wonderful guy. Very impressive. He would hit 460-foot fly balls that were caught and never bitch. Batters who would hit .230 would fly out 400 feet and scream. He did a lot of favors for people, but he never wanted to be thanked. One time I needed theater tickets. I think it was *South Pacific*. I couldn't get them, though.

Frank Shea said, "Ask Joe. He'll get them for you." So I asked him.

He said, "Let me make a phone call."

I went to the theater. The tickets were at the

window. Two tickets in an envelope reserved for "Bob Kuzava."

"How much?" I asked.

"No charge," I was told. "If you want to pay for them, you can't have them."

George Solitaire, the ticket agent, was his friend. He was connected with Lionel trains, too. I know Joe was instrumental in getting trains for his teammates' kids at Christmas. At maybe cost. He was a super guy.

The highlight of the 1951 season for me came in the final game of the World Series. Against the Giants. Casey brought me in to relieve Johnny Sain in the top of the ninth inning. We were winning 4–1, but the Giants had the bases loaded and no outs. Monte Irvin hit a long fly ball to Woodling in left. One run scored and the other two runners advanced a base. Bobby Thomson followed with another long fly to Woodling. Another run scored. Both balls were well hit. But this wasn't the Polo Grounds. In Yankee Stadium they were just long outs. The score was now 4–3 with the tying run in scoring position. Sal Yvars pinch-hit for Hank Thompson and sliced a low line drive to right. He hit the ball good. But Bauer made a sliding catch. The stars were with me.

I felt great. It's hard to describe the feeling to a layman. I was happy to get the Giants out, help my teammates out, and collect the $5,000 winning share. Of course, after Uncle Sam got his share, there wasn't too much left. But it was pretty good on top of the $13,000 I was paid that year. My top salary was $20,000. That was pretty good money in those days.

Of course, it's not much compared to today's ridiculous salaries. I don't blame the players, though.

Who would say no to a one-million-dollar contract? But California, with all the money Gene Autry has put out, hasn't won yet. He lays it out, but they can't put it together.

In 1952 I thought I had a good year, too. I was healthy and I finished 8–8. I was mainly a short reliever and a spot starter in doubleheaders. I was the fifth starter, along with Johnny Sain.

We had a tremendous Series that year. It was probably my greatest thrill. The Yankees that year were one of the best clubs I ever saw or played on. They had just about everything: pitching, hitting, power hitting, and defense. Those players went on to win five world titles in a row. That's pretty tough to do when everyone's shooting for you. Brooklyn had a terrific club. But so did Cleveland during the regular season.

Whenever we played the Indians, we always saw the same three guys: Bob Lemon, Early Wynn, and Mike Garcia. Whenever we played Detroit, we never saw a second-line pitcher. If a Yankee of those days hit .290, he was really a .330 hitter.

Everyone talks about the seventh game of that year's World Series. With one out and the bases loaded in the bottom of the seventh, Casey called me in from the bullpen to face Duke Snider. On a full count Duke popped out. Jackie Robinson was the next hitter. I ran the count to three-and-two on him, too. Then he hit a pop fly directly over my head. It was tough to get out of the way. I yelled for someone to get it. Finally I called for Joe Collins. But he had lost the ball in the sun. And there's no way I should have been there. Suddenly here comes Billy. I'm thinking there's no way that ball's going to drop.

Then I'm thinking maybe there is. But Billy catches the ball at his knees to end the seventh inning. If he didn't catch that ball, three runs would have scored, and the Dodgers would have won both the game and the World Series.

Looking back, I remember I had good stuff. I wasn't worried too much about Snider. I always had pretty good luck with him. I got away with Robinson, though. The curve was up. He probably wanted it up. He was too anxious, though. Jackie was a great second baseman. He could beat you in so many ways. He didn't have great leg speed, but he worked at it. He was a competitor who wanted to win. In short, he was a great athlete. I'm glad I didn't have to face him again. I worked hard at not seeing him again. I retired eight batters in a row. That was the second year in a row I saved the final game of the World Series. That was a record at that time. What was more important, though, was we were world champs again. Everyone was tickled to death. It meant a lot of money for us.

Casey never got too close to anyone. But he was good to me. Once in a while he would do you a favor. Casey was a psychologist. He would treat everyone differently. And he surrounded himself with good coaches: Bill Dickey, Frank Crosetti, and Jim Turner. He knew who to pat on the back and who to prod. Who can argue with his success? But you had to have the horses. His track record in the National League wasn't so good.

Every once in a while he played hunches. Left-handers were not supposed to win at Ebbets Field. But with the World Series on the line, he brought me in with the bases loaded and one out. And I got them out. He must have known something.

That Stengelese was a media-type thing, though. When he wanted to chew you out, he talked like you and me. One time we had a bad night. Everything went wrong. He's sitting on the bench, and he says to no one in particular, "Instead of reading the sports pages, you guys should be reading the want ads."

Irv Noren and I were roommates. He was a Baptist, I was a Catholic. There were no problems. He was a great guy, hell of an athlete. Good hitter, good fielder. He didn't have a strong arm, but he had an accurate one. He was so good in the minors that Clark Griffith paid $80,000 to Hollywood for him.

My biggest regular-season thrill was a one-hitter I pitched at Yankee Stadium in 1953 against the White Sox. Bob Boyd, a left-handed-hitting outfielder, got a double with one or two out in the ninth. I probably would have made some money if I had gotten the no-hitter. I might have been a guest on the Ed Sullivan *Talk of the Town* show.

I had a good fastball and a good curve that day. I always tried to get ahead of the hitter. First I tried to get strike one on the hitter. Then I tried to make him hit my pitch. In a jam I'd go to the fastball. I stayed in good shape and gave a good effort. That's the way I'd like to be remembered: as a guy who went out every day, and gave one hundred percent, and took pride in being a professional baseball player. And as a good hard-working human who was proud to be a contributor to those clubs.

It's ironic that I wasn't happy when I was traded to the Yankees, and I wasn't happy when I was traded away from the Yankees. The Yankees made a mistake when they traded me. I was hurt; I had pulled a rib-cage muscle when I was hitting fungoes to the outfield one day. The team was on the road, and I was home, taking whirlpool treatments, when I was traded. I should have been on the disabled list. As it turned out, it was ironic that I was hurt when I came to the Yankees, and I was hurt when I was traded away.

You hate to leave such a great group of competitors. Hank Bauer, for example. He was a brawler, a former Marine drill instructor. He was very vocal. You had to know him to like him. He loved life and he lived it to the hilt. But he had great legs and he kept in shape.

Whitey Ford was a mechanic who knew how to pitch. He knew what he was doing all the time. He had a reason for every pitch he threw. He was Irish and he had guts. He was cocky, but not a braggart. Eddie Lopat helped Ford a lot. But Ford was smart enough to listen to Lopat. Whitey was one model being groomed by another.

Allie Reynolds was a real fierce competitor with a great fastball and a great curve. He was mean on the field but he was the opposite off it. He was a first-class guy who was always in condition.

Vic Raschi was a quiet man who on the day of a pitching start was very intense. He wouldn't let anyone take his picture on the day of a game. Casey would nod to Billy Martin, "Go to the mound."

Vic would say, "Go back to second. You have enough trouble playing your position. Don't ever tell me how to pitch."

Billy would plead with Casey. "Don't ever tell me to go to the mound again. He'll punch me in the head."

Mickey Mantle was cut out of the same mold. I

watched his 565-foot home run go right past me in the bullpen at Griffith Stadium. I was sitting with Ralph Houk and Charlie Silvera. The wind was blowing out and he hit a blast across the street. We couldn't believe the shot he hit. Red Patterson, the traveling secretary, claimed he found it three or four yards across the street. I never saw a ball hit so far. You could have cut it up into 15 singles.

Yogi Berra

Yogi Berra never led the American League in any conventional single-season offensive statistic. But he was consistently solid.

Career-wise, he batted. 285, hit 358 homers, and drove home 1,430 runs. In single seasons he hit 20 or more home runs in each year from 1949–58. He clubbed a career-high 30 round-trippers in both 1952 and 1956. During the 1949–53 world title run, he averaged a .292 mark, 26 home runs, and 102 RBI. His best all-round season was in 1952 when he batted .322, banged 28 circuit clouts, and scored 124 runs. Overall, he hit more career home runs as a catcher than anyone except Johnny Bench.

Despite getting off to a rocky start behind the plate, he was a steady defensive player too. Many people know he failed to throw out Al Gionfriddo at second base to lock up Bill Bevens' no-hit bid in the 1947 World Series, and many people know he failed to catch Ted Williams' first foul pop to nail down Allie Reynolds' second no-hitter of the 1951 season. But not too many people know he played a record 148 straight games behind the plate in 1958 and 1959 without an error. He fielded an incredible 1.000 in

1958 and an almost equally remarkable .997 in 1959. In two seasons he made two errors. Ironically, those were his last two full seasons behind the plate.

Yogi Berra never led the American League in any single-season offensive category. But he was, according to Paul Richards, the best eighth-inning hitter in baseball. And he did play on a record 14 pennant winners.

Yogi Berra never led players in any single-season World Series offensive category, either. But he did get a lot of all-time firsts.

In 1947 he became the first rookie in the history of the Fall Classic to hit a pinch-hit home run. Overall, he played in a record 14 World Series, participated in a record 75 games, went to the plate a record 259 official times, delivered a record 71 hits, and banged a record 10 doubles.

He also produced a couple of seconds and thirds. His 41 runs scored and 39 runs batted in rank second on the all-time list; his 32 bases on balls and 12 home runs rank third on the all-time list. He was, according to Gil McDougald, the best hitter in baseball when the game was on the line. And he played on a record 10 Fall Classic winners.

Since his playing days, Yogi has managed and coached successful teams in New York, where he led both the Mets and the Yankees to the World Series, and Houston, where he is still a coach with the Astros. He's even started a career as a television film critic. Always accompanied by Carmen, his loving wife of over forty years, Yogi has become a unique repository of winning baseball knowledge.

Which brings to mind something that John Thompson, the basketball coach of the United States' 1988 Olympic Team, recently said during the team's tryouts: "We have a number of all-star players trying out for the team. But I don't want an all-star team. I want a winning team."

Yogi Berra was unique. He was an all-star. But more importantly, he was a winner.

The "Peer of the Nation's Sportscasters," Mel Allen has coined some of the most descriptive player nicknames during the modern era.

Bucky Harris was fired as the Yankee manager when his team lost the 1948 pennant race in the last weekend of the season. If the Yankees had won that pennant, Harris, not Stengel, might have been the manager of the 1949–53 Yankees.

Casey Stengel doesn't look happy about his seventieth birthday party at Yankee Stadium on July 30, 1960. Perhaps he knew it was a farewell get-together.

(Left) Mickey Mantle, a nineteen-year-old phenom during spring training of 1951, looks ready to measure off 536 regular-season home runs and a record 18 World Series clouts. *(Right)* Joe DiMaggio fights back tears during his retirement announcement following the 1951 season. In the background a younger "Yankee Clipper" looks toward personal and team success: a .325 lifetime batting average with 361 home runs and nine world championships.

(Above) In eight seasons with the Yankees, Vic Raschi never missed a starting turn. Consistency was his trademark; from 1949–51 he won 21 games each year. *(Below)* Allie Reynolds was at the top of his form in World Series play. He won seven games, saved four, and finished with a 2.79 ERA in six successful World Series.

In his eight seasons with the Yankees, Eddie Lopat won 113 games and lost just 59, an average of just seven defeats a season. His best season was in 1953 when he posted a 16-4 record while leading the league in winning percentage (.800) and ERA (2.42).

(Left) In his nine-year major-league career Tom Ferrick spent back-to-back full seasons with only one club, the 1947–48 Senators. Overall, he posted a 40-40 record with 56 saves. Eight of those wins and eleven of those saves were recorded with the 1950 Yankees, with whom he pitched the better half of a season. *(Right)* Whitey Ford pitched and won the final game of the Yankees' 1950 sweep of the Phillies in the World Series. In that season, rookie Ford won 9 of 10 decisions. Overall, he won 236 games and lost 106 for a winning percentage of .690, tops for any pitcher with 200 or more lifetime wins.

Tommy Byrne first caught Yankee attention when he was a pitcher at Wake Forest College in Winston-Salem, North Carolina. Here he is as a sophomore in 1939.

One of the reasons Casey Stengel liked Charlie Silvera as a backup catcher to Yogi Berra was that he didn't mind putting "his nose in the dirt," as he did in this play against the Senators.

(Left) Charlie Silvera. *(Right)* Yogi Berra batted .293 and averaged 26 home runs per season during the Yankees' 1949–53 era. In his career he hit .285 and slugged 358 round-trippers.

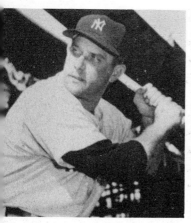

(Left) Gene Woodling played in five world championships during his six years in the Bronx. After a sub-par year in 1954, he was traded to the Orioles in a deal which gave the Bombers Bob Turley and Don Larsen. Woodling went on to have his best seasons when he was between 35 and 40. *(Right)* Bobby Brown has risen from World Series hero to president of the American League. Brown hit a record .439 over four World Series.

Billy Johnson was a big RBI man for a hitter with average power. He drove home 94 runs with five home runs in 1943 and 95 runs with ten homers in 1947.

Phil Rizzuto *(left)* and Gerry Coleman, both of whom played on each of the 1949–53 teams, made up one of the best double-play combinations of their time. In 1949 Coleman fielded .981 and Rizzuto .971, league bests at their respective positions.

(Left) Cliff Mapes may be the only player in major-league history to throw out a runner on third base at the plate on a solid hit to right field. He is the only player to have two of his uniform numbers retired. *(Right)* The Yankees traded Frank Shea, Jackie Jensen, and others to the Senators for Irv Noren in 1952. Noren went on to play on three pennant winners and two world championship clubs with the Yankees.

(Left) Billy Martin was the type of player who could get the jump on the opposition. In his three full seasons with the Yankees, he averaged only ten errors a season and never fielded below .980. *(Right)* Johnny Lindell's game-winning home run on the next-to-last day of the 1949 season put the Yankees' five consecutive pennants and world titles into motion. In the 1947 World Series manager Bucky Harris inserted Lindell in left field, and John responded with nine hits in 18 at bats.

Whitey Ford *(left)* and Gil McDougald celebrate a 1951 Yankee victory.

Johnny Sain has been the only pitcher to lead one league in wins (24 with the 1948 Braves) and another loop in saves (22 with the 1954 Yankees).

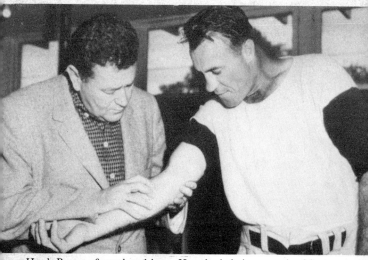

Hank Bauer often played hurt. Here he is being examined by team physician Sydney Gaynor. In fact, just about the only thing that kept Bauer out of the lineup was Stengel's platoon system. But when the money was on the line, he was on the field; the Yankees played 50 World Series games from 1950 to 1958, and Bauer played in 49 of them.

(Left) Joe Collins had a swing tailor-made for Yankee Stadium. During the 1949–53 years, he hit a total of 62 home runs. In Series play, he hit another four. *(Right)* Gil McDougald came up to the Yankees in 1951 with an unorthodox batting stance, but he followed through with a .306 batting average and the Rookie of the Year Award.

Four good gloves in the Yankee lineup belonged to *(from left)* Billy Johnson, Hank Bauer, Gerry Coleman, and Joe Collins, seen here during the 1951 spring training season.

(Left) Many of the Yankee players of the time call Joe Page one of the best relief pitchers they ever saw. In 1947 and 1949, he led American League relievers in wins (a total of 27) and saves (a total of 44). His ERA in those years was 2.48 and 2.59, respectively. *(Right)* Phil Rizzuto *(left)* and George Stirnweiss talk baseball at second base. Stirnweiss was a good wartime player. In 1944 and 1945 he led the league in triples, runs scored, and stolen bases. In 1945 he led the league in batting average and slugging percentage.

(Left) By the time Joe Ostrowski got to the majors, he was thirty-one years old. His best season in his five-year career was 1951 when, as a spot starter and reliever with the Yankees, he posted a 6–4 record with five saves and an ERA of 3.49. (Right) Frank Shea broke into the majors with a bang. In 1947 he won fourteen games and lost five for a winning percentage of .737. In addition, he was the winning pitcher in the All-Star Game, and won both of his decisions in the World Series.

Johnny Mize, Allie Reynolds, and Joe DiMaggio after a 4–2 victory over the Senators in 1951. Mize tied the game, DiMaggio drove in the winning run, and Reynolds allowed only four hits.

The Yankees' broadcasting crew included *(from left)* Phil Rizzuto, Mel Allen, and Red Barber.

(Left) Johnny Mize as a coach for the Yankees in the '50s. He is the only player to have played on five consecutive world championship teams in his last five years in the big leagues. *(Right)* Bob Kuzava had a total of only five saves in the 1951–52 regular seasons. But in the World Series of those years, he became the first of only two pitchers to save the final game of back-to-back Series.

Joe DiMaggio, Mickey Mantle, and Whitey Ford *(left to right)* have many great moments to look back upon at an Old Timers' Day Game at Yankee Stadium. Together, the three played on 21 different pennant winners and 15 different world championship teams.

I got the nickname "Yogi" from a run-of-the-mill movie that took place in India. One of the characters was a sad Hindu monk who was called a yogi. Jack Maguire, the son of the Cardinal scout and later the player with the Giants, said to our friends when we came out of the movie theater, "Look at him. He walks like a yogi and he looks like a yogi. That's a good nickname for him—'Yogi.'" From that day on the name stuck.

My family was against my playing professional baseball. Dad thought any young man who didn't go to work when he got out of school was lazy. I said I would work nights and odd jobs. But I wanted the chance to play baseball. Finally we had a family meeting. The parish priest was even invited. He convinced my family that I should be given a reasonable time to try what I wanted to do. But he got me to agree that if I didn't make it, I would try something that was not baseball.

Joe Garagiola and I were scouted by the Cardinals. The scouts wanted Branch Rickey to sign both of us. He offered Joe a $500 bonus, but he wanted me to sign a contract without a bonus. I refused. First, I wanted at least the same money they offered Joe. I wasn't jealous of him. He lived right across the street from me, and he was my best friend. But on the team we played on, he batted third and I batted fourth. So I figured I was worth at least the same money he was. And second, I knew that if Joe signed for $500 and I signed for nothing, my dad would be convinced that I was following a worthless profession. When I turned down the Cardinal offer, I remember saying, "Joey's good. I'm glad you signed him. But I don't know why you don't want me, too."

I was discouraged. But something that I didn't know anything about happened. Leo Browne, an umpire in the Eastern League, wrote to George Weiss of the Yankees about me. He told him I would sign for $500. After the Yankees lost the 1942 World Series to the Cardinals, Weiss sent Johnny Schulte, their bullpen coach, to see me. I signed for a $500 bonus and $90 a month to play for Norfolk, Virginia, in the Piedmont League. Just before I left for training camp, I received a telegram from Branch Rickey, who had just left the Cardinals to take a similar job with the Dodgers. He asked me to report to Bear Mountain, New York, where the Dodgers were training. He wanted me to sign a bonus contract. Some people said he hadn't wanted to sign me to a Cardinal contract because he'd known that he was switching to the Dodgers. I don't know about that. All I know is that I never found out what the bonus figure was. I already belonged to the Yankees.

But World War II was going on, and I spent the next three years in the service. In 1945, before I got discharged, I was playing for the base team in New London, Connecticut. One day we played the Giants, and I got three hits off Ace Adams. Mel Ott, their manager, was impressed. He offered Larry McPhail $50,000 for me. McPhail didn't even know who I was, but he figured if Ott thought I was worth $50,000, I must be somebody. He called me to New York, talked to me, and assigned me to the Newark Bears in the International League for the 1946 season. I batted .314, hit 15 homers, and was called up to the Yankees for the last week of the season. In my first game I hit a home run off Jesse Flores of the Athletics. In the seven games I played, I hit two homers, drove home four runs, and batted .364. I went home to "The Hill" in St. Louis pretty happy. Joey did, too. In 1946 he was the starting catcher for the world champion Cardinals. He batted .316 against the Red Sox in the World Series. In one of the games he got four hits. That was a record for a rookie.

The Yankees had a lot of depth at catching when I reported to training camp in 1947. They had Aaron Robinson, Charlie Silvera, Gus Niarhos, and Ralph Houk. But I was lucky. I could play the outfield and some of the regulars were hurting. Joe DiMaggio had a sore heel and Tommy Henrich had a bad knee. My timing was right. With my manager, too. Bucky Harris was the new manager of the Yankees. The year before, when I was at Newark, he was the general manager at Buffalo in the International League. He knew I could hit. That spring the Yankees picked up Joe Medwick, the old Cardinal who was reaching the end of the road. He had just been released by the Dodgers. Harris asked Medwick to give me some tips in the outfield to prevent me from getting killed out there. It's funny the way things worked out. When I was a kid on "The Hill," Medwick used to buy papers from me.

We were supposed to open the 1947 season in Washington on a Monday; but it rained, so we returned to New York for the home opener on Tuesday. Former President Herbert Hoover threw out the first pitch. That was the best pitch I saw all day. I played right field and went oh-for-four against Phil Marchildon of the Athletics. He beat us 6–1. In the postponed opener, which we played on Friday, I did much better. President Harry Truman threw out the first ball that day. I don't know if I could have hit that pitch, but I did pretty well against Bobo Newsom.

I tried to go with the pitch, and I got four hits: one to left, one to center, and two to right.

In the World Series that year I had a tough time. I batted just .158 with only three hits in 19 at bats. Bucky Harris decided to put me behind the plate, and play Johnny Lindell in the outfield with DiMaggio and Henrich. That was a good move on Bucky's part. Johnny hit .500 in six games. But the other part of the move wasn't so good. I struggled behind the plate. In Game One I went oh-for-four, and Jackie Robinson and Pee Wee Reese stole off me. In Game Two I didn't do much better. But at least we won both games. Bucky sat me down in Game Three. He used Sherman Lollar instead. We lost a wild game. I closed the score to 9–8 when I pinch hit a home run in the seventh inning against Ralph Branca. Then Hugh Casey came in and closed the door on us, but I was happy that I had finally done something right. The hit set a record. It was the first pinch-hit home run by a rookie in World Series history.

But I was back in the dumps the next day. That was the game that Bill Bevens lost his no-hitter and the game on the last pitch to Cookie Lavagetto. We got a run in the first and another in the fourth. They got one in the fourth on two walks and a steal by Pee Wee. On the play I threw the ball into center field. So it was 2–1 going to the bottom of the ninth. With two outs and a runner on first, Al Gionfriddo stole second. My throw to Phil Rizzuto was high. Then Bucky decided to walk Pete Reiser, who had a bad ankle. Bucky was criticized later. You're not supposed to put the winning run on base. But Bucky knew they didn't have any more lefties on the bench and Eddie Stanky, a weak hitter, was at the plate.

Burt Shotton put Lavagetto up as a pinch-hitter. Cookie was the most surprised guy in the park. He thought Shotton wanted him to run for Reiser. During the season he played in only 41 games. He batted .261 and hit only one double. So what'd he do? He doubled off the right-field wall to end one of the most dramatic games in World Series history.

I sat out Game Five. Aaron Robinson started in my place. We won 2–1. In Game Six I got in when Lindell got hurt, and I got two hits. But we lost 8–6. I was happy that Bucky started me in Game Seven. I didn't do anything, but Joe Page came on in relief for Bevens, who had relieved Frank Shea, and pitched strong relief in a 5–2 win. It was old hat for the Yankees. It was their eleventh world championship. But it was a big thing to me. It was my first. My World Series check was for $5,830, which was $830 more than I had gotten for the entire season. It was a lot of money. I took the check home to St. Louis and showed it to Mom and Dad. Suddenly baseball no longer seemed like a worthless profession to them.

In 1948 I had a tough time behind the plate. But in 1949 Casey Stengel became the manager, he brought Bill Dickey in with him, and Dickey turned things around for me. He worked on my mechanics and my confidence. He told me, "Take pride in your position. It's the best job in baseball. Look at all the .220 hitters who have been in the league for over 10 years. The way you can hit, you can last forever behind the plate. All you have to do is learn the mechanics." Right away he noticed I was standing too far behind the batters, and I wasn't shifting my weight right on my throws. He showed me how to judge pop flies hit directly over my head and how to gauge the movement of throws from the outfield.

He also got me off my heels on throws to the bases. That's why my throws were sailing. He taught me to get up on my toes and take a short step forward before I released the ball. He also showed me how to throw the ball from behind my ear with lots of wrist action on it. And for the first time in my life, I knew where the ball was going before I released it.

Dickey was always telling me to be heads-up behind the plate. On July 4, 1949, I made a play that made him proud of me. I was pretty proud myself. It happened in the first game of a doubleheader against the Red Sox. In the top of the ninth inning, the Red Sox loaded the bases against Vic Raschi. Then Al Zarilla lined a single in front of Cliff Mapes in right field. Johnny Pesky, who was on third, thought Cliff was going to catch the ball, so he held up. When the ball dropped, Pesky broke for the plate; but Mapes, who had a powerful arm, threw a bullet to me. It sailed so I had to catch it like a first baseman, but I grabbed it before Pesky's foot hit the plate. There were 63,000 people in Yankee Stadium that day, but it seemed like I was the only one who knew that it was a force play. "He's out!" I screamed at home plate umpire Joe Paparella. "It's a force play. I don't have to tag him. The throw beat him. He's out."

Paparella seemed confused. He hesitated. Finally he said, "By God, you're right. He is out." Raschi then got Bobby Doerr to fly out to Mapes to end the game.

Until that day I was known as a good-hitting catcher. But after that play I gradually began to get the reputation as a good defensive catcher, too. Dickey reminded the reporters after the game, "I've been telling you that Yogi's going to be the best defensive catcher in the game. He might be right now."

When we beat the Red Sox in that doubleheader, they were 12½ games back. We were coasting. It continued that way until August 7, when we trounced the Browns in the first game of a doubleheader, 20–2. But a beanball war erupted. Dick Starr and Karl Drews of the Browns hit me, Henrich, Gerry Coleman, and Gus Niarhos. Starr's pitch broke my left thumb. Tommy Byrne, our pitcher, tried to retaliate, but he was so wild that he couldn't hit anyone.

But Casey acted like I got hit on purpose. Every day he was on my case, making sure I ran in the outfield and telling me to make sure that I shook hands with all of my fans with my left hand. That way, he said, I would get some exercise for my bad thumb. While I was out of the lineup, big stories about me appeared in *Life, Look,* and *Collier's.* That made Casey even madder. His needle got sharper. The players picked up on it. Billy Johnson suggested that maybe I should get only a half-share of the World Series cut that year. Finally I got back in the lineup on September 7. Good thing. The Red Sox had closed our lead to 1½ games, and Henrich, DiMaggio, and Mize were hurting. That Sunday I got three hits, including a homer and a double. I was relieved. For the first time in a month I had made a contribution, and Casey wasn't on my back anymore.

The season came down to the last two games. The Red Sox had taken a one-game lead with two games to play at the Stadium. It was very dramatic. Saturday was "Joe DiMaggio Day." Joe came out of a sick bed for his day and to play. In the ceremonies before the game, Mayor William O'Dwyer said, "You came here from San Francisco, but after today you will never leave New York."

Then it was Joe's turn. He said, "I thank the good

Lord for making me a Yankee. Lefty O'Doul told me many years ago, 'Don't let the big town scare you. New York is the most generous town in the world.' Well, this day proves it. . . ." Then he nodded to the Red Sox dugout and said to Joe McCarthy, his favorite manager, "If we can't win, I'm glad you will."

But we were fortunate enough to win both games. Each of them went down to the final out. After the last game McCarthy came in to congratulate Casey, Joe, and some of his former players. He was standing right by my locker. A writer said to him, "Too bad you had to lose the pennant in one game."

"Yes," he said, "but we had 153 games to win it."

In 1950 I had maybe my best all-round year. I batted .322, I drove home 124 runs, and I hit 28 home runs. But as a team we had to battle from behind. Until the All-Star Game, the Tigers led by three to four games. But a few things turned us around. Johnny Mize had been sent to Kansas City for a month to work out his bad shoulder. When he came back, he got hot for a month, and Casey put him in the cleanup spot, dropping Joe to fifth. Johnny really had an easy swing, but he had pop in his bat. But then Joe got hot and no one could get him out. And Whitey Ford came up from Binghamton and won nine of 10 games. We beat the Tigers out by three games.

In 1951 we finished five games in front of Cleveland. We clinched the pennant in a doubleheader victory over the Red Sox at Yankee Stadium on September 28. Allie Reynolds clinched a tie for the pennant, and Vic Raschi wrapped it up in the nightcap. It's the first game that I'll never forget, though; Reynolds pitched his second no-hitter of the year. I caught his first one in Cleveland, too. He beat Bob

Feller, 1–0. Gene Woodling won it with a home run. In the second no-hitter Allie had to get Ted Williams for the final out—twice! The first time Ted hit a towering pop foul over by our dugout. But I dropped it. I wanted to crawl into a hole and die. Then Ted hit one in the same spot again. I prayed all the time the ball was coming down. At the last second I lunged and grabbed the ball. My prayers were answered.

What did I say to a pitcher who got in trouble? Well, it depended on who was pitching. If it was Vic Raschi, I would try to get him mad. I'd say, "You're supposed to be a pro. But you can't throw a strike when you need one." Vic was a competitor. You wanted to fire him up. Whitey Ford, too. I'd say, "You're supposed to be our stopper, but you can't throw a strike. Get the goddamn ball over the plate." He'd yell back at me and I knew the batter was in trouble. Bob Turley was different. You had to baby him. I'd say, "C'mon, Bob, you still have your good stuff. Let's get this hitter out and get an early dinner tonight." You had to reassure Bob. He needed encouragement.

One day Tommy Byrne had a shutout late in the game when he walked a couple of consecutive batters. Casey came out to the mound and asked Tommy how he felt. Tommy said, "I'm okay. I can finish." Casey wasn't sure. But I thought Tommy still had good stuff, so I said, "He's okay, Case."

The Old Man turned to me and said, "If you think he's all right, that's all I need to hear." Case left Tommy in and he completed the shutout. But I was a little nervous afterwards, hoping that my word and Tommy's arm would be good enough.

In 1953 I had a good all-round year. That's the year when we won our fifth consecutive World Series. I batted .296, I hit 27 homers, and I drove home 108 runs. Also, I batted .429 in the World Series. Until that year I had never batted well in the World Series. That was the first time I batted over .300. I made two big plays, too. In Game One I threw out two consecutive runners at third base on sacrifice-bunt attempts. It was demoralizing to the Dodgers. They didn't seem to get over it.

That year we beat the Dodgers in the World Series for the fourth time during my career. It didn't seem that they would ever beat us. They were always saying, "Wait till next year." Well, "next year" came in 1955. I guess they were due. We played most of the Series without Mantle and Bauer. That's no excuse, though. The Dodgers played well and deserved it. They made great plays and capitalized on opportunities. And Johnny Podres was sensational. Personally I had a good Series. I batted .417 and got 10 hits, but I would have traded all of them for a little luck on the ball Sandy Amoros caught. But give Podres and Amoros credit. They did what they had to do to win. And they came up with two of the greatest performances in World Series history.

The Dodger lineup was tough from top to bottom. They liked the ball up high so we tried to keep it down. We tried to pitch Hodges away all the time. When we did come inside, we made it a bad pitch. He was a strict pull hitter. We kept the ball down on Jackie and changed up on him. He held his hands up very high and had trouble getting them down to hit the low pitch. Pee Wee was tough to pitch to. He had a good eye and would wait for his pitch. So we mixed up the pitches and tried to move it around on him. We gave Billy Cox breaking pitches, too, trying to keep him off balance.

Snider took big swings and tried to hit everything for distance. He liked the ball out over the plate and had good power to left center. We pitched him in tight and tried to shorten up his swing. But he hit over .300 in four consecutive World Series against us, so I guess we weren't too successful against him. Furillo could hit to all fields, but he had better power going the opposite way. We tried to pitch him inside. Campanella liked the ball up around his eyes. We would pitch him tight and then pitch him away. We wanted him to go reaching. We were pretty successful with him.

I called the signals in the only perfect game in World Series history. But give Don Larsen the credit for that one. He was the guy who was perfect that day. He got pretty good support, too. McDougald made two good plays and Mantle made one, too. But Don had a great fastball and pinpoint control. He showed that to Dale Mitchell, the last hitter. We went fastball, slider, fastball, fastball, curve. Before the last pitch Don shook me off twice. That was set up in advance. We had Dale guessing. He was looking fastball and Don gave him a curve. It was still pretty amazing. Dale only struck out about 10 times a year. And we got him to look at a third strike. As I said, give Don credit!

I had good success against Don Newcombe. I hit three home runs against him in the 1956 World Series. But make sure you say he was a good pitcher. He won 27 games that year. They say I hit two bad pitches for home runs in Game Seven. But I don't know. Newk made two good pitches. They were pitching me outside, because they didn't want me to pull the ball. But I adjusted my stance and was able to get around on pitches that were away. Trotting around the bases the second time, I yelled at him, "Don't hang your head, Newk. It was a good pitch." But I don't think he felt any better about it.

After Larsen pitched his perfect game, I called home. Mom asked me to hit a home run in Game Six. I said I would. But Clem Labine shut us out in 10 innings, 1–0. So my promise was one day late, but I hit two home runs instead of one. Mom was doubly proud of me!

Looking back on my career, I'm proud, too. The writers described me as a funny person. But that wasn't the case at all. No one was ever more serious about baseball than me, and no one in baseball ever worked harder to succeed. Dad thought that baseball was going to make me turn out bad. But I don't know. I think baseball helped me to turn out pretty good. Some people thought that I was going to remain a bad catcher. But I think I turned out pretty good there, too. It didn't happen by accident, though. It happened through hard work. Also, professional pride. I was proud to be a major-league player, and I was proud to be a Yankee. All of my teammates were proud of our winning tradition. We wanted to continue it. In order to do it, we knew that we all had to contribute. We had to do our part. When I look back, I like to think that I did mine.

Cliff Mapes

      The father of Cliff Mopes, like the fathers of
many players in this book, made tremendous personal sacri-
fices to give his son the chance to play baseball. Cliff's dad,
who loved baseball, didn't get a chance to pursue it because
he was the oldest of ten children and he had to work to help
support the family, But he vowed that if he ever had a boy,
he would move to California because of the favorable baseball climate. Well, soon after Cliff was born his father
pulled up stakes and moved to California. Father and son
would play catch until dark every night. And while they
played, they would dream of Cliff's playing in bigger parks
in bigger cities.

    Then one day in 1948, Cliff came up through the tunnel
at Yankee Stadium, looked up in awe at the three-tier park,
and realized the stadium was bigger than any of the ones he
had imagined. "It was unreal," Cliff mused. "But it was
real, too, because I got there. I was living my dreams."

    He soon came back to reality though. He had to beat out
some big names for a spot in the lineup—names like Joe
DiMaggio, Charlie Keller, Tommy Henrich, Johnny Lindell,
and Hank Bauer. Later the names of Gene Woodling,

Mickey Mantle, and Jackie Jensen. But Cliff got good playing time. In 1949 and 1950 he played in 111 and 108 games, respectively, Followers of the sport remember him for two defensive plays in two big games against the Red Sox in 1949. In one of them, he threw out a runner from third at the plate on a single to right field. In the second game, with the pennant at stake on the final day of the season, Casey Stengel inserted him in centerfield as a defensive replacement for the ailing DiMaggio.

Today he's best known for an often-asked trivia question: "Who was the only player to have two of his uniform numbers retired?" The answer of course, is Cliff Mapes. He wore #3 after Babe Ruth and #7 before Mickey Mantle.

But Cliff is proud of his contributions to the Yankees, especially in 1950 when he batted .247, hit 12 home runs, and drove home 61 runs. Sometimes he thinks he might have done better. From a distance the game looks easy, he says. But somehow it's hard to put it all together.

I finally caught up with him in the summer of 1987. I wanted to talk to him about two-platoon baseball. It wasn't Cliff's favorite subject. He didn't like it or Casey Stengel, the manager who popularized it. But he still feels fortunate.

After Cliff left baseball, he worked for a chemical company for 24 years and the state of Oklahoma for five more. Today he's retired, and lives in Pryor, Oklahoma. But one day a week he works for "Meals on Wheels," bringing food to shut-ins. The glow on their faces gives Cliff a bigger thrill than he used to get when he hit the "short porch" at Yankee Stadium. Cliff is once more a part-timer, but this time he loves it.

My dad was a baseball nut. He was the oldest of ten children. Because he had to work to support his family, though, he wasn't able to pursue a baseball career. But he vowed if he ever had a boy, he would move to California because of the good baseball climate. One year he pulled up stakes and we went. He worked with me from the first time that I can remember. After eight hours of hard labor, he would come home and play with me till dark. He was a big, big influence on me.

When you're young, you have so many dreams. My dreams were about making the big leagues. One day in 1948 they came true. I came up through the tunnel at Yankee Stadium and looked up at the three-tiered park. I was in awe. I couldn't imagine a park like that. Yankee Stadium was much larger than my dreams.

In 1948 I didn't think I had a chance to break into the lineup. There were so many great outfielders on that team. Joe DiMaggio ... Charlie Keller ... Tommy Henrich ... Johnny Lindell ... Hank Bauer. But there were a few injuries and I got some playing time. In 1949 and 1950 I got even more playing time. I played in 111 and 108 games. In 1950 I hit 12 home runs and drove home 61 runs. I feel pretty good about that. I made a contribution to those five consecutive world titles.

In 1949 I played a part in two big games with the Red Sox. That year, you'll remember, we beat the Red Sox out for the pennant by one game. On the last day of the season. So every game with the Red Sox was the equivalent of two games in the standings.

Most of the players you talk to will remember the big hits they made. But my biggest thrill was a defensive play. On a single to right, I threw out a runner who was on third at the plate. The Red Sox, in a key play, had the bases loaded with less than two outs. Al Zarilla lined a one-hop single to me in right. Johnny Pesky was the runner on third base. I didn't even think about him. But Ted Williams was on second. As I charged the ball, I thought, "I got him easy." I got rid of the ball quickly, and Yogi Berra caught the ball like a first baseman. I don't know why Pesky didn't score on the play. Maybe he thought I was going to catch the ball. Joe Paparella, the plate umpire, was confused, too. He called Pesky safe, not realizing that Johnny was out on a force play. Yogi was probably the only one in the park who knew that Pesky was out. He yelled at Paparella, "Force out."

Paparella said, "By God, you're right. He's out."

The second big game against the Red Sox took place on the last day of the season. In a sudden-death situation, with the pennant on the line, we carried a 5–0 lead into the ninth inning. But Vic Raschi tired and Joe DiMaggio failed to catch a ball that was hit by Bobby Doerr. DiMag usually has that ball in his back pocket, but he was hurting. He was battling a bout with pneumonia. Then he signaled to the bench. He couldn't go anymore. So Casey walked over to me and said, "Go out and take Joe's place. He's hurting." I went out there and caught a fly ball. Then, with the tying run at the plate, Vic got Birdie Tebbetts to pop out to Tommy Henrich at first for the game and the pennant. It felt pretty good running off the field that day.

I dressed next to Joe for three years. He was hard to get to know. He was kinda shy. A loner, you know. But a heck of a nice guy. After he got to know you, he would talk with you for hours after the game. Every year at spring training, you couldn't help but be amazed by him. He would pick up a bat for the first time, and you would swear he had never been away.

Keller, Henrich, and Bauer were great guys, too. Three of the greatest I ever met. Henrich didn't have that much natural ability, but he played a long time without it. He compensated for his lack of natural ability with intelligence. He was always thinking, especially in right field. He could play that position blindfolded. He always knew what to do with the ball. Bauer was my buddy with Kansas City in the minors. He gave me my nickname, "Tiger," when I was with Kansas City in 1947. I had a good year and the name stuck.

In the 1949 World Series Hank and I platooned in right field. I played four of the five games. Hank played when Preacher Roe pitched for the Dodgers. I got only one hit in 10 at bats, but it was a double that drove home two runs against Don Newcombe in Game Four. It helped to get Newk out of the game, and we went on to win, 6–4.

I wore two numbers that the Yankees later retired: #3 and #7. But not because of me. Pete Sheehey, the long-time Yankee clubhouse man, liked me. In 1948, when I came up, he gave me #3. That was Babe Ruth's number. I guess Pete figured that we were both right fielders. But the Yankees retired it on June 13 of that year. We beat the Indians that day, 5–3. It was Babe's final appearance at Yankee Stadium. He died on August 16.

Pete gave me #7 when they retired #3. That was the number Mantle made famous. They retired that one, too. But when he came up in 1951, I had #7, so Pete gave Mickey #6. He was just a spindly kid when he came up. But after I was traded to St. Louis, he really developed. And he switched to number #7 and developed that number, too.

The Yankees of those years were as good as they had to be. The tougher the situation, the better we played. We took advantage of mistakes by the other team. If we needed a run, we could get one.

It's no secret that Casey and I didn't get along. I always thought that he favored some players. I guess I was just jealous. But I know I didn't like platoon baseball.

I wasn't the only player who didn't like him. Joe didn't care for him. Phil Rizzuto and Billy Johnson didn't either. There were others, too.

Johnson was a good guy. A good player, too. He had a good glove and a rifle for an arm. He was a good contact hitter, too. He hit into a lot of double plays. That's because he hit the ball so hard. He would hit four line drives in a game and get only one hit. He was the unluckiest hitter I ever saw.

Casey looked better when I got to St. Louis and Detroit, though. Zack Taylor of the Browns didn't know baseball. He was a good boy but he wasn't a baseball man. When I got to Detroit, the Tigers fired Red Rolfe and replaced him with Freddie Hutchinson. Boy, he was a character. He would tear up the clubhouse after a loss. He lived seven miles north of the park, and he would walk home, cussing every step of the way.

After I retired from baseball, I worked for a chemical fertilizer plant for twenty-four years. Then I worked five years for the state. Now I'm enjoying retirement. But one day a week I work for "Meals on Wheels." I bring meals to shut-ins. If you could only see the looks on their faces when I come. They make my day.

Sometimes you wonder why you didn't play better. It looks so easy. But for some reason you just can't put it all together. Still, I've got no regrets. I did my best.

It's like those dreams of youth that I was talking about. Everything comes out right in your dreams. But for me it came out right in life, too. I lived my dreams. I got there.

Johnny Mize

Johnny Mize won four home run races, four slugging percentage titles, and three RBI crowns. Yet Casey Stengel once said, "He hits like a leadoff batter" He was the only player to hit 50 or more home runs and strike out less than 50 times in the same season. Johnny Mize was not baseball's typical player and he did not have baseball's typical career.

He batted .300 nine times in the National League. It could have been more, but he spent three years in the service during World War II. His lifetime average was .312. But in his five years with the Yankees, he hit no higher than .277.

Mize won two home run crowns with the Cardinals and two home run titles with the Giants. His 43 homers in 1940 were the most ever by a St. Louis player. His 51 homers in 1947 were the most ever by a New York Giant player (Willie Mays also hit 51.) In his career he hit 359, including 25 for the Yankees in 1950.

However, in 11 seasons in the National League, he never played on a pennant winner. In five seasons in the American League he played on five world championship teams.

He had better personal success in the National League, but better team success in the American League. Actually, he was the victim of fate in the Senior Circuit. In the six years before he joined the Cardinals, St. Louis won three pennants and two world championships. In the five years after he left the Cardinals, St. Louis won four pennants and three world titles. His timing was no better with the Giants. In the five years after he left the National League, New York won two pennants and one Fall Classic.

In the American League he was the beneficiary of fate. He played on five pennant winners and five world championship teams in his five years with the Yankees—his last five years in the major leagues.

The Johnny Mize who played with the Yankees was not the Johnny Mize who had played with the Cardinals and the Giants. Slowed by age and a bad shoulder, he had to make adjustments, something he had always been able to do. When he played at Sportsman's Park in St. Louis, he tried to hit straightaway because the corners were deep. When he played at the Polo Grounds in New York, he tried to pull the ball because center field was spacious. When he played with the Yankees in the Bronx, he hit according to the situation. He made adjustments. Johnny Mize with the Yankees was no longer a .300 batter. He was no longer a consistent long-ball hitter. But he was still an RBI threat. In 1950 he got 76 hits and 72 RBIs. One year later he had 49 RBIs with 86 hits. He drove home 29 runs with 36 hits in 1952. The following year he scored 27 runs with 26 hits. Overall he drove home 177 runs with 224 hits. And many of those runs were scored in pinch-hitting assignments. In his last three seasons (1951–53) in the major leagues, he led the American League in safe pinch-hits each year.

In his last two years (1952–53) in the majors, Mize hit a total of only eight home runs. But in Game Four of the

1952 World Series, Stengel called on the thirty-nine-year-old veteran to replace the slumping Joe Collins, and "Big John" responded to the challenge. He hit a homer in each of three consecutive games to set a record that has been tied only by Yankees Reggie Jackson and Hank Bauer.

Johnny Mize had to wait 11 major-league seasons before he played in a World Series. But once he got the chance he capitalized on it. He became the only man to play on five consecutive world championship teams in his last five years in the major leagues. After he retired from the game, he had to wait twenty-eight years before be was inducted into the Baseball Hall of Fame.

The first time I contacted him, he said, "I don't have to speak to you writers anymore. I'm in the Hall of Fame now. We did all the heroics on the field, and you guys make all the money writing about it."

A little later I made Johnny Mize the subject of one of the poems in my book about the World Series. I sent him a copy and I guess he liked it. A few days later he called. "I'm ready to talk," he said.

Johnny Mize is proud of his records. He hit at least one home run in every major-league park in use during his playing career; was the only left-handed hitter in the history of the National League to hit 50 or more home runs in one season; was the only batter to hit 50 home runs and strike out less than 50 times in the same season; hit three home runs in a game six times; and bowed out of the majors by playing on five consecutive world championship teams.

"They're records," he said. "Some of them may never be equaled again. That makes me feel very good. If you play the game the way it should be played, you always want to be the best."

Yes, it's nice to look back once in a while, and, yes, there have been some thrills along the way.

Take the 1947 season with the Giants, for example, when I hit 51 home runs. I became the first—and remain the only—left-handed hitter in National League history to hit 50 or more home runs in a season. Roger Maris and Babe Ruth have been the only lefties to do it in the American League. Of course, they both hit 60. And, yes, there is a family connection between Ruth and me. His wife, Clara, was my cousin.

I'm also proud of the fact that during my time I was one of only three players to hit home runs in every major-league park. Including old Baker Bowl in Philadelphia. But Griffith Stadium in Washington was my toughest fence. The distance was 405 feet to the corners, and there was a big wall in right. Finally I got one. Walt Masterson was beating us, 1–0. Casey Stengel sent me up to pinch-hit for Gil McDougald with the bases loaded. I hit a grand slam and we went on to win, 5–1. Never before had I hit one off the wall. Not even in batting practice.

I set another major-league record that I'm proud of: six times I hit three home runs in one game. Five times in the National League and once with the Yankees. The time I did it with the Yankees we lost to Detroit, 9–7. The Tigers had a real good team. One of the homers was off Art Houtterman. He was real tough.

My toughest was Russ Bauers of the Pirates. For a while. He was real tall, and I didn't like to step in against him. But then he hurt his arm and he became real easy to hit.

In fact, it was sort of odd. In the six games in which I hit three home runs in one game, my team lost five times and tied once. One of the times I got all three homers off Cincinnati left-handers. Two of them came off Johnny Vander Meer, and one of them came off Milt Shoffner. The first time I hit three homers in a game came against the Braves in St. Louis. Within a week I did it against the Giants, too.

A couple of World Series highlights stand out, also. In 1949 I got the game-winning hit against the Dodgers in Game Three. At Ebbets Field. The score was tied going to the top of the ninth when we loaded the bases against Ralph Branca. Cliff Mapes was the hitter. He was halfway up to the plate when Casey turned to me and said, "Go up and hit for Mapes." I hit a two-run single off the right-field wall. It was important, because in the bottom of the ninth, Roy Campanella and Luis Omo hit home runs off Joe Page, but we hung on to win, 4–3. Someone said to me afterwards, "Weren't you nervous when Casey sent you up there?"

I answered, "No, there wasn't enough time to be nervous. I was in too much of a hurry to get up there."

My biggest World Series thrill came in 1952. I was thirty-nine at the time. It's funny, too, because I didn't think I would get much of a chance to play. Joe Collins started at first base the first three games. But he was having troubles with the bat. In Game Three Casey sent me up as a pinch-hitter in the bottom of the ninth. I hit a home run but we lost to Preacher Roe, 5–3. Casey started me every game for the rest of the Series, and I took advantage of the opportunity. The next day Allie Reynolds beat Joe Black at the Stadium, 2–0. In the bottom of the fourth, I lined a home run into the lower right-field stands to give us a 1–0 lead. That hit turned out to be the game-winner, too. Black got me out the first time that day. He didn't get me out again. Later in the game, I hit a double off him. In Game Seven I got an RBI single off him. It gave us a 1–0 lead.

In Game Five I hit a three-run homer off Carl Erskine. But we eventually lost that game in 11 innings, 6–5. In the bottom of the ninth I almost won it. I hit a ball to the bullpen fence in right. But Carl Furillo braced his right hand on the fence and leaped high to make a game-saving catch. That home run off Erskine, though, gave me homers in three consecutive World Series games. No one had ever done that before. Not too many people know that.

Let's go back to the beginning. The person who had the biggest influence on my baseball career was Harry Forrester, who was the baseball coach at Piedmont College down here in Demorest, Georgia. I played for the college team three years while I was still in high school. I went to Piedmont Academy, which was connected with the college. Around that time the city took over the college. I guess I looked promising, because the city officials came to me and said they would fix it up so that I could take a subject at the college. At that time a high school student could go out for college sports if he took a course at Piedmont. Well, I played three years and the city officials never brought the subject up. I never did, either.

Frank Rickey, the brother of Branch, signed me to a Cardinal contract. From 1931 till 1933 I played Class C ball in Greensboro, North Carolina, and Elmira, New York. I had good years. In 1934 they moved me up to Rochester, New York, which was a

Double-A team. I hit over .300 for the fourth year in a row.

After the 1934 season the Cardinals sold me to Cincinnati for $55,000, which was a lot of money at the time. But before the season ended, I pulled a muscle loose in my pelvic bone while running out a double. First base slipped under me as I rounded the bag. Larry McPhail of the Reds said, "We'll take Johnny, but if his leg bothers him, we'll want our money back." The Reds had just bought Ival Goodman, Lew Riggs, and Billy Meyers, so they couldn't take a chance on me.

But Branch Rickey told McPhail, "No way, if you buy Mize, you gotta keep him."

So the sale was canceled and I returned to Rochester in 1935, and hurt my other leg in the same spot. Discouraged, I retired from baseball, but eventually I checked with doctors in Atlanta, and finally I was sent to Dr. Robert Hyland in St. Louis. He found a growth on my pelvic bone in both legs and did corrective surgery. Later I enjoyed saying, "I became the only guy who played in the major leagues who couldn't play in the minors."

In 1936 I came up to the Cardinals and stayed. All six years with them I hit .300. In fact, I batted .300 my first nine years in the majors. In my rookie year I drove home 93 runs with only 414 at bats. The next six years I drove home 100 or more runs each season. Then I spent three years in the Navy during World War II. When I got out of the service, I had 70 runs batted in with two months to go in the season. But I broke my wrist and was out for the season. I followed up with RBI years of 138 and 125, so, under ordinary circumstances, I might have driven in 100 runs in each of my first fifteen years in the majors.

Though I had good personal success in St. Louis, the team could have done better. Before I came up, the Cardinals won three pennants and two world titles in the early '30s. After I left, they won four pennants and three world titles in the early-to-mid '40s. While I was there, we seemed to lose out in the final days of the season every year. We'd lose by three or four games. There were reasons for that. Branch Rickey was known to say, "I'd rather finish second than first. If we can stay in the race until the last week of the season, we can draw big crowds and pay small salaries." Then he'd tell the players, "We didn't win the pennant so we can't pay you a big salary."

St. Louis owned a lot of players in the minors at that time. They sold Bill Lee to the Cubs. We could have won three or four pennants with him. That's the way the Cardinals operated. Stan Musial said later, "The sale that killed us in the 1940s was sending Walker Cooper to the Giants. The front office got $175,000. The team got nothing. Not even a player to be named later. We could have won five or six straight pennants if we had still had Walker Cooper."

Also, in those days, they didn't bring players up from the minors late in the season. It's a shuttle bus now. Back then they'd say, "We can't take anyone off the minor-league teams. If we do, the fans won't support the club."

Look at Louisville today. Earlier in the season, when I visited the city, the team was in first place. Then St. Louis raided the club. Remember when they brought up Willie McGee a few years back? The White Sox even took Louisville's manager, Jim Fregosi. Recently I looked at the standings. They were in last place.

By way of contrast, we had Stan Musial in the minors in 1941. We could have won the pennant if they had brought him up. But they didn't bring him up until after the minor-league season was over. In fact, I didn't even see him when he came up. I was out with a shoulder injury, the one I re-injured with the Yankees in 1949, when I made a rolling slide into second against the White Sox.

I'll tell you another way they operated. In 1939 I won the batting title. I hit .349. You know what they told me at contract time? "You should have hit more home runs." You know how many I hit? *Twenty-eight.* Good enough to lead the National League in home runs. The next year I led the National League with *43* home runs. That's the most in the history of the St. Louis Cardinals. That's also the last time a Cardinal won a home run title. You know what they said when we talked contract: "Well, John, your home runs went up, but your batting average went down. We want you to take a cut."

I said, "Trade me." They did, after the following season. But they didn't exactly give me away. They got three players and $50,000 for me.

I thought I would go to the Dodgers rather than the Giants. On Pearl Harbor Day I was quail hunting. When I got home, I was told that Leo Durocher had called and wanted me to call him back. I did and he said, "Would you be interested in playing for me and the Dodgers?"

I told him, "It doesn't make any difference where

I play." As it turned out, though, the Giants had had a meeting with the Cards the previous day and had gotten the inside track. That's how I ended up with the Giants.

Even though I was a good long-ball hitter, I was a good contact hitter, too. I don't know, I was just good at getting the bat on the ball. Casey used to say, "He hits like a lead off batter." Did you know I'm the only hitter to hit 50 or more home runs and strike out less than 50 times? I struck out 41 times in 1947. The next year I hit 40 homers and struck out 37 times.

Yes, I played in three different parks. In St. Louis I would swing straightaway and hit to all fields. That's why I hit more triples and doubles at Sportsman's Park. In 1938 I led the National League in triples with 16, and in 1941 I led the league in doubles with 39. In 1940, when I hit 43 homers, they put up a temporary mesh screen above the fence. If it hadn't been there, I would have made a serious run at Ruth's record. At the Polo Grounds I changed my stance to become a pull hitter. It had a long right center and a deep center. It was the worst possible park for me to play in. And yet I had some good years there. My power alley was right center, so I had to hit the ball either in the bullpen or over the center fielder's head to get a triple. At Yankee Stadium, from right center on back to the foul pole wasn't too bad. I might have put some big numbers on the board if I had played my entire career at Yankee Stadium. But you just don't know, do you? I do know that the Polo Grounds hurt me, though. I hit a lot of 430-foot outs there.

The Mayor's Trophy Game was when the Yankees

and Giants played to benefit inter-city charities. Two of those games were very important to my career. In 1946, the first time, I was leading the National League in home runs when Joe Page hit me on the right hand and broke a bone. The umpire called the pitch a strike. A few seconds later, the spot had ballooned into a knot. The first-base umpire looked at my hand and said to the home-plate umpire, "Can't you see the swelling? He had to be hit with the pitch."

The home-plate umpire grudgingly said, "Okay, you can take first, but I still say the pitch didn't hit you."

They took me to the hospital for X-rays and found out the wrist was broken. I came back later in the season. On Friday the 13th. Mel Ott, my manager, gave me a four-leaf clover. It didn't bring me good luck, though. I ran into a fence and broke my toe. I was out for the rest of the season. Ralph Kiner beat me out for the home run title, 23–22. I should have ended up in the thirties that year.

Three years after I broke my wrist, the Mayor's Trophy Game worked in my favor. The Giants had just come back from a road trip. I wasn't playing regularly but I was in the exhibition game. Casey came up to me before the game and said, "How are you doing?"

"Well, I'm not playing much," I said.

"How would you like it if we got you over here?"

"It would probably be hard to get me," I said. Later I learned that the Red Sox were trying to get me, too. That might have been the reason why the Yankees were interested in me. The Yankees and the Red Sox went down to the last day. We won by one game. The Yankees might have felt that I could make the difference.

In 1950 my shoulder continued to bother me, so the Yankees sent me down to the Kansas City Blues to get some playing time and to work out my shoulder. It worked. Toward the end of my absence, the Yankees experimented with Joe DiMaggio at first base. When that didn't work out, they recalled me, and I got hot. For the season I hit 25 home runs and drove home 72 runs with 76 hits.

But when I talked to George Weiss in-between seasons about contract, he said, "Well, John, you played only part-time."

"I played every time they put my name in the lineup," I said.

They didn't put me in the lineup against any softies. I rarely played against St. Louis. When we played the Browns, they said, "Let someone else play." I didn't play in too many laughers, either. But when we were playing a big game or against a tough pitcher, my name was always in the lineup.

For example, pinch hitting. It was tough pinch hitting with the Yankees. You might go three or four games without getting an at bat. But I always got along very well with Casey. I got along with him very well when I was playing against him in the National League. He'd say to me with the Yankees, "I'd like to put you in there, but if I do, I won't have you on the bench to pinch-hit. So I think I'll keep you on the bench until I need you." But, of course, you didn't get into any lopsided games. You were always hitting against a pitcher who was throwing well. You had to be patient at the plate, look for a pitch, and wait on it. I used to think ahead. I would keep a bat in my locker. When I knew Casey would need me, I would go into the clubhouse and swing the bat. Consequently, when I went up to home plate, I was ready to hit. I didn't take 10 minutes stretching and swinging before I stepped into the box.

Then I hit according to the score. If there was a man on third with one out, I would try to hit a fly ball. If we needed a single, I would look for a big hole in the infield and go to left or through the middle. If we needed the long ball, I would wait for a pitch I could hit. I would also study the left-handers in the game and see how the pitcher was working them. If the pitcher was working inside, I would go to right field. If he was working outside, I would go to left field.

One day in the clubhouse, Pete Sheehey, the long-time clubhouse man, saw me practicing with a golf swing. He said, "Why are you swinging like that?"

"Mike Garcia's pitching," I said. " He's throwing fastballs low and inside." I hit his first pitch into the right center-field bleachers to win the game and clinch a tie for the pennant. The next day we won the pennant.

So I guess I could handle the bat. I led the league in home runs and slugging average four times each. Overall, my slugging average was .562, eighth on the all-time list. I won three RBI titles and three championships for safe pinch-hits. In addition, I led the league in doubles, triples, and runs scored.

And I wasn't as bad on defense as some of the writers reported. Twice I led the league in fielding. In fact, that's how I got my nickname, "The Big Cat." Joe Orengo, a utility player, gave it to me. It was one of those days when every ball that was hit was taking a bad hop. But I was coming up with everything. All of the throws were bad, too. But I was coming up with them, too. Orengo said, "You're like a big cat out there." In later years the reporters thought I was called that because of my *bad* fielding. But it was because of my *good* fielding.

I would have to say that my best year was my second season in the majors, 1937, when I collected 204 hits and batted .364, my all-time high. But would you believe I finished second in batting to Joe Medwick, who won the Triple Crown that year? The next year I went down to the last day of the season before Ernie Lombardi beat me out. In our final game we were playing the Cubs, who had already clinched the pennant. Their starting pitcher said to me before the game, "If you want to win the batting title, all you have to do is to bunt the ball to third. I'll tell the third baseman to play deep, and I'll break to the first-base side. It'll be a sure thing." But I didn't want to win the batting title that way, so I swung away. Tony Lazzeri, the one-time great Yankee second baseman who was coming to the end of his career, was playing second because they were resting Billy Herman for the World Series. The first time up, he was playing towards second, and I ripped a one-hopper right at him. The next time up, he was playing towards first, and I hit another one-hopper right at him. If those two balls had gone through, I would have won the batting title. On my own! But as it turned out, I went oh-for-four, and Ernie won the title by five points.

The next year I hit .349 and won the batting crown by 17 points. That's the year the front office said to me, "You won the batting title but you didn't hit enough homers." Only enough to lead the league!

How good were the 1949–53 Yankees? Well, we

were good enough to win. We played one year to make a salary for the next year. We were hoping for a raise. When you drove home 72 runs with 76 hits and it wasn't appreciated, you never knew.

The Hall of Fame, well, that took a long time. Twenty-eight years. The year I retired, they established a new five-year waiting period. When I went into the Old Timers' Group, after twenty years, they established another five-year waiting period. Then they added five players to the panel. That held me back even longer.

When you start in baseball, you have three goals: one, win the pennant; two, win the World Series; and three, get to the Hall of Fame. I've been fortunate. I've achieved all three of those goals. But it takes a little of the glamour away when you wait twenty-eight years and some of your contemporaries, with whom you played even-to-better, make it much sooner.

But, overall, I have no regrets. I enjoyed playing with all three teams: the Cards, the Giants, and the Yankees. I wasn't too crazy about the Polo Grounds. But my teammates were great. And the fans were, too.

Every day I get letters from fans who say that I'm worthy of every honor I've received. It makes me feel good. That's the way I played. I tried to do my job as well as I could. And I tried not to make enemies. I played to win but I played fair.

That's why I'm proud of playing on five consecutive world championship teams. I'm the only one who's played on them his last five years in the majors. It's a record. It may never be done again. That makes me feel very good.

That's why I retired. In the last game of the 1953

season, Casey didn't put me in. I had a chance to tie a record. I had 19 pinch-hits, and the record at the time was 20. After the game Casey explained to me, "You were going up next. But Billy [Martin] made out."

Heck, we won the pennant by 13 games. I could have broken that record easily. When that happens, you have to say to yourself, *If they don't want you to be the best, then why play for the best?* So I retired.

Irv Noren

Most of the Yankee players from the 1949–53 era feel that the 1952 team was the best. Irv Noren agrees. In fact, he goes one step further. He says that the 1952 Yankees were the best team he has ever seen. That's a revealing statement, because Irv Noren coached third base for the 1972–74 Oakland A's, who won three consecutive world championships. The 1972–74 A's have been the only team, in addition to the 1936–39 and 1949–53 Yankees, to win as many as three consecutive world titles.

Noren sees some striking similarities between the 1952 Yankees and the 1972–74 A's. Both teams had good leaders, bear-down players, and regular guys who pulled for each other. That's important to Noren, a .275 lifetime hitter who tried to get along with his teammates and tried to give one hundred percent every time he took the field. When he matches up the personnel on the two teams, however he gives a strong edge to the Yankees.

Today he sighs with regret that it all came to an end. He didn't appreciate all of it then, he says. He does now. He's happy that he fulfulled the dream of his father's, who groomed him to be a major-league ballplayer and got to see him play *throughout his career. He's proud of the fact that he was an outstanding minor-league player who won two batting titles. He must have been a great minor-league player. Thrifty Clark Griffith purchased him for $80,000 from the Hollywood Stars. He's thrilled to be able to say that he was the roommate of three players who were elected to the Hall of Fame: Whitey Ford, Mickey Mantle, and Stan Musial. Not too many players can say that. He's also honored that in his five years in New York he played in the World Series four times.*

And he had the best season of his major-league career in New York. In 1954 he batted .319. That's the year the Yankees won 103 games, the most they ever won under Casey Stengel's guidance. That's also the one year that Irv Noren as a Yankee failed to play in the World Series.

Irv's dad was a baker who, when his son would play a night game for the Santa Barbara club in California, would interrupt his work to see Irv play. Then he would return to work and bake until 2:30 in the morning, and then all the next day, to make up the time. In 1960, when Irv was playing for the Dodgers, his dad was driving cross-country from California when he had a heart attack and died on the highway in Arizona. The Dodgers were going to be in Pittsburgh in three days, and he was heading to see his son play.

Irv got into the liquor-store business before he got out of baseball. Eventually he became a coach for the Cubs and later the third-base coach for the Oakland A's. Then he ran a trophy shop, but the hours were too long.

When I hooked up with Irv, he was into horses. He bought his first one in 1957. Over the years he has been in and out of the business. About nine years ago he got back into it. He owns brood mares which he races at the Santa Anita Racetrack, not far from his home in Arcadia, California. He also breeds them, shares in the stud profits, and sells them. I spoke to him quite late in the evening. Lee, his wife of forty-three years, told me that he's at the track "all day and night." It doesn't matter how many hours you put into your work, it appears, as long as you love what you're doing. Irv Noren loves what he's doing.

My biggest thrills in baseball were putting on a major-league uniform, playing in the World Series, and having my father with me at that time. I knew that a ballplayer was what he wanted me to be. To make it and to accomplish what he desired was my goal.

He was a baker. Boy, did he work hard. I didn't realize how hard he worked at the time. He would take time out from his job to come home and play catch with me. At my junior high school games, he was always there, giving me pointers. We moved out to Pasadena in 1936. When I played for Santa Barbara, in Class C ball, he would bake till game time, drive up there, drive back, bake till 2:30 in the morning, and bake the whole next day.

His hard work paid off for me. I won the MVP Award of my league twice in the minors—with Fort Worth in 1948 and the Hollywood Stars in 1949. Batted .330 with the Stars. Bucky Harris, who had just been let go by the Yankees, was managing at San Diego in 1949. He saw me play and urged Clark Griffith of the Senators to buy me. Griffith paid $80,000 for me. He wasn't known to spend that much money too often.

The next year Harris was managing the Senators, and I was playing for them. In spring training, he came up to me and said, "You're my center fielder." That was important to me, because I had never had good springs when I was with the Dodger organization. So I didn't have to press that rookie spring. Harris got me started on the right foot. He gave me confidence that I could play in the American League. Instead of coming up where no one knew me, I had the right guy in my corner. He was the key to my success with Washington. If you couldn't play for Bucky Harris, you couldn't play for anyone.

Griffith called me the day I was traded to the Yankees and said, "I just traded you upstairs." I was to report to Yankee Stadium the next day for a doubleheader. My wife was expecting at the time, so I called her mother and my folks, who flew out to be with her. I joined the Yankees on a Sunday. When I entered the clubhouse, I had goose pimples. Raschi, Reynolds, and Rizzuto were there. It was a great feeling but I was a little scared. I was never worried in Washington. There was an adjustment to be made in New York, though. In Washington you played loose. In New York you had to produce.

The Yankees traded Jackie Jensen for me. He was playing center field and was one-for-40, or something like that. I got two hits in my first game, against Billy Pierce of the White Sox. I always hit Pierce well. One day I went oh-for-four. Casey started platooning me after that. It was like he was waiting for me to have a bad day.

One game in 1952 stands out in my mind. It was the last series in Philadelphia. We needed to win one game to clinch the pennant. They had Harry Byrd and Bobby Shantz pitching. I hit a home run in the eighth inning of the first game to tie the score, 1–1. We won in the 12th or 13th to clinch it.

The 1952 club was as good a team as I ever saw. Remember, I was the third-base coach for the 1972–74

Oakland A world title teams, too. The World Series in 1952 was something special. The Yankees and the Dodgers. Wow! They were two great teams. I remember when Reynolds struck out Jackie Robinson three times in one game. Looking! Robby never took the bat off his shoulder. He would go back to the dugout and yell at Reynolds, "Throw that fastball again and you'll regret it." Reynolds would reach back a little further and throw the ball a little harder each time Robby came up. Jackie'd look again. He never saw the ball. Boy, we got on him. There was a lot of bench jockeying going on that day. There doesn't seem to be as much today.

I remember another World Series well. The 1955 one. I hit into a record five double plays. But I was playing hurt. I had two bad knees. I hurt one when I ran into the wall at Yankee Stadium one night. The walls were all concrete then. There were no pads. I hurt the other sliding into home. But you have to hit the ball hard to ground into a double play. I remember one play, Gil Hodges was holding the runner on. He never stepped off the base. I hit the ball right at him, and he threw the ball to second for an easy double play. Two of the others were hit hard. The other two I could have beaten out if I had had good wheels.

My top salary was $27,000. The players today, in my opinion, are definitely overpaid. But if I were playing today, and the owners offered me that kind of money, I'd take it, too. The owners are at fault. Especially George Steinbrenner. He's afraid that someone is going to outbid him. No one is worth $2 million. If players today are worth $2 million a year, DiMaggio, Williams, and Musial would be worth $8 million. Superstars in our day had to do it all: they had to play defense, hit home runs, drive home runs, and hit .325.

I hit .319 in 1954. That was my best season. Bill DeWitt, who used to be with the Browns, was then assistant general manager to George Weiss. He offered me a $1,000 raise for 1955. I sent the contract back. The second contract he sent me called for a $2,000 raise. I sent it back again. I told him, "That's no raise after hitting .319."

He said, "Well, that's what we're paying you." He hung up. Three weeks went by. Then he called. "That's a good raise," he said.

"Bill, you're not with the Browns now," I said. "You're with the world champs."

He hung up again.

Weiss called me three days later. "What's the trouble?" he said.

"Money," I said.

"What would satisfy you?"

"An $8,000 raise," I said. "To $27,000." I got it.

The 1952–53 Yankees were great. Everyone played together. No one worried about what the next guy was getting. We just worried about doing our job. We went out and won pennants and World Series. That was our job.

Casey was the perfect manager for that team. He was a great guy. I got along with him fine. He was always two steps ahead of the game. With the Mets, later, he might have been different. But he wasn't afraid to make a move with the Yankees. One game he pinch hit Johnny Sain for Joe Collins, who already had two hits in the game. Sain hit a line drive to win the game. That was Casey. Not afraid to make a move.

There were no bed checks on the Yankees. He

treated us like grown men. It was up to you to keep yourself in shape. He would often say, "If you don't do the job, we have a lot of guys to take your place."

During spring training, I used to go to the dog track at St. Pete every night. Everyone did. I didn't miss a night. Casey knew that. One day I'm standing in the outfield before a pre-season game. Casey came out, hands in front of his pants.

"You go to the dog track a lot," he said, "don't you?"

"Yeah, every night," I said.

"Bit much?"

"I see Weiss and others out there."

"Not every night."

"If you want me, you know where to find me."

"By God, you're right," he said, slapping me on the back. "Keep it up."

That Stengelese was a lot of fun with the press. But in the clubhouse you understood him thoroughly. One time I was up with a 3–2 count. Just as I got set, I heard a big yell. Casey was on the front step. I walked over and he said, "If it's a strike, swing; if it's a ball, take it."

I walked away, shaking my head. *My father taught me that when I was eight years old*, I thought. Well, the pitch came in letter high, and I swung and missed. I looked over at the bench and saw Casey. He had thrown a towel over his head. It was like he was saying, "That stupid son of a bitch doesn't know a strike from a ball."

I roomed with three Hall of Famers. Ford and Mantle with the Yankees. And Musial with the Cardinals. Three of the greatest guys I ever met. Don't believe what they wrote about Whitey Ford. He would lay up in his room the night before a game and try to figure out how to win the next day.

"All I've got is a little curve and not much of a fastball," he'd say.

If Whitey was going to pitch the next day, he would have room service. He took care of himself. The night of a game he would go out for a few drinks. Maybe.

Mick, deep down, was sort of a loner. But he was a super guy. I really enjoyed him. I hadn't seen anyone with his ability. He was a super competitor. I saw him come back to the bench many times with tears in his eyes, he was hurting so bad. But he had that great desire. He wanted to play.

We'd go up every morning to the Stage Deli on Seventh Avenue. Bauer and some of the guys lived above the Stage Deli the year before. All of the entertainers, guys like Jackie Leonard and Danny Kaye, would be there, waiting for us.

The night Mick hit the 565-foot homer, I was in the outfield with him before the game. The wind was blowing out a little. He'd just hit two good shots in batting practice. I said, "Mick, you can hit one over the back wall tonight." It was a coincidence that I said it and he did it.

One day he hit one clear up in the center-field bleachers off Alex Kellner. I saw the pictures the next day, and he was on his back knee when he hit it. That's how strong he was.

Another day he hit the facing, way up on top, against Pedro Ramos. One more foot and it would have gone out of Yankee Stadium.

He also hit one right-handed off the facade between the two decks in Detroit. The second baseman turned around and caught the ball on the first bounce. Every day you played with Mantle, you thought he would hit one further than the day before.

Today, they compare Reggie Jackson and whoever to him. But there's no comparison. I was a coach with Oakland for four years when Reggie was there. He didn't compare. No one else today does, either.

I hooked up with Musial in St. Louis. Fred Hutchinson, the Cards' manager, had played against me, so he knew what I could do. He told me later, "If the pennant came down to the wire, you were the guy we were looking for." The Cards stayed in the pennant race, and they needed a left-handed-hitting outfielder, so they picked me up. I had a good year for them. Hit .367 in 17 games. Hutch said to me one day, "If you had gotten here earlier, we would have won the pennant."

Musial is one of the finest gentlemen anyone could ever hope to meet. I was his answering service on the road. People would walk up to him in a restaurant and say, "Heh, Stan, remember me?"

Stan would say, "How's the family?"

He never bad-mouthed anyone. He'd make a guy walk out of a restaurant ten feet high.

Ford, Mantle, and Musial for roommates. How many players can say that?

But, geez, there was a big difference between playing for the Yankees and for the other teams I was on. With the others it was a little harder to get up for each game. The seasons were longer. They dragged when you were 30 games out. You played more for yourself. You tried to improve your batting average 10 points at the end of the season for next year's contract. Of course, you still tried to win the game any way you could. You have to play the game right. Get the man from second to third. But it was more of a challenge and more fun with the Yankees. Every game meant so much more.

With the Yankees there was that extra World Series money, too. For example, after the 1952 World Series, I used the winners' share to put a down payment on a house in Arcadia. Everything I have I owe to baseball. But whatever I got, I earned. I always tried my best. Maybe it didn't work out right. But I always came to play.

I wasn't a guess hitter, a pull hitter, or a home run hitter. I looked for a strike and basically hit the ball where it was pitched. Like most lefthanded hitters, I was a low-ball hitter. But if I hit a home run, I would forget about it and go back to hitting the ball where it was pitched. I'd just like to be remembered as a guy who got along well with his teammates, and who gave a hundred percent.

Bobby Brown was that type of player. He made himself a major-league ballplayer. When he was on the road, he would call up the visiting team to find out if he could come out to hit. For an hour-and-a-half he would hit. He wanted it.

But it always comes to an end, doesn't it? I remember a day, speaking of that, when a minor leaguer thought Eddie Lopat had come to the end of the road. Going north from spring training, we were playing a Yankee farm team. I was playing first base. Boy, they were raking Eddie. It was a get-in-shape day for him. But the kids didn't know that. Major-league hitters were always guessing with Lopat. Not the kids, though. They were swinging from the heels—and connecting. Finally, this one kid comes down to first base and says to me, "Is that really Eddie Lopat out there? He doesn't look like Eddie Lopat."

Well, he was wrong and he was right. It was Eddie Lopat, but he wasn't pitching like Eddie Lopat. Eddie Lopat was working on his timing so that he would look like Eddie Lopat once the season started.

You know, the Oakland A's 1972–74 world title teams had more fights in the clubhouse than the 1952–53 Yankees. But once they passed the white lines, they were the same type of team. Everyone pulled together. I was back this year for Old Timers' Day. Everyone was buddy-buddy. Especially Catfish Hunter. There were no big shots there. We had the same feeling on the Yankees. We pulled for each other, too. That mutual feeling made us all champs.

But raw talent-wise, there's no way you could compare the A's with the Yankees. Would you compare Bill North with Mantle? Gene Tenace with Yogi? Catfish and Joe Rudi, yes. Dick Williams, too. You know how I feel about Casey. I'm a Dick Williams man, too. He is as smart a manager as any manager I've ever seen. But that's where the comparisons end. The Yankees win the matchups, hands down.

It's nice to go back for Old Timers' Day. It's nice just to run into old ballplayers again. I was recently playing in a Ladies Professional Celebrity Golf Tournament. Joe DiMaggio was playing with a foursome in front of me. He waited for me to come off the eighteenth green.

"Let's go up and have some hors d'oeuvres and a drink," he said.

On the way to the dining room, a kid ran up to us and said, "Hey, Mr. Coffee, can I have your autograph?"

"Can you beat that?" Joe said to me after the kid ran off. "He probably doesn't even know that I was a ballplayer."

As I said, it comes to an end, doesn't it?

Billy Martin

Occasionally, an average regular-season ballplayer turns into a superstar in the World Series. Billy Martin was that kind of player.

A .257 lifetime hitter with a career high of .267 for a full season in 1952, he hit the ball at a .333 clip in five World Serits. He batted a post-season high .500 in 1953. In his last three Fall Classics—1953, 1955, and 1956—he hit .500, .320, and .296.

During regular-season play he hit 64 home runs in 3,419 at bats, an average of one home run every 53 times he went to the plate. In World Series play he ripped five home runs in 99 at bats, a rate of one home run every 20 plate appearances.

Considered a clutch performer he was at his best in the 1952–53 World Series. In the second game of the 1952 Fall Classic, he hit a three-run homer that broke open a 2–1 game against the Dodgers. The Yankees went on to win, 7–1. He started and ended the 1953 World Series, also against the Dodgers, in grand fashion. In the first inning of Game One, he tripled with the bases loaded to catapult the Yankees to a 9–5 victory. In his final at bat of the Series,

*in the sixth and deciding game, he singled home Hank
Bauer with the game-winning and championship-clinching
run. Overall, he got 12 hits in 24 at bats for a .500
batting average. That mark tied him with Davis Robertson
of the 1917 Giants for the highest average in a six-game
Series. His 12 hits put him in a class by himself. No other
player has ever recorded 12 hits in a six-game Series.*

*In addition to batting .500 in the 1952 World Series, he
hit two home runs, two triples, and two doubles to compile
an incredible .958 slugging average.*

*But another aspect of his World Series play—his defense—
has gone virtually unnoticed. He did not make an error
over a stretch of 23 consecutive games, a World Series
record for a second baseman.*

*The most important play he made came in the seventh
inning of the final game of the 1952 World Series. It
should have been a routine play for the Yankees, but it
almost lost the Series for them. With the bases loaded and
two outs, Jackie Robinson lifted a high pop fly near the
pitcher's mound. Joe Collins, the first baseman, lost the ball
in the sun; Bob Kuzava, the pitcher didn't react on the
mound. Two Brooklyn runners had already crossed home
plate and a third one was rounding third when Billy
Martin bolted from second base and made a knee-high catch
to prevent the Dodgers from scoring three runs and winning the World Series on a ball that was hit sixty feet from
home plate. Instead, the Yankees held on to win, 4–2.*

*Yankee general manager George Weiss ungratefully said
later, "Billy Martin made an easy play seem difficult."*

*A strange comment. First, the catch was not Billy Mar-
tin's play to make. Second, if Billy Martin didn't make the
play, no other pin-striped player would have, and the Yankees might have lost—rather than won—the World Series.*

*It wasn't easy getting hold of Billy Martin—when he's
not managing the Yankees he's involved with a host of other*

activities—but with the help of his charming wife, Jill, I finally spoke with him one fall morning a year ago. He was in Oakland, California, where his mother lives, and was congenial and considerate, in true Yankee fashion.

I set a major-league record in my first game. I got two hits in one inning. It was Opening Day in 1950 and we were playing the Red Sox. We fell behind 9–0. Mel Parnell was pitching for the Red Sox. Gerry Coleman started at second base. But the Old Man put me in. Jackie Jensen, too. He wanted to give us some playing time. In my first at bat there were two men on, and I doubled off the left-field wall. Later in that inning I singled with the bases loaded. That was some way to break into the major leagues!

You're right, I was a big-game player. But when we played, they didn't keep records on game-tying and game-winning hits. There's more emphasis on that now. If some people did their homework, they world find that Mickey Mantle, myself, and some others got a lot more game-winning hits than they do now. There were four or five occasions when I got game-winning hits that cinched the pennant. But I still haven't read about them.

I remember my first World Series home run. I remember *everything* about *every* World Series game I played. Vic Raschi pitched for us, Carl Erskine for them. It was Game Two in 1952 and we won 7–1. I hit a double, a three-run homer, and got four RBIs. Charlie Dressen, the manager in the other dugout, said I couldn't hit a high fastball. That's what I hit for my home run. But basically I was a good breaking-ball hitter, and Erskine was a good breaking-ball pitcher. But he couldn't get me out. The Dodgers had the right pitching book on me, but they threw me the wrong pitches.

I hit a home run off Preacher Roe, too. It was in Game Two of 1953. I walked up on a screwball and hit the ball out of the ballpark. Later in the game the score was tied, 2–2, in the bottom of the eighth inning. Preacher threw a great pitch to Mickey, down and away. But Mickey muscled the ball out of the park. It was a two-run homer. It won the game for us. Eddie Lopat beat Preacher, 4–2.

Ebbets Field was a bandbox park. If we played there, you could add 15 to 20 home runs to everyone's stats. Mickey Mantle? God only knows how many home runs he would have hit at Ebbets Field. We used to run out of balls in batting practice there. The last couple of World Series we played against them, we didn't even try to hit singles. We tried to hit the ball out of the park.

I remember another 4–2 victory over the Dodgers in the World Series. It was in the seventh game of 1952 at Ebbets Field. The Dodgers had loaded the bases with one out in the bottom of the seventh inning. We were winning 4–2, but they had Duke Snider and Jackie Robinson coming up. That's when Casey made a bold and a brave move. He brought Bob Kuzava in. Kuzava was a lefty. The move left Casey open to the second guess. No one else brought a lefty in with the game on the line at Ebbets Field. But Casey knew what he was doing. He figured that Kuzava could get Snider. And he did. He got Duke to pop up. But when Casey left Kuzava in to pitch to Robinson, he really left himself open. Jackie could have done some damage in that situation. But

Casey knew that Robby was a good fastball hitter, and he knew that Bob was a good breaking-ball pitcher. On a three-two pitch Kuzava threw a curve. At the time, I was playing very deep. Then when I saw the breaking pitch, I broke towards second. I expected Robby to pull the ball. But he popped it up between first and the pitcher's mound. Joe Collins lost the ball in the sun. Fortunately, though, I broke toward home plate and caught the ball below my knees on the dead run. If the ball had dropped, the Dodgers would have scored three runs, and we would have lost the World Series. But my play didn't impress George Weiss. After the game he said I made an easy play look hard. Thanks, George!

Give Casey credit, though, for making a gutsy move with the World Series on the line. Kuzava retired all eight batters he faced, and we won our fourth consecutive world title. Yes, Casey was the best manager I ever played for. No doubt about it. One of the reasons was he was so hard to figure out. For example, during the regular season he batted me first, second, seventh, or eighth. But in the World Series, for some reason, he batted me third, fifth, and sixth. One day he played me at third base in a World Series game. I had never played third base before. But that's how much confidence he had in me.

I didn't talk to Casey for many years after the Yankees traded me in 1957. I was hurt and I blamed Casey for the trade. But I was wrong. George Weiss was responsible for me leaving the Yankees. He thought I had been a bad influence on DiMaggio, Mantle, and Ford. But they're all in the Hall of Fame. I'm not. Maybe they were a bad influence on me. On the contrary, though. Joe DiMaggio, for example, is a very nice gentleman. He befriended me once. I appreciated it then. I appreciate it now. And I'll never forget it.

Well, anyway, I wouldn't talk to Casey for many years. Then when I was a scout with the Twins, both of us were at the winter meetings in Houston. Some mutual friends told me Casey was hurt that I wouldn't speak to him. They said he wanted to patch things up. I did, too. When we finally bumped into each other, we talked, and he carried on in front of a group of people, making me sound like the greatest second baseman since Rogers Hornsby. But because I love Casey so much, a lot of people think I've modeled myself as a manager after him. That's not true. I've learned from smart, mediocre, and stupid managers. I've learned from them all.

But we were talking about the World Series. I had a big one in 1953. I batted .500 and got 12 hits. That's the most hits anyone's ever gotten in a six-game series. And we won a record fifth consecutive world championship. For a short time I was on top of the world. *Very* short. I got called into the Army and spent two years in the service. The real downer was the pay of a corporal. At least Ted Williams and Gerry Coleman got captain's pay.

There was another downer when I returned to the Yankees in 1955. The Dodgers finally beat us. But it took some great performances to do so, and we carried them to the wire. Johnny Podres pitched a great game, and Sandy Amoros saved him with a sensational catch. Walter Alston made a great defensive move, too. He inserted Sandy Amoros in left field as a defensive replacement. Junior Gilliam never would have caught Yogi's fly ball. Amoros did. Gil surprised me, though. He had more time to get back

to first than I did to second. But give Reese credit.
He made a great play on the relay.

We got back at them in 1956, though. Once again
the series went seven games, but this time we beat
them by a shutout. Johnny Kucks won a 9–0 three-
hitter. And once again Casey made a couple of good
moves. This time he got some help, though. He
replaced Joe Collins with Bill Skowron at first base,
and he replaced Enos Slaughter in left field with
Elston Howard. I like Enos but he blew three plays
in Game Six. He let three balls drop. He took a pop
fly over shortstop on one hop, he let a fly ball down
the left-field line drop, and he misplayed Jackie Robinson's line drive, which turned out to be the game-
winning hit. Bob Turley pitched a great game. But
he lost 1–0 in 10 innings—on a ball that should have
been caught. After the game I went up to Casey's
locker and said to him, "I don't care if Enos told you
he slipped on Jackie's hit. He blew three plays. I
know he's your National League buddy, but if you
play him tomorrow, you're going to blow the World
Series. If you're smart, you'll put Howard in left and
Skowron at first. Then we'll win it." And that's exactly what he did. Bill hit a grand slam and Ellie hit a
solo shot, and we won it.

Casey made another gutsy move in the seventh
game. He picked a kid to start it. As it turned out,
Johnny Kucks pitched a great game. He had a great
heart and Casey knew it. I know that Jackie Robinson said after the game that the Dodgers got beat by
a second-rate pitcher. But I disagree. Casey made
the right choice. Speaking about "second-rate" players,
though, how many times did Jackie get beaten out by
a "second-rate" second baseman in World Series play?

But don't get me wrong. I have a lot of admiration for Robby.

That was my last World Series as a player. But it was a memorable one. There were a lot of dramatic moments. Don Larsen's perfect game, for example. In the bottom of the eighth inning the infielders got together in the dugout and said, "Keep the ball in front of you, knock it down, and don't let them get a cheap hit." We weren't concerned about the perfect game, though. Winning was the important thing. We had to win to take the lead in the Series. But we ended up getting both: the lead in the series and the perfect game. The key hit in the game was a home run by Mickey. It gave Don the only run he would need. What a clutch hit! But that's what Mickey was all about—clutch hits! If you added up his game-winning hits, the total would be awesome.

Yes, I know that some of the Yankees from our era think the Dodgers had a better lineup, man-for-man, than we did. But I don't agree. Phil was equal to Reese. Overall, our defense was better than theirs. They had a great first baseman in Hodges. Snider was a great hitter, too. But he was very fortunate. He was the only lefty in their lineup. They were loaded with right-handed hitters. So he faced nothing but right-handed pitchers. But he couldn't compare with Mickey anyway. Yogi could hit better and throw better than Campy. Bauer had a quicker release, a better arm, and a more accurate one than Carl Furillo. And Furillo had a *great* arm. Overall, we had better speed, too. We had seven guys who could outrun any of them. Erskine and Podres were two outstanding pitchers. Newcombe was good, too. But we knew we could beat Brooklyn if we could keep Newcombe in the game. Newk couldn't beat us. Raschi, Reynolds, and Lopat could beat anyone. They were three of the best money pitchers of all time. And we had a few players on the bench who were outstanding. Jackie Jensen, for example. He was a great player. But he couldn't even get into our lineup.

Brooklyn was one of the best baseball machines that ever played at Ebbets Field. Out of their ballpark, though, they were just another club. They couldn't beat us at Yankee Stadium. On the other hand, *we* could win *anywhere*.

Charlie Silvera

Charlie Silvera was a role player. His role was backup catcher to Yogi Berra. If Berra got hurt, Casey Stengel knew he had a dependable number-two man. Silvera was an insurance policy.

Like many of the players on the 1949–53 Yankees, Silvera came from the San Francisco area. Other players who came from the Bay Area included Joe DiMaggio, Bobby Brown, Gerry Coleman, and Gil McDougald. Frankie Crosetti, who was the third-base coach, came from there, too. When Silvera came up to the Yankees from the Pacific Coast League late in the 1948 season, he made an instant impression. In four games he got eight hits and batted .571. Charlie always did a good job when he got a decent chance. When Berra broke a thumb in 1949, Silvera filled in admirably. He batted .315 that year. It was his only season with more than 100 at bats in the majors. In the two other seasons in which he had a respectable number of at bats, he hit .327 and .280.

By way of contrast, when he had 25, 26, and 9 at bats in three different seasons, he had batting averages of .160, .192, and .222, respectively.

Silvera's role epitomized Stengel's theories of specialization. Casey implemented the two-platoon system, alternating players like Hank Bauer and Gene Woodling in the outfield. He purchased National League players such as Johnny Mize and Johnny Sain for a September stretch drive, and quite often those players ended up contributing to many more. He used players as alternate starters and pinch hitters. Mize and Bobby Brown are two examples. He used certain pitchers in spot starts, middle relief, and save situations. Sain and Bob Kuzava wore those many hats well. And he hung on to reliable backup players like Silvera.

Casey often referred to Silvera as the best backup catcher in the major leagues. But when one was a backup player to Yogi Berra, that is exactly what he was—backed up. In seven World Series, Silvera played in just one game and batted only two times. Charlie got paid $16,500 in 1956. That was the most he was ever paid with the Yankees. But that season he batted just nine times, the least number of plate appearances that he ever had in a season. There must have been a good reason why the Yankees kept him around.

Joe Collins says the 1949–53 Yankees were a well-oiled machine with 25 smooth component parts. For the machine to run smoothly, each of the parts had to perform its role. Charlie Silvera performed his admirably.

Charlie and Rose Silvera, his wife of forty years, live in Millbrae, California. When I last spoke with him two summers ago, he was a West Coast scout for the Yankees. As we concluded the interview, he told me he was going to Candlestick Park to see a ballgame. He was doing what he always enjoyed more than anything else: he was going out to the ballpark.

When Billy got his job with the Yankees in 1984, I got my present job as their West Coast scout. I'm 63 now and still doing what I always wanted to do. I'm on my way to Candlestick Park right now. If I weren't working, I'd be there anyway.

I grew up in the San Francisco area. Joe Devine signed me right out of St. Ignatius High School. Gerry Coleman, Bobby Brown, and I went to high school together. There's only one month's difference in our ages.

In 1947 and 1948 I spent the first two weeks of the season with the Yankees, when there was a 40-man roster. Then I was optioned to Portland in the Pacific Coast League. In 1948 I batted .301 for Jim Turner. Casey was at Oakland that year, and I had great series against him. The following year, both of them were with the Yankees, so I *had* to make the club. Actually I was recalled for the final four games of the 1948 season. Gus Niarhos was hurt and Yogi was in the outfield at the time. So I caught the final four games, and I got eight hits.

My first game in the majors was in Philly. That day Joe dropped a fly ball, probably the first one in his life. My first day was also Frankie Crosetti's last day in the majors as a player. And I got three hits that day. One of them was a triple, one of only two that I hit in my major-league career. I hit it off Dick Fowler. I got three hits in my second game, too. And I got two hits in my last game. I remember that last game for another reason. Joe hit the wall at Fenway four times. In the ninth inning Bucky Harris put in a pinch-runner for him. The Boston crowd gave Joe a standing ovation as he ran off the field. That's pretty hard to conceive. Joe had done everything humanly possible that day to knock the Red Sox out of the pennant race. And the fans wanted him to know that they applauded his effort.

At the end of the 1948 season, I got married. My wife, Rose, broke in with five consecutive world championship clubs, too. She was never in the *minors*. In 1954, when we lost to Cleveland, she said, "Where's my World Series check?"

I said Yogi was in the outfield when I caught my first game in the majors. He had lost his confidence behind the plate in 1947 and 1948. So in 1949 the Yankees brought in Bill Dickey to groom Yogi. He put Yogi behind the plate and said, "C'mon, kid, you can do it. You're going to be a great catcher." And Yogi became a great catcher. He had those quick feet and that good arm. Dickey built everything else around those assets.

In 1949, my rookie year, I batted .315. Joe and I were the only ones to hit .300 that year. Yogi broke his thumb and missed six weeks. I took his place. On the next-to-last Sunday I pulled a groin muscle, and Yogi was forced back into action. We ended up winning the pennant by one game. I haven't been given much credit for the role I played in 1949. I'm going to blow my own horn a little bit here. I didn't hang around all those years because I was Casey's illegitimate son. Without me the Yankees wouldn't have won five straight. There wouldn't have been any dynasty.

Tommy Henrich had a great first half in 1949. Then he got hurt. But Johnny Mize came along. It was a patchwork team. We set very few records. Boston had all the .300 hitters and all the pitchers with the big winning percentages. We had a real team effort. We had something like 77 injuries that year. Casey did a great job of juggling. That's how the two-platoon system started. We had Woodling and Bauer, Lindell and Mapes, Brown and Johnson, Coleman and Stirnweiss. Another reason Casey platooned was because of our youth. Gerry, Gene, Hank, and I were all rookies. Mapes was in his second year. Cuddles Marshall and Duane Pillette were young, too. But everyone contributed.

There was a carnival atmosphere surrounding those last two games with Boston in 1949. Most of the players lived in apartments on 158th and Girard Avenue. The Boston people came down for the two games. There was a boxing ring on the corner. Jake LaMotta, the fighter, used to stage fights there. Those Boston people partied all night. We enjoyed the whole scene, watching the fights from our fire escape and drinking our juice.

I got two at bats in that year's World Series. In Game Two. The first time, I hit a ball in the hole at short, but Reese threw me out. Then I popped a foul ball to Billy Cox at third. Mize pinch-hit for me the next time. But Preacher Roe beat us, 1–0. Overall, I played on seven World Series teams, but I got into only that one game. They used to call me the "Arndt Jorgens of the '50s."

In 1950 I didn't get my first at bat until June 17. I pinch-hit a ground-ball single up the middle. That's the day my first child was born. By 1951 I knew my role. No one was going to take Yogi's job. But I figured it wasn't so bad to catch behind a Hall of Famer. I was the number-two catcher. Houk was number three. I was a better defensive catcher than Houk. They used him for pinch hitting. They saved me for defense. But I'd do anything to hang around. I got to the park early. I'd pick up bats if I had to. It was great. Everyone said it was the best time to play ball and be a Yankee. I didn't like sitting around but I didn't want to be traded, either. In those days the Yankees traded you to the Browns, the Senators, or the A's. At trading time we'd always be waiting for the announcement of a big deal, especially if we got off to a bad start. The deal would be dictated by the press. I escaped all of that. Some thirty catchers were traded away during Yogi's time. Guys like Gus Triandos. I did the job I had to do. I doubt if I could have been a regular at Yankee Stadium. I wasn't a lefty and I didn't have power. But Casey said, "He's the best backup catcher in the major leagues." I think I proved that.

In 1951 I hit my first-and-only homer in the majors. On July 4 at Yankee Stadium. Yogi was hurt. I hit it down the line off Fred Sanford of Washington. That day I caught a doubleheader. It was the only time I ever did with the Yankees. Ironically we lost both games. But I never tried to hit the ball out. I was a slap hitter with a short swing. I tried to make contact. It helped me with "Death Valley." There was a lot of area to drive the ball around.

There was so much talent on the Yankees of that era. Just look at our bench: Mize, Coleman, Brown, Carey, myself. We could have played with just about any other team and held our own, especially against teams of today's standards. No team today will monopolize like the Yankees and Dodgers of those days. There's too much flux. Today's players, when they someday go to Old Timers' Day games, will have fifteen different hats to wear.

Also, the pride is missing. We had a lot of pride. We policed our own. When I came up, Lindell, Stirnweiss, and Johnson took me aside. "We play for all the marbles here," they said. "We play to win every day. Then it becomes a habit." But they were great supporters, too. When you were playing, they were pulling for you all the time. We traveled on trains. We were like brothers. We respected each other. I roomed with Collins. We didn't know what the other guy made. We didn't care, either. We were just happy to be Yankees.

In 1952 Yogi got hurt, so Casey used me more against left-handed pitchers. The following year, I batted .280. We won the pennant easily, so I got a lot of playing time at the end of the season.

Sometimes we didn't understand Casey's moves. Sensing our feelings, he'd say, "You don't like me now. In October, when you get your World Series checks, you will." He was right. In spring training I'd sit next to Woodling and say, "Well, Gene, how are you going to spend your World Series money this year?"

One day Yogi didn't show up for a game. He called Gene Mauch, the trainer, and said, "I've got a cold."

Casey told Mauch to tell Yogi, "Get your fanny out to the park in case I need a pinch-hitter." Mauch did. And Yogi won the game for us.

The Old Man knew how to get the most out of his players. Take Bauer and Woodling, for example. He'd get them riled up and they'd bust their asses. They'd say to themselves, "I'll show that old buzzard I'm not going to sit down."

One day he took Jensen out after Jackie had hit two home runs. His defense was, "Well, the odds were against his hitting three." You could never rest on your laurels with Casey. I said before that we didn't get a World Series check in 1954. The Indians won. For one year they were a great club. They beat all the second-division clubs. We split the season's series with them. No club ever beat us in a season's series when I was there. But they had a great pitching staff and all their regulars had a superb year. That was our only team that won 100 games. And we finished *eight* games out!

In 1955 Elston Howard came up. So I got less playing time. Houk went to manage at Denver. But Elston could catch and play the outfield. So in 1955 and 1956 I was the number-three catcher.

They used me in the bullpen. It would get hot out there. We used to sit in a cubbyhole in the back. There was a phone there. Houk, Sain, and I would talk strategy. You learn a lot as a reserve. Look at Houk's record as a manager. Look at Sain's record as a pitching coach. We'd look for visual signs from Casey. A lot of bullpens didn't have phones. For example, if Casey wanted a pitcher who wore glasses, he'd point to his eyes. If he wanted a fat man, he'd make a round circle with his hands.

Joe Page would throw 10 pitches and he'd be ready. He had a strong arm and a strong heart. He didn't have much breaking stuff. He'd simply say, "Here it is. Let's see if you can hit it." For two years he was unbeatable. Then it caught up to him. Johnny Sain believed in throwing every day. In fact, he'd throw three times a day. And he did a great job. So did Ferrick, Morgan, and Ostrowski.

I warmed up Don Larsen the day he pitched his perfect game. I still have the glove. He has us down every five years for a get-together. Everyone who's around shows up. Warming up pitchers at Yankee Stadium and Ebbets Field, you had your back to the diamond, so you didn't see much of the game. I watched the last inning of his perfect game from the bullpen. It was so tense. The Series was tied at two games apiece. The score was 2–0. The no-hitter was on the line. The perfect game was on the line. The game was on the line. You've got to give Don credit. He handled the pressure well. On that day he was *perfect.*

By late 1956 I wasn't doing enough to merit what I was making. On the last day of the winter meetings I was sold to the Cubs. You know who told me? A guy who ran a hock shop on 42nd Street. He was a good friend, so he called. I couldn't believe it. He told me to go down and buy a paper. Sure enough. I had been a loyal Yankee for sixteen years, and they didn't even have the courtesy to tell me themselves. Same thing with Vic Raschi. No one from the front office told him. I did. They said to me, "You've been around with Vic for a long time. Go over to him and smooth things over." *Very* cold.

Vic started the Stengel dynasty. In 1949 he pitched on three days of rest 10 consecutive times. He always took the ball when they asked him. He always pitched against the best, like Lemon and Parnell, who were just great. Isn't it ridiculous, though. The "Big Three" were three of the greatest clutch pitchers of all time. And they get three or four votes for the Hall of Fame each year. Well, I'll tell you something: they're in my Hall of Fame.

I'm pretty proud of my .282 lifetime batting average. I was a .290 hitter with the Yankees. Deron Johnson took my place at half my pay. I made $16,500 in 1956. The Cubs gave me $20,000 in 1957. It was an incentive deal. But I sprained my ankle on Memorial Day. Inactivity caused it. I was sitting around too long with the Yankees. The doctor said I would have been better if I had broken it. I tried to rush back and I hurt it again. It still hurts thirty years later. But I have no regrets. I probably got more mileage as a second-string catcher than any reserve on any other club. The Yankees treated me well. And I played with them when they accomplished something that no other team in the history of major-league baseball has done.

People often ask me, "Why don't you wear your 1949–53 World Series ring with the five stones?" That ring symbolizes the five consecutive world championships we won. But I wear my 1949 World Series ring instead. That was the year I played on my first winner. That was the year when I played in my only World Series game. And that was the year when we showed the most heart because there was so much adversity to overcome.

Overall, I played in seven World Series in my eight full years in New York. It's pretty amazing how successful we were. Against great competition, too. But I'll tell you something: DiMaggio was my yardstick of success. When I was a kid, I used to watch him at Seals Stadium in San Francisco. That's when he hit in 61 consecutive games. Many years later I'd be catching in the bullpen up in the Bronx, and I'd look at him in center field and say, "Holy Christ, here I am. Yankee Stadium. Pinch me. My dreams have come true."

Billy Martin's had a big influence on me, too. He, Bauer, and I roomed together one year. Billy and I wouldn't play. One day he said, "If I ever manage Oakland, you'll be my bullpen coach." Well, when he got the Twins' job in 1969, he called me. When he got the Detroit job in 1971, he called me. When he got the Texas job in 1974, he called me. When he got the Oakland job in 1980, he called me. When he got the Yankee job in 1984, he called me again.

People say, "Billy's gotten you fired a lot."

I say, "Yes, that's true, but he's gotten me hired a lot, too."

Gil McDougald

Gil McDougald, when he came up to the major
leagues, had something to prove. The Yankees had established stars at his regular position, second base, and his
adopted position, third base. Gerry Coleman and Billy Martin were at second, and Billy Johnson and Bobby Brown
were at third. But Gil won a spot in the lineup, playing 82
games at third base and 55 at second. In the process, he
batted .306 and was named the American League's Rookie
of the Year.

In that year's World Series, with the Yankees and the
Giants tied at two games apiece, Gil broke open Game Five
with a grand slam home run. The Yankees won 13–1. He
was the first, and is still the only, rookie in the history of the
World Series to hit a grand slam home run.

Casey Stengel periodically taunted Gil, and McDougald
repeatedly vowed to show the Old Man a thing or two.
Casey just smiled, knowing that Gil played better when he
was mad. Gil, the Old Man knew, had something to prove.

In 1955 Casey got mad about Gil's batting stance. He
told McDougald that he wouldn't be playing anymore if he
didn't change his stance immediately. Once again Gil fumed.

But he responded with batting averages of .285, .311, and. .287 in the three years that followed. The .311 season in 1956 was, according to Gil, his best season in the major leagues.

In 1958 he didn't want to go to the All-Star Game because he was upset with the voting and his backup stature. Gil's votes had been spread over three different positions on the All-Star Game ballots. If they had been concentrated into one position, he would easily have been the starting shortstop. But Casey told Gil that he was going no matter how he felt. Grudgingly, McDougald sat on the bench for seven innings, got into the game in the eighth inning, and delivered the game-winning hit.

That year, in the World Series, the Yankees were down three games to one to the Milwaukee Braves, who had defeated the Bronx Bombers in seven games in the previous Fall Classic. The experts didn't give the Yankees any chance to come back. But Gil did. In Game Five he homered and doubled with the bases loaded. In Game Six he hit a home run in the top of the tenth inning to give the Yankees the lead in a game they won, 4–3. In Game Seven he got two hits in a 6–2 Yankee win. Gil wound up with a .321 average and two home runs. It was his best World Series. And the Yankees became the second team in history to rebound from a 3–1 deficit in games to win the Series.

In his career Gil batted .276 and hit 112 home runs. In the World Series he batted just .237, but he hit seven home runs. The seven home runs is the second-highest number by a right-handed batter in the history of the Fall Classic. And he did something, in addition to his rookie grand slam, that no one else has ever done: he played three different positions in three different series on world title teams.

During his major-league baseball career he and general manager George Weiss had some heated negotiations. One of them proved to be pivotal to Gil's post-baseball life. Weiss told McDougald, "You need me. You can't make a living without me." That was the wrong thing for Weiss to say and the right thing for McDougald to hear. He quickly decided to get into another business. Today that business is flourishing.

At the end of the 1960 season, with expansion coming in and nothing more in baseball to prove—he had played on eight pennant winners and five world title teams in ten years—he retired from one career and started another.

In 1958, during a pre-game batting practice at Yankee Stadium, he got hit on the left ear by a line drive off the bat of Bob Cerv. The force of the blow it is believed, drove Gil's ear drum partway into his skull. Over the ensuing years, including a seven-year stint as the head baseball coach at Fordham University, Gil's hearing has progressively deteriorated. Dr. Bobby Brown, Gil's good friend, keeps in close touch with him. Two weeks before I spoke with Gil, Dr. Brown had advised him that the timing for the type of surgery he needed was not quite right yet. Perhaps in a couple of years, he said.

Gil lives in Spring Lake, New Jersey, and I spoke with him at his office in Nutley, New Jersey. He is executive vice-president of the Metropolitan Maintenance Company. Seated across the desk from him, I spoke into a microphone that was wired into an electronic keyboard. Another wire ran from the keyboard to Gil's hearing aid. Gil measured the modulation of my normal speaking voice, set it on the right frequency on the keyboard, and from that point on, handled my questions as deftly as he had gloved Rocky Colavito's drives down the third-base line thirty years before.

When the interview was over and I got set to go, Gil said to me, "Don't go making my physical problem more than it is. Just say that Gil has a minor communication problem."

Proving himself is nothing new to Gil McDougald. In

business, as well as baseball, he has succeeded in doing just that.

Back in San Francisco, my brother Bill and I both played high school basketball and baseball. Actually I was better at basketball than I was at baseball. I got a few scholarships and I pursued the sport. But suddenly the Yankees decided they wanted to sign me in '48. At the time, I didn't know whether I had the ability or not. But we decided to give it a shot.

I say *we* because I got married before I went out to Twin Falls, Idaho, where the Yankees assigned me. My wife and I proceeded to have four children rather quickly. It was great in one respect: we were young and growing up with our family. Later we would be growing older with another family.

Joe Devine, the scout who signed me to the contract, took a personal interest in most of the players he signed. He was very close with his players, and he stayed in touch with them. I think that has changed over the years. Today scouts sign you and forget about you, because they're afraid you might not turn out too well, and they don't want to be known as the scout who signed you. But in the old days it was a lot different. They treated you more like family, and if you were having problems, they would talk to you, and they would talk to your manager, and they would try to help you out.

My rookie year was '51. You might remember that the Yankees and Giants switched camps that year. We went to Phoenix, Arizona, and they came to Florida for the first and, I think, the only year. I particularly enjoyed it, because it was only a short hop from Arizona to California. We were invited to the rookie camp which Casey had run every year since he came to the Yankees. It was an exceptional spring, because Mickey Mantle joined the Yankees that year, and he proceeded to have one of those springs that Babe Ruth must have dreamt about. Everywhere we went, they'd point to a spot where so-and-so hit one, and he'd proceed to hit one farther. We barnstormed all the way up the West Coast, playing in all the towns of the Pacific Coast League. San Francisco, Oakland, Los Angeles. They're all in the major leagues now. In L.A., Mickey hit a couple of home runs in one game. One of them was hard to believe. It was one of those two-iron shots he'd hit to center field. The center fielder broke in quickly and cut over, but the ball just took off and kept going. It landed at least 40 to 50 feet behind the center-field fence.

I remember another day we were at USC, the university. They had a field house beyond the snow fences that represented a homer. He hit a ball right over the field house. I believe it was the farthest he ever hit a ball. But you'd have to check with him. He hit so many that one might not have impressed him at all. But, really, I've never seen anyone move a ball like that. Then we went up to San Francisco, where I was born, and we played at Seals Stadium, where there had been only 10 or 12 balls hit over the right-field wall until that time, because there was a perpetual wind blowing in from right.

Well, that night Mick first went up right-handed, and he hit one across Guerrero Street so fast that you wouldn't believe it. The people were shocked. All the years that I played in that park, I didn't see left-handers hit balls over that fence. Then I see a right-hander, who was only nineteen, rifle one over it. Then he got up left-handed and hit one out in left center field. But that was the way that spring went for Mickey Mantle. He got $20 million worth of publicity in two months. He overshadowed everyone else, including Joe DiMaggio, who was reaching the end of the line.

The Yanks were desperately trying to find a spot for him. He broke in as a shortstop, you know. When I saw him play short, however, I said, "Well, he may be able to hit, but he better be able to drive home seven or eight runs a game, or there might be a deficit at the end of the nine innings." He had one of those scatter arms. He would clear out the players in the dugout, and the people in the box seats weren't too happy to see him out there, either. It was another adjustment for me. After watching Joe—you never saw him make a tough catch—I'd watch Mickey, because every catch was a sensational one. First, he'd misjudge the ball. Then he'd outrun it. Finally, he'd catch it. It was like watching two movies at the same time.

I remember other players with reputations who joined us that spring. There was Jackie Jensen, who was an All-American football player at the University of California, and a heck of an athlete. Later he won the MVP Award with the Red Sox. But he had a tough time cracking our lineup, because our outfield was loaded. Cliff Mapes and Hank Bauer were in right field, Mickey and Joe were in center, and Gene Woodling was in left. Jackie needed playing time. The Yanks traded him off to Washington, and that's where he established himself. He had speed, a great arm, and a good bat. All he needed was playing time.

Of course, the competition in the infield was no easier. Bobby Brown and Billy Johnson were my competition at third. Gerry Coleman and Billy Martin were at second, and Phil Rizzuto was at short. When I went to spring training, I didn't see much of a chance for Gil McDougald to go anywhere. At that time, I had never played any position except second. Finally Casey told me to take some grounders at third. I guess in the back of his mind, he thought, "If you have good hands and you can field the ball, what difference does it make what infield position you play." I totally agree with that philosophy.

Also, Casey must have thought Johnson was reaching the end of the trail, as far as he was concerned anyway. The Yanks traded him before the cut-off date to the Cardinals. I became the regular third baseman or second baseman, depending on who was pitching. If a left-hander was pitching, I played third; if a right-hander was pitching, I played second. It was a case of whether Billy or Gerry played second when I played third. When I played second, Bobby would play third. I was more confident at second base, but I realized I wouldn't be in the lineup if I didn't switch. I was always fairly confident in my hitting, so I said, "What the hell, if you make an error, so what." Basically, I felt if they'd give me a chance, I would prove I could play. It wasn't a case of being cocky In the minors I proved myself everywhere I played. Over three years I averaged .340. I didn't see why it would be any different up here. I guess you might say I had inner confidence.

I probably ruined more players who tried to emulate my batting stance than any other player. It was an odd stance. The more that I look at it on film, the odder it becomes. But when you use something through high school and the minors, and no one comments on it, you feel it's natural. But the more exposure I got, the more people zeroed in on it. When I got to Beaumont, Texas, under Rogers Hornsby, I could see him look at me and in his own mind say, "No way." But he played me and I had one of the best years I ever had in baseball. When I went to Phoenix with the Yankees—he was at Seattle at the time—he came into L.A., and he couldn't understand why Casey wasn't using me, and, sure enough, that afternoon I played my first game. From that day on, I was a fixture in the starting lineup. Evidently, Rogers told Casey, "Give the kid a chance, and you won't take him out of the lineup."

I changed that stance in '55. It was a good stance until the pitchers realized I had trouble hitting the outside pitch. I had trained myself to hit pitches on the inside half of the plate. If the pitch was on the outside part, I would let it go up until two strikes. If the pitcher had good control and threw it on the outside corner, you would see Gil McDougald go down on strikes. It happened many times.

When I changed my stance, I switched from an open one, with my bat hanging down behind me, to a closed one, because we were in Chicago, and Casey was tired of looking at my .170 batting average. "If you don't change that stance—and I mean today— you won't be playing here," he said. I got mad, but I did change my stance. I never had so many sore thumbs from hitting the ball on the handle and on top of the bat, but before I knew it, I was hitting .300. I wasn't hitting the ball hard, but everything was dropping in. With the old stance, I thought

I could hit the ball harder, but the defense was bunching me, and I was trying to hit through too many players. In changing my stance, I was able to hit the ball everywhere on the field and still pull the ball. With the old stance my back foot would be up on the plate and deep in the box. Jim Hegan of the Indians would bark at the ump, "Get him in the batter's box." The ump would draw a line, but I'd inch back again, because I wanted the pitcher to throw right at me. Same as Don Baylor today. He does the same thing. He hits a lot of foul homers. If they turned the diamond around, he'd probably hit 70 homers, because he has a lot of power.

Being able to float around the infield really helped me. It didn't matter to me. There was no pressure at any position. I'm the only infielder to play three different positions on three world title teams, but it didn't impress me at the time. When you're young, you're so jazzed up. Afterwards, when writers recall it in print, you say, "Oh, my God!"

The year Casey turned over shortstop to me, '56, I really enjoyed the most. That was my best year in baseball. I thought I contributed from the field, and I had my best year with the bat. Batting averages never worried me, though. I wasn't conscious whether I batted .250 or .300. I would rather hit .250 and drive home key runs than hit .300 and fail to deliver in the clutch. Good managers aren't deceived by batting averages. When I first came up to the majors, there were certain outfielders we called "Percentage Petes." They'd hit .300 but drive home less than 30 runs. You can't win pennants if outfielders don't drive runs home. Excepting first basemen, you can't expect your infielders to be your RBI men.

All the Yankees of that era thought that way. They

were great players and great guys. Hank Bauer was my roomie for ten years. We got to the World Series eight of those ten years. Close friends were Gerry Coleman, Gene Woodling, Yogi Berra, and Eddie Lopat. At that time we had a golf circuit that we called the "Pro Tour." We all played out of different golf clubs, so we wound up playing a lot of golf between the four clubs. But I only single them out because they lived closer. I consider all the Yankees my friends. The Kubeks, the Richardsons, the Silveras. We were all family.

Yes, the Yankees liked the night life. But no more than any other athletes. You find in any form of athletics that the thing that draws players out at night is the four walls. You look at them constantly during the day waiting for a night game. I think it's sheer boredom rather than the routine of chasing. When you have time on your hands, you can get into trouble. You can drink too much, carouse too much, do a lot of things. The individual needs a lot of self-discipline. One can be very disciplined on the field and very poorly disciplined off it, but on our club the players exercised great self-control. Of course, when you have seven or eight newspapers analyzing your every move, it might not seem so. Take the Copa incident. It was very unfair. Hank got a lot of exposure out of it. They said he clobbered a guy. Later they found out a bouncer did it. Hank handled it well, though. He said, "If I had hit the guy he would have looked a lot worse."

It's true that Casey would criticize me to get at Phil. I was Casey's whipping boy. It took me five or so years to realize what Casey was doing, though. I don't think Phil ever did. No matter what I'd do, good or bad, he'd chew my ass out. I'd get mad and storm out of meetings. Later, when I'd cool down, I'd say, "Well, Gil, you won't be playing today." But when I'd look at the lineup, I'd always be in there.

One day he batted me fourth, in front of Joe. I didn't want to go up there. I didn't know how Joe would take it. I thought he might harpoon me with a bat. Casey understood personnel better than anyone I ever came across. He shook up Joe, because Joe was going bad for him. I got three or four hits in the first game. Feeling somewhat self-important, I said, "Shit, I'll be there in the second game, too." Well, I batted eighth. You talk about killing a dobber quick. He did a good job of that. But he shook up Joe and Joe started to hit and he continued to hit down the stretch.

He told me in '56, "I found out a long time ago that you're a better player when you're mad."

I said, "Casey, how can you bear down all the time? We play 154 games. Most of the time you stand out there and nothing happens. You have to save yourself for the times when it does."

"Yes, but you could have been a very good hitter."

It made me feel good. Yes, I've heard Ted Williams say the same thing. But I wasn't blessed with his vision, his wrists, his power.

Ted used to call me a "shit hitter."

"You're goddamn right," I'd say, "but you'll never beat us a goddamn game as long as I'm with this club."

We'd talk hitting for hours, and I'd come away thinking he didn't understand hitting in the true sense of the word. People who are blessed and never have to struggle don't understand the fundamentals. It's the same in other sports. I remember listening to Arnold Palmer give a clinic in golf. My reaction was,

"Wow, this is the best golfer in the world? I understand how to attack a ball better than he does."

The best coaches don't stay in baseball. The guys who are there belong to a mutual admiration society. The manager fills his staff with buddies. That's sad. I really think that the best coaches should be in the minors where they can help young players develop. They should get paid better than major-league coaches, too, because the players in the majors say, "Hey pal, I got here without you. I don't need you now."

I remember my grand slam home run in the World Series. I was the only player to hit one as a rookie. I've looked at a million pictures that fans have sent me to autograph. Yogi was on third, Joe on second, and Mize on first, if I remember right. Larry Jansen was the pitcher for the Giants, and I think the score was tied 1–1 at the time. Jansen threw me a slider. It looked like a 450-foot homer in the pictures in the papers the next day. It probably traveled all of 330 feet, if it was lucky. The thing that I particularly remember about it was that Casey called me back from the batter's box before the pitch. I said, "Why, that SOB's going to pull me for a pinch hitter. I'll wrap this bat around his neck if he does."

He called me over and said, "Hit one out." That's the truth. That's what happened, so help me God.

I remember one time in Washington, too. Johnny Mize had never hit a home run at Griffith Stadium. He had hit one in every other park in the majors. I had two or three hits in the game. But Casey took me out for a pinch hitter against a right-hander with the bases loaded. I was so goddamn mad. All the way down the dugout, I rapped the bat on the steps. I didn't know what to do with the bat. I guess a lot of

guys could have told me. Then Mize hits a grand
slam home run. What the hell can you say about
that? I was mad at Mize for three weeks. "The least
you could have done," I told him, "was hit a triple."

Casey had a feel for situations and people. Bobby
Brown used to study him. He knew Casey like a
book. We used to sit together on the bench. In a
certain situation, I'd say, "Grab a bat, Brownie, you're
up there."

Brownie would say, "Not yet. The Old Man's going
to come down here, look in my eyes, and say to
himself, 'Not yet.' He'll use me later." That's exactly
what would happen. He knew every one of Casey's
moves.

That's what made playing for the Yankees of that
era fun. The people who played for them loved to
win. Gerry Coleman was a beautiful friend of mine.
I could hear him, when he wasn't in the game, root-
ing for me all the time. Billy too. It's easy to sit on
the sideline and say, "I hope the SOB kays. I'll be in
there then." That I never saw on the Yankees. We
put the game above ourselves. I appreciated that
more than anything else.

I remember Allie's two no-hitters. The one in Boston, I didn't have too much to do with. There weren't
too many tough plays. Except the final out, when
Yogi dropped Ted's towering pop fly near the dugout. Phil said to me, "Now the you-know-what's going
to hit the fan."

I replied, " Phil, you've got to be kidding. With
Yogi's luck, the ball will come up to him in the same
spot, and he'll catch it this time." Sure enough, that's
exactly what happened.

I remember vividly the one in Cleveland. With two
outs in the ninth, we were winning 1–0 on Gene

Woodling's home run. The situation called for me to play back. But Bobby Avila, who was leading the league in hitting, was a great bunter. Hell, I didn't want Allie to lose the no-hitter on a bunt, so I moved up.

"Get back," Allie said.

I just stayed there.

Allie stared at me and snapped, "Get your damn butt back." I ignored him again and started to walk to the mound to explain when Casey came running out and yelled at Allie, "What the hell's wrong with you!"

"I want Gil back."

"Gil plays where I want him. I want him up. You don't run this team. You don't have 37 on your back. Just throw the ball." Then Casey walked back to the dugout.

Allie's mad as hell. The count runs to three-and-two. Avila keeps fouling pitches off. Every one looks like it's coming right at me. Sweat's pouring into my glove. Then I say to myself, "Well, whatever's going to happen will happen." Then Bobby swings at a bad pitch and misses. It's the only high pitch I see him swing at all year. Allie has his strikeout and his no-hitter.

That same year I got in the record books during the regular season, too. In St. Louis I drove home six runs in one inning. I hit a home run and a triple. Jensen, who batted behind me, hit a homer and a triple, too. But he got only two RBIs. I said, "Jensen, what can you do, you're an All-American." All it is, though, is opportunity and having a hot hand that day. It's no big deal. It can happen easily.

Eddie Stanky—that happened in '51, too. In the World Series. The play probably gave us the incentive to turn the Series around. Stanky was that type of player. He liked to take advantage of any opening. He wasn't blessed with natural ability. But he made up for it with heads-up play. Yes, he kicked the ball out of Phil's glove. I never saw a ball go so far on a play like that. Our guys said to each other, "These guys are playing hardball. Let's go get them." The next day we had a meeting. Casey mocked us out. "You let them show you up." That was one of the things that helped us win the '51 Series.

The next year we won 18 games in a row. One short of the American League record. Every day Casey held a meeting and told us what rotten ballplayers we were. We said, "What do you have to do to please the Old Man? Shit, he's impossible." Then we turned around and lost nine games in a row, and he was the most beautiful guy in the world. We said, "Maybe we should lose 18 in a row and have peace in the dugout." But that was his psychology. Don't whip a man when he's down. If you're going to get on someone, do it while he's going well. I think it's a good philosophy.

I was playing third when Billy made that catch in the '52 World Series. It would have been a hell of a way to lose a World Series. Billy was a hell of a competitor. In '53 he had another super World Series. He was chirping all the time. He got on all the players on the Dodgers. We said, "Billy, you might get a chance to get in there to pinch hit. Don't jazz them up too much." Well, Billy got into the lineup and hit a three-run triple off Don Newcombe. He got hot with the bat, played great defense, and had a super Series.

Billy had a couple of run-ins with Clint Courtney. I did, too. Two consecutive nights I bowled him over at the plate. Perfectly legitimate plays. He dropped the ball both times. Well, evidently he thought retaliation was in order. In a subsequent at bat, he hit a ball off the screen in right, and, instead of settling for a single, which it was, he raced to second. Hank's throw had him by thirty feet, but he came into Phil spikes high. Well, we all looked upon Phil as our meal ticket in the infield. In a flash Reynolds, who was pitching, was on top of Courtney. Joe Collins and I were, too. But no one could hit him. There were too many guys trying to get a pop at him. He was way off base. Sure they fined us. But the most important thing I remember about the incident is there weren't too many people from St. Louis in a hurry to get out there.

Sandy Amoros? I knew you were going to bring that up. When I look back upon that incident, I can't fault myself with bad base running. But it was the seventh game of the World Series, and some newspaper writers said that I cost the Yankees the Series. In my own mind I could say, "Yes, I blew it." But I don't feel that bad about the play. I've looked at the play many times. There are some gray areas. We had first and second in the bottom of the seventh with no out. The Dodgers were winning 2–0. Johnny Podres was pitching. Sandy Amoros was playing left field. Yogi hit a high, slicing fly ball towards the left-field line. I represented the tying run, so I got down to second as quick as I could. Amoros was playing too far towards center. Yogi was a good left-field hitter. He ran like hell, but the ball kept fading away from him. I watched him and I saw him put on the brakes. As soon as I saw him brake, I took off for third. I said, "He's dead." From the angle he put on the brakes, there seemed no way he could catch the ball.

But he shot out his glove and the ball landed in it like an Easter-egg catch. I said, "Oh, shit." Cutting across the infield seemed to be my only chance. I busted my butt, retracing my steps. But they made a good relay: Amoros to Pee Wee Reese to Gil Hodges. They got me by a couple of feet. Sandy Amoros made a hell of a play. But I always thought he played the ball poorly. If it were me, that's the time I would have run into the fence and hurt myself. There's no way I would have slammed on the brakes. But it worked out well for them. He decoyed me. Give Podres credit, too. He pitched a hell of a game.

The next year, Don Larsen pitched a perfect game. Three things stand out about that game. One, Dale Mitchell pinch hit with two outs in the ninth. My experience with him at Cleveland was he could hit .300 with his eyes closed. I thought sure he'd plunk one in somewhere. But it was Don's day. Two, I remember Mickey making a hell of a play in left center against Gil Hodges. He simply outraced the ball. Three, Jackie Robinson hit a ball that ricocheted off Andy Carey's glove at third. I was playing short and didn't think Andy could reach the ball, so I was behind him. I caught the deflection. Jackie had bad wheels. I had a rotten arm. But I threw as hard as I could. It was a race between my arm and his legs. We just did get him.

We won big in the seventh game, 9–0. Yogi hit two homers. He owned Newk. But he owned a lot of pitchers. Yogi's batting average, though it was good, didn't truly display how good he was. Many people ask me, "Who's the best hitter you ever saw?"

"It all depends," I say. "Are you talking about batting average, home runs, or who you would like to see up there with the game on the line in the ninth inning?" If they mean with the game in the balance, I say, "Give me Yogi any time."

Yes, '57 was a turning point for me, and, yes, Casey did say I didn't become the player I could have been because of Herb Score. But you would have had to live through that in order to understand. That night Herb was really firing, as he always was, and I would say he was the fastest pitcher I ever saw. Faster than Sandy Koufax. He had to be throwing at least a hundred miles an hour. That was all I remember about the game. I just flicked my bat at the ball. The ball shot back at him. Herb didn't have time to get into his follow-through, because the ball hit him on the wrong eye. I saw the blood spurt. I didn't know whether to run to first or run to the mound. After the game I made a statement to the press, "If anything happens to Herb, I don't want to play anymore." The press blew it up. But that's the way I felt. It couldn't have happened to a nicer guy. He's such a beautiful person. C. I. Thomas, his doctor, called me in every town that I traveled to, to let me know Herb's condition. His mother called me the next day and said, "Gil, you had no control over what happened. Don't ever think of quitting." When people are that nice to you, you say, "Hell!" But it took the starch out of me.

When I went from Cleveland to Detroit, I hit a ball off the knee of Frank Lary, who was one of the best pitchers of the day. They carried him off. In the papers they were calling me, "Killer McDougald." Then when we went to Baltimore, Skinny Brown was pitching. He was a knuckle-baller. But he tried to slip a fastball by me, and I came close to decapitating him. His cap flew off, and the ball went right between his cap and his head, and I could see the look on his face, and I could tell he didn't want anymore of pitching that day. That's when I really thought of quitting. People would say, "You're 11 of 13. You're really thinking of Herb, aren't you?"

That hurt. All I could say was, "That's the funny thing. When you go up there, and you don't give a damn, it seems everything hits your bat well." And I hit the ball very good.

When I almost hit Brown in the head, I said, "Screw this. I'm going to pull everything from now on." Within a month and a half my batting average dropped 40 to 50 points. I really didn't care. All of a sudden, it seemed like you could hurt people. My vivid thought was I had hurt three people within a short period of time. I knew you don't have any control of the ball when it leaves the bat. But I also knew that you could pull the ball into outs, and that's what I started to do.

I had a few highlights left. In '58 I thought I should have started in the All-Star Game. I said to Casey, who was managing, "Screw it, if I can't start after three trips here, what's the honor?"

"You're going," he said. We had words. But I went. I sat on the bench until the eighth inning when Casey put me in to pinch hit and then put me at shortstop. Luis Aparicio was the starter. He made it every year. I don't think he had a ground ball hit to him all night. When I got into the game, I wasn't loose, but I got three ground balls in the eighth and two in the ninth. Initially, he put me up to pinch hit. Though I didn't hit the ball hard, I hit it in the right spot. My hit won the game for us. I notice a lot of guys today make comments about playing or not. Sometimes I can understand. You might have the better year, but they still pick the Williamses or

DiMaggios. That's an inequity. When they did that to me that year, they had the fans voting for me at three different positions. With all my votes, I was way ahead of everyone else. I didn't have enough at one position, though. But it turned out all right for me in '58.

That October I had a really good World Series against the Braves. The preceding year, Milwaukee beat us in seven games when our left-handed hitters didn't produce. But in '58 they were ahead 3–1. The writers were burying us. Before Game Five I said to them, "Right now, I guess nobody's betting his check against mine. But I'm saying we'll win three straight games." Nobody took me up. Good thing. We won three straight games. In Game Five I had a home run and a double with the bases loaded. The next day, I homered and made a key play in the field. It was a good Series for me and the Yankees.

The person on the Yankees whom I most admired was George Weiss. He talked me out of baseball more than anyone else. In '51 I thought I had a pretty good year. But Weiss didn't think I was half as good as I thought. He told me once, "You can't make a living without me." That stuck with me. I mean it hit way down deep.

I said, "I'll prove to him someday that I can make a living without him." What he really did was force me into business.

My highest salary was $40,000. I could have gotten that in my fifth year. Joe Cronin of the Red Sox wanted me real bad. That's the year he offered $1 million for Score. No one was talking those figures at that time. When the Indians said, "No," he said, "I'll get Gil." I would have loved to play in that park. The fans were super. The infield was great, and I loved the park. I know I could have hit 30 home runs a year in that park. I probably never would have changed my stance if I had been traded there.

When I reached the point of retiring in '60, I said, "I've got nothing more to prove. I've done everything I've wanted." Expansion was coming in in '61. I was guaranteed, "You're on the protected list."

Then I got a call from one of my buddies. He said, "Gil, I'm telling you, you're Washington's first pick. I can negotiate for you. Are you interested?"

"No way," I said. "I'm not interested in playing in Washington. They could offer me $10 million. I don't like the city and I don't want to play there." Then the offer switched. Gene Autry of the Los Angeles Angels called me four straight nights. That bothered me, because he offered me more money than I had ever made with the Yankees, counting World Series money. It also bothered me, because I knew I was no longer a good ballplayer. I started to think that maybe the Yankees had shortchanged me along the way. But the most important thing was my family. I got tired of traveling and putting on the uniform. When you get to that stage, you better get the hell out. The children were growing up and they didn't have a father. I said, "Hell, it's time to get out and start a business." I started it in '57. I'm still in it today, with a few different wrinkles. I made a clean break. There has been no adjustment. I don't miss the game. I've seen only two, not counting Old Timers' Day games, since I've retired. I'm not much of a baseball fan.

I enjoyed coaching Fordham University's baseball team for seven years. The kids were different. They weren't there to make money. They accepted advice and looked up to you. I never had any problems, though there was a lot of trouble on campus at the time. It was a case in life where you had to make up your mind what you wanted to do.

My wife and I decided we wanted to raise another family. Our first family had grown and moved to various parts of the country. We adopted three children. My girl's finishing up in college. She's twenty-one. My two sons are fifteen. I'm once again at the stage of looking at kids in college and collecting mortgage books. And I love it.

Joe Collins

Joe Collins was a true Yankee. He did whatever had to be done to win. And quite often it wasn't easy. Before he got to the Bronx, he sandwiched many years in the minors around World War II. The Yankees had fifteen to twenty first basemen in their farm system, so Joe climbed the ladder to the majors one classification at a time.

When he finally got to Yankee Stadium, after a ten-year investment of time, he found that the competition at first base was even more intense than it had been in the minors. First basemen who shared the position with him during his ten years with the Yankees included George McQuinn, Tommy Henrich, Dick Kryhoski, Johnny Mize, Bill Skowron, Eddie Robinson, and Harry Simpson. But from 1950–56 he managed to play a hundred or more games every year. Though his lifetime batting average was a modest .256, he was a winning ballplayer. He was deft at hitting behind the runner and scoring a runner from third base with less than two outs. One year he even led the Yankees in game-winning hits.

In his 10 seasons with the Yankees, they won eight pennants and six world championships. In his eight full *seasons with the Bombers, they won seven pennants and five Fall Classics. In addition, he was one of the 12 players who was a member of the five consecutive world title teams.*

In World Series play, Joe's batting average was deceiving. He batted just .163. But four of his hits were home runs that led to Yankee wins. In Game Two of 1951, he hit a home run off Larry Jansen en route to a 3–1 Yankee win over the Giants. Against the Dodgers, in Game One of 1953, he smacked a game-winning four-bagger against Clem Labine. Two years later, again in Game One, he belted two round-trippers, including the game-winner against Brooklyn's Don Newcombe.

Joe Collins got into business toward the end of his baseball career, as a public relations director for People's Express. He looks forward to the summers when some of his former teammates work their vacations around golf get-togethers on the Jersey courses. Frank Shea comes down from Connecticut. Joe DiMaggio comes in from California. Other Yankees of yesterday congregate, too.

Joe and I got together at his office in downtown Newark around nine o'clock in the morning four summers ago. Joe's a big favorite in the Newark area. A year or so before we met, the people of Union, New Jersey, his hometown, honored him with a "Joe Collins Day" for his decades of commitment to the community's youth and sports. The city even named a field after him.

It's pretty difficult to get into a storytelling mood at nine o'clock in the morning, but by the time we parted, Joe was leaning against a street pole, outside on the pavement, swapping humorous stories with me about Lefty Gomez.

Joe was proud to play with the Yankees. They knew how to win, he said. He knew how to win, too. He also knew how to leave the game. When the Yankees sold him to the Phillies after the 1957 season, he retired from baseball. He said that if he couldn't play with the Yankees, he no longer *wanted to play the game. Joe Collins was a true Yankee in every respect.*

The beginning of my professional baseball career and the end of it are connected by a telephone pole. But that's long distance. Let me begin at the beginning.

My dad changed his original name, Kollonige, around the time that he got married. No one knows me by the original name. I had to use it in the service. But I changed it right after the war. It was tough for the kids going to school. No one could pronounce it.

While I was in high school, in Scranton, Pennsylvania, I was invited to try out with the Wilkes-Barre Barons. In the meantime, my dad ran into Bill Schroeder of the Yankees, who steered me to Binghamton. I worked out with Binghamton and was invited to join the club for a ten-day home stand. That was in 1939. In that same year I was sent to Butler, Pennsylvania, and Easton, Maryland, two Class D teams.

Did you ever hear of a professional baseball player who ran into a telephone pole? Well, I did. It stood between the stands and the playing field. I tore my shoulder apart. Almost half my face and ear, too. That shoulder would come back to haunt me. They sent me home in the latter part of May. I was still in high school at the time. I didn't graduate until January 1940.

At the age of 17, I was a professional ballplayer. But I didn't reach the majors for another decade. The competition was intense. Even if you were good, you moved up only one league classification each year. Of course, the service came along, too. I enlisted in the Navy Air Corps in December 1942. I got my wings at Pensacola. Years later, Ted Williams, Gerry Coleman, and I would get together to talk about our flying days.

After I got separated from the Navy, I was assigned to Newark in the International League. George Selkirk was the manager of the Bears at that time. He liked pull hitters. Fortunately I was that kind of hitter. In order to get me in the lineup, he put me in right field. That helped my career, especially when we had Johnny Mize with the Yankees. Two years later, I was playing center field between Lou Novikoff and Ted Sepkowski. They were slow. What was worse, they never moved. Novikoff would say to me, "You've got it, kid. There's lots of room."

In 1949 I hit .323 for Kansas City playing first again. I made the All-Star team. At the end of the season, I came up to the Yankees. In 1950 I went to spring training with them, and I stayed.

The competition was still intense. The only guys I had to beat out were Johnny Mize and Tommy Henrich. Still, I thought my chances were good so long as I got a chance to play. I ended up playing some outfield and defensive first base the latter part of a game.

The Yankees were a great group of guys. Everyone talks about Pittsburgh: "Family, family family!" I don't think any team ever had a greater group of fellows than we did. Casey didn't have to do too much managing. We policed ourselves. If someone didn't run a hundred percent, someone in the dugout would yell, "If you're too tired, you should get more sleep."

Casey started the two-platoon system. He alternated Gene Woodling and Hank Bauer. Both were very good fielders and very good clutch hitters. But Hank will tell you Casey prolonged his career, even though he didn't like it at the time. Casey kept the players angry at him, knowing that they'd play harder. Gil McDougald was a key example.

Outside of Billy Martin, I was Casey's number two Bobo. I never moaned or bitched, I played any position, and I played hurt. You could never figure Casey out, though. One day in 1951, he batted me fourth in the first game of a doubleheader. I got three hits. In the second game, I batted eighth.

One year we clinched the pennant in Boston on an off day. I was hurting, nursing a pulled groin muscle. But Casey asked me to play the next day. I did. That night at the pennant-victory party, he embarrassed me by saying, "Collins, I don't want to see you at the park tomorrow. You've got the day off." I took a lot of heckling from my teammates over that one. The next day he saw me in the hotel lobby. He knew what I was thinking. "If you go to the ballpark," he said, "it's going to cost you $500. I don't want to see you until Tuesday for the team picture."

Another time we were playing in St. Louis. He sent about five of us by plane ahead of the train. The other guys, I think, were Vic Raschi, Allie Reynolds, Phil Rizzuto, maybe, Eddie Lopat, and Coleman. Meanwhile, the train arrived just in time for the game. That one backfired. Phil and I played five innings, and both of us went hitless in three at bats. Everyone else got three hits. They took out their anger on the Senators. We won 18–1. I ended up sorry I missed the train ride. I heard they had a hell of a time.

Casey's edge was psychology. The way he handled certain players. He would direct remarks at one player to get to another. Take Rizzuto. He was sensitive. So Casey wouldn't criticize him directly. Instead he would direct the remarks intended for Rizzuto to McDougald. Casey knew McDougald could take it. He also knew Phil would get the message.

Once in a while in spring training, Casey would sleep on the bench. When he was out with "his writers" till three in the morning. He'd be up at seven, though. He needed very little sleep. But sometimes he would snooze on the bench. Then he'd look up and see something he didn't like and let the player know in no uncertain terms what he thought.

He could always get out of a mistake, though. One day in spring training he looked up and said, "Now where's Collins? I know he's up to something." Bill Dickey whispered in his ear, telling him I had played five innings and gone home, which was customary. Then Casey pointed to someone and said, "I don't mean Collins. I mean you."

The first game I ever played for the Yankees, Raschi was on the mound. It was the eighth inning, as I remember. The first man got on. The next guy bunted the ball to me. I tried second and pulled Phil off the bag. (All my errors were throwing ones.) Now there are first and second with no out. The ball was bunted again. This time I pulled the third baseman off the bag. I walked to the mound and said, "Vic, I sure screwed this game up for you."

He snapped, "Just give me the ball."

Well, he struck out the next two hitters and got the third batter on a pop-up. In the ninth I hit a pitch into the stands to win the game. What a reprieve he gave me!

My first good year was 1951. I hit .286 and nine home runs. In addition, I stole nine bases. That was the year Joe D retired. When he started hitting good fastballs to right field, he felt he had had it.

Yeah, I remember the time in Detroit when he miscounted the outs. He caught a fly ball and ran to the dugout. All hell broke out in the Tigers' dugout. Some wag said, "We get three outs. Let's count them. One, two. That's not enough." He was very embarrassed.

He was the best player I ever saw, though. He did everything well. He was the best I ever saw going from first to third, and he was the best I ever saw at stretching hits. He always made the right play at the right time. I never remember a ball in left center going to the wall.

That same year Bobby Thomson hit the pennant-winning home run for the Giants. Phil and I were at that game. We left early because of the crowd. A half-hour later, we were parked at a red light on Tonnele Avenue in Jersey City with the radio on. There was a guy in the car next to us. When Thomson hit the home run, I said, "How about that!"

He said, "Fuck you!" and sped away. I guess he was a Dodger fan.

Yankee fans got mad at the Giants in that year's World Series, too, when Eddie Stanky kicked the ball out of Phil's glove at second base. But I thought it was a good heady play A very clever play. I didn't hold anything against him.

The next two years were good ones for me, too. I hit 18 and 17 home runs. But that was no big deal. With the Yankees you were supposed to contribute. Everyone else was hitting home runs. The World Series those years were evenly matched. Either team, the Yankees or the Dodgers, could have won.

Of course, when you talk about the 1952 World Series, you think of Billy's catch in Game Seven. If he doesn't make it, three runs score on a pop-up to the mound, and we lose the Series. I never did see the ball. Jackie Robinson's pop-up was right in the sun. It looked like a foul ball in the stands to me. Bob Kuzava should have made someone aware where the ball was, or caught it himself. I remember one time when Lopat had a ball hit directly above the mound. Andy Carey, Coleman, and I were surrounding it. Lopat tackled me and knocked me out of the way so that the play could be made.

Eddie was a take-charge guy. So was Reynolds. When Allie came out of the bullpen, I felt sorry for the Dodgers. He was throwing so hard, and his curves were breaking so sharp, they didn't have a chance. Whitey Ford was a guy who was in command on the mound, too. When he came up to the major leagues, he was a pro. He was always poised on the mound. Dwight Gooden came up the same way. Same composure, same poise.

In the 1953 World Series I had a tough afternoon against Carl Erskine. I struck out four times. That's the day he set a World Series record by striking out 14 batters. Mickey went down swinging four times, too. I couldn't pick his ball up. He was coming overhand right out of the center-field bleachers. He had a great curve and change that day. But I complained and Mickey complained. Mize, who wasn't playing that day, was busting us. "Why can't you hit him?" he'd say. "The man's meat." But in the ninth inning he pinch hit and looked at a third strike.

"Why couldn't you hit him?" we wanted to know.

"The pitch was this much outside," he said, pressing his thumb and forefinger together.

Mize tried to bring the St. Louis Cardinals to New York. Enos Slaughter, too. "This is the way we did it with the Cards," they would say.

"You're not with the Cards anymore," we'd reply It didn't work, though. Once a Card, always a Card, I guess.

The Dodgers finally beat us in 1955. Sandy Amoros' catch was the difference. That was the game. A memorable one. I still think he was out of position, though. He was too far over in left center for Berra. Yogi was a good left-field hitter.

Don Larsen's perfect game in 1956 was memorable, too. Before we went out for the ninth inning, everyone in the infield talked about getting a glove on any ball that looked like a base hit. The scorer would probably call it an error, not a hit. We weren't thinking about a perfect game. We were thinking about a no-hitter.

I didn't hit for average in the World Series. But I got some big hits. Four of them were homers. My first came off Larry Jansen of the Giants in 1951. I hit it off the end of the bat, right down the line. My second came in the opening game of 1953. It turned out to be the game-winner against Clem Labine. My last two were hit in the opening game of 1955. Off Don Newcombe. The second one was also a game-winner.

I always hit Newk good, even when he was with Montreal in the International League. Another guy I wore out was Bob Lemon. How can you account for that? You hit some so easy and you can't buy a hit off others. A fellow by the name of ["Wild" Bill] Connelly had a good curve against me in the minors. But he couldn't throw it over to anyone but me. I didn't see him again for five or six years. One night we're playing the White Sox, and I'm batting with the bases loaded. Connelly comes out of the bullpen, and he spots three curves on the outside corner. I was the last guy he got out in the majors.

Looking back, I have to say that those Yankee teams from 1949 to 1953 were great clubs. We knew how to win. It wasn't conceit or ego. It was inbred from the time you joined the franchise. It permeated the minor leagues. We were expected to win and we did.

It was a class club. Especially the pitching staff. I never remember any pitcher saying anything about an error. They'd try as much as possible to get you off the hook. They didn't want anyone to look like the goat.

We had so many guys who could win a game for you. Billy was a little pepperpot who was tough in the clutch. Gerry was the best double-play second baseman I ever saw. The ball never hit his glove. It was just deflected to first. Gil was the best all-round player on the team at that time. Gene was very underrated. He won more games than they gave him credit for. Hank was hard-nosed and good in the clutch, too. They were all winners.

You take Mick. He was awesome. In his first spring training he was phenomenal. I never saw anyone hit the ball so high and so far in my life. He was an unbelievable hitter. He came up as a shortstop, you know. There he was something else. He was more likely to hit the stands than the first baseman. He was what you would call "wild high."

The only negative thing I can remember was negotiating a contract with Roy Hamey, who was the assistant to George Weiss. I wanted $25,000 for what I had thought was a pretty productive year.

"We're only going to give you $18,000," he said.

"Why?" I said. "I had a pretty good year."

"You didn't hit .300."

"I never hit .300."

"Those are the guys we pay the big money to."

"I thought the idea was to win games. I led the team in game-winning hits. I thought the idea of the game was to give yourself up, to get the man from second to third, to score the runner from third with less than two out."

"You didn't hit .300."

"Well, I'll tell you what I'll do," I said. "I'll make a deal with you. If I hit .300 this year, you pay me $25,000. If I hit below .300, you pay me $18,000. It's only a matter of another 18 to 20 hits. I can get them. But I'll tell you what. I'm not going to play for the Yankees. I'm going to play for Joe Collins."

"That's a selfish attitude," he said.

Can you believe that? I couldn't. But you can believe I got the $25,000.

After the 1957 season I got into the trucking business. It was time to get out. My shoulder was bad. I was still paying for that long-distance call I made in 1939. I could play only three or four times a week. Ironically the Yankees sold me after the season to the Phillies. Hamey had moved on to Philadelphia before me as the general manager. Why'd he buy me? He couldn't have been looking for a .300 hitter.

But he offered me $25,000. I said, "No, if I can't be a Yankee, I don't want to play this game anymore." I hung up my spikes.

I think he understood.

Gene Woodling

In 1948 the Yankees could have gotten Gene Woodling for virtually nothing. Instead, one year later, they paid the San Francisco Seals of the Pacific Coast $100,000 for him.

That pretty much typifies Woodling's career. He was never properly appreciated by the front office. He batted .300 for four major-league clubs, but each of the four got rid of him.

In 1952–53 he put together back-to-back .300 years with the Yankees. In fact the Yankees won five world titles in Gene's first five years in New York. Yet after one substandard year, in 1954, the Yankees sold him to the White Sox.

Still, according to Woodling, the best was yet to come. "I had my best years between the ages of thirty-five and forty," he says. During that span he batted .321 for the Indians, .300 for the Orioles, and .313 for the Senators.

He was a .300 hitter in World Series play, too. In 1949 he batted .400; in 1950, .429. In 1952 he hit .348; in 1953, .300. Overall, he batted .318.

One of the reasons Woodling got traded so much was because, in his words, he was a "red-ass." That is, he said what he thought.

Casey Stengal didn't always like Woodling's opinions. But they didn't affect his regard for Gene.

"Gene Woodling had more good years after he left the Yankees than any other player we traded away," Stengel once said. "We really made a mistake there. And I'm honest enough to admit it. I really liked Gene. We had our disagreements. But they balanced out."

The night before I spoke to him, from his home in Medina, Ohio, he and his wife, Betty, had attended their forty-fifth reunion at Akron East High School. In the midst of their reminiscing, he said to her, "How could I be so lucky, to be the one who made it?" In high school he had liked every sport—except baseball. Gene Woodling says that Bill Bradley had to be the most perceptive scout in the world to see a baseball future in him. Although Gene could play the game, he didn't know anything about it. In the minor leagues he once led the Ohio State League with a .398 batting average, but his manager said he couldn't hit. And Gene believed him.

But he was a quick learner. And every success he had on the playing field he parlayed into future success off it. Charlie Silvera used to sit next to Gene Woodling at spring training every year and say, "Well, Gene, what are you going to do with your World Series check this year?" Gene always knew exactly what he was going to do—save it to buy land. In 1957 he bought a farm in Medina. He, his wife, and his son restored a 127-year-old house together, and he raised Appaloosa horses. Today he has thirty-eight acres of land that he says he's going to hold while he does a lot of traveling. In fact, when we spoke, he had a forty-day trip to China planned for the fall.

Gene is appreciative of the good life. Once in a while when he's alone on his tractor, he looks up and says, "Thanks, God, for you and for baseball. You've given me everything I've got."

Regrets? Heck, no, I'd do it over a thousand times. My wife, Betty, and I were high school sweethearts. We went to our forty-fifth reunion at Akron East High School last night. During the evening I said to her, " How could I be so lucky, to be the one who made it?"

I must have been good at horseshoes. My timing was perfect. I came from a wrong-side-of-the-track neighborhood. Thank goodness. That's why I became an athlete.

It's a funny thing. I didn't even like baseball back in those days. Everything but. It was a family tradition that we all be top swimmers. My brother was a national champion. He would have gone to the Olympics if it hadn't been for the war.

Bill Bradley had to be a super scout to see me. It amazes and scares me to think how easily I could have been missed. I owe everything to baseball.

My top salary was $40,000. Two years in a row, when I was thirty-six and thirty-seven, with Baltimore. I have no regrets salary-wise, though. I wouldn't trade my success for today. I hope today's players end up like me. We hear gross, not net. How about Uncle Sam? The car I used to pay $1,800 for is now $22,000. The acres I paid $200 for are now $15,000.

I bought the farm in 1957, when I was with Cleveland. It's thirty miles from Akron, about forty to fifty from Cleveland. I've got thirty-eight acres. Sold some away. The rest will stay with me till I die. I did have horses. Appaloosas. My wife always wanted them. They're tremendous show and riding horses. Good quarter-milers, too. At one time I had thirty-eight of them. My wife, my boy, and I worked the farm. We restored a 127-year-old house together. Right now, I'm going to hold the land I have and do a lot of traveling. In fact, in the fall, Betty and I are going to China for forty days.

I did a lot of traveling in my baseball career, too. I played in four different minor leagues. And with seven different major-league teams. In the minors I led three of the leagues in batting. I batted .280 for Newark in 1947. That was my *one* bad year. In 1940 I led the Ohio State League with a .398 batting average. But, after the season, my manager said, "Gene, you can't hit." I didn't know anything about baseball back then. I thought he was right.

I was up for cups of coffee with Cleveland and Pittsburgh before the Pirates dealt me to the San Francisco Seals in 1948. That was my big break. I got a raise to go back to the minor leagues. The Seals were an independently owned club. Paul Fagin, who made his money in the sugar market, treated his players much better than major-league owners. He owned his own airplane and flew his players before major-league clubs did. He owned limousines, too. We traveled first class. And Seals Stadium was a beautiful park. Why the Giants ever bought Candlestick Park, I'll never know. We drew 692,000 people in 1948. It was a wonderful year for me. I batted .385 and was named the Minor-League Player of the Year by *The Sporting News*. I played for Lefty O'Doul, who was a great guy, the best. He came as close to being a hitting coach as anyone could be. There is no such animal, though. No one helps anyone to hit. Hitting is a God-given talent. The title *hitting coach* simply creates jobs.

Well, we were in Portland at the end of the year, and Lefty called me to the front of the bus. He said, "We finally sold you. Are the Yankees okay?"

I said, "Sure, they're great." Then I thought, *Where am I going to play? They've got Henrich, Keller, and DiMaggio in the outfield. Where am I going to play?* I got worried. I had already been up for a couple of cups of coffee. In those days you just got two or three chances. I worried that if I failed with the Yankees, I wouldn't get another chance.

It was ironic that the Yankees bought me. Casey and I both came to the Yankees in 1949. The year before, we were both in the Pacific Coast League. He managed Oakland and had a heck of a year. As I said before, I hit .385 for the Seals. So I think he had a big influence on my becoming a Yankee. Then we went on to win five consecutive world titles together.

It's also interesting that the Yankees had to pay the Seals $100,000 for me. They had to give up two players, too. In 1947, when I was with the Newark Bears, Bill Skiff, who was my manager, told George Weiss of the Yankees, "Get Woodling. You can get him for nothing."

Weiss said, "No, we're not interested in Woodling."

Just goes to show you how smart they can be. In later years, whenever Skiff got a few belts in him at a social get-together, he loved to remind Weiss of his costly mistake.

"Heh, George," he'd say, "remember Woodling. You could have had him for nothing. What'd we eventually pay for him, $100,000?"

Well, anyway, the Yankees bought me. In 1949 we won the pennant and World Series, of course, and I received 10 percent of the sale price at the end of the season. That's the kind of guy Paul Fagin was. He took care of his players. I also got $6,000 for my World Series share. Never before in my life had I seen so much money at one time.

I was never secure, though, in my career with the Yankees. They had 20 left fielders every spring. I don't know why. I didn't mind the competition, though. I had more trouble in other areas. I was too much of a red-ass. I always said what I felt. Once I said that the Yankee uniform didn't make me a ballplayer. That was sacrilegious in those days. And I said I didn't care for the platoon system. I still don't. I always felt that I could hit any pitcher. I had my job and I did it. A lot of guys got me out, but I wore some guys out, too.

Hank Bauer used to say to Casey, "When you're five games ahead, you platoon. When you're one game ahead, both Gene and I play."

That first season with the Yankees was special, though. The 1949 World Series was a big thrill for me. Those bus rides between New York and Brooklyn were something special. Those fans were really into the World Series. All the people who crowded round were so knowledgeable. The New York fans knew so much more than any other fans in the country at that time. And no one was booed in New York. Mantle got booed later for some of his antics. But, generally speaking, they even cheered the opposition. I never heard anyone booed in New York.

Speaking of Mantle, I was there the day he hit that ball out of Griffith Stadium. He hit one farther the next year at Sportsman's Park in St. Louis. But he got so much publicity the year before that they couldn't surpass it. No one, including Babe Ruth, hit them consistently as far as Mantle did. Mantle was unbelievable. I don't think he ever realized the talent he had. He was just a small-town boy who came to New York to swing a bat.

I remember the night Allie Reynolds threw a no-hitter in Cleveland. Why wouldn't I? Late in the game I hit a home run to give him a 1–0 win over Bob Feller. Feller, you know, once threw a 1–0 no-hitter against the Yankees. In 1946. Well, anyway, there were 80,000 people in Cleveland's Municipal Stadium that night. It was a ballplayer's dream. Ballplayers are no different than other people. We all want to do something special in front of the hometown folks. It made me feel very proud.

I hit well in Cleveland. It was my favorite park. And against that pitching staff. Feller, Lemon, Wynn, Garcia. Why? That's one of the nice things about baseball. You never know.

We were talking about Reynolds, though. When he was with Cleveland, he was just a young man. He was just a thrower. Boy, could he throw, though. He and Virgil Trucks could put the ball up to the plate about a hundred miles an hour. They could fire. Reynolds later relieved in a lot of clutch games. He loved big-game situations. By that time he had developed a curveball. A good one. Experience made the difference. He was just like Feller. Each of them had a great fastball and a great curveball. You couldn't sit on a pitch with those guys on the mound.

Playing with the Yankees was like a dream come true. There I was, playing next to DiMaggio, who was one of my favorites when I was a little kid in Akron. I'll never forget that weekend in Boston when Joe returned to the lineup after missing the first 65 games. He demolished the Red Sox, single-handed. It was unbelievable that he could bounce back the way he did. The fans were awed. We were, too. Like Ted Williams taking batting practice. It was a special treat for us.

When I played with Joe, I had the left-field line,

Hank had the right-field line, and Joe had everything in between. Joe could go get them. Actually, my strong side was my left side. Joe noticed that. One day he said to me, "Gene, if you can get it, go get it." Of course, you didn't run over Joe. He made it easy to play next to. The bottom line was he *loved* to win.

In truth, I was a good fielder. They said I was the best to play the sun field at Yankee Stadium. I led the league in fielding one year. [Actually he led the league back-to-back in 1952 and 1953, with identical .996 averages. In fact, during the Yankees' five world title years, he committed only nine errors, an average of less than two miscues a season.] I guess I knew how to get out of the way of the ball.

Speaking about the sun field, I lost a ball in the sun in the fourth game of the 1950 World Series against the Phillies. That was one of our toughest World Series. We beat them in four games. But look at those scores. They were all decided by one run, except the last one. Anyway, I lost a ball in the sun. You've heard about that sun field in October. Well, the newspapermen played it way out of proportion. They made me look like a fool. But they made me a lot of money, too. Everyone wanted to hear about the play on the banquet circuit that winter. The next spring I told the writers, "Thank you."

I didn't let newspapers, or writers, get to me. I felt that I was given a job, and I did it the best that I could. Baltimore booed me out of town once and I came back to do a great job the second time the Orioles got me. I couldn't blame the first Baltimore experience on anyone except me. I didn't hit in the spring. Paul Richards, the manager of the Orioles, wanted me, but just before the June 15 trading deadline, he came to me and said, "I better get you out of town." It was the only place that I didn't do well. But he brought me back later and I turned it around.

No one likes to be traded. The phone rang for twenty-four hours on the day that the Yankees traded me. I just took the phone off the hook. But I wouldn't roll over and die. I went on to play some good baseball. In fact, I became a better ballplayer after I left New York.

Actually my best year was with Cleveland in 1959. I won a lot of ball games that year. I guess they were throwing where I was swinging. But I had my best *years* in Baltimore, when I was thirty-five to forty. I can't explain that. Can you?

One of the nicest compliments I ever got came from Casey. He said, "We traded a lot of guys away. How many of them have lasted so long and played so well in the same league as Woodling?"

One year Casey and I fussed a lot. About playing time. All to do with baseball. He accepted it. One day he sent Frankie Crosetti to Bauer and me. Crow said, "You guys don't play well unless you're mad." Casey understood us. We were a couple of square-heads. When I was with Baltimore the first time, and I wasn't hitting, one of the writers asked Casey, "Heh, Casey what's wrong with Gene?"

Casey said, "He's not mad enough to hit."

He knew who to stir up and who to leave alone. Looking back, he got good baseball out of us. I didn't pout. Hank, neither. We got stirred up. We played hard. We hustled. That was the Yankee way. The worst insult on the Yankees was if someone said, "Nice hustle." It was expected. We ran hard. We played hard. There were no ground-ball double plays on that club. We had a lot of talent. And we were a regular group of red-asses. We got mad and we played hard.

We were fast, too. We didn't steal bases. But who didn't go from first to third or second to home? Guys today steal third base with two out in a tie game. I'd be mad if I were the batter. They'd be taking the bat out of my hands. Casey didn't take you out of the game. His favorite remark was, "I don't want guys who give you one swing and two outs." He got rid of Billy Johnson and Jackie Jensen for that reason. Jim Rice? He'd never play for Casey.

The year that Casey and I fussed a lot, we won the pennant and World Series, as usual. After we won the Series, I went into his office and said, "Hey Casey?"

He cut me off quickly. "Hey, don't come in here and apologize for making me look good all year," he said.

He didn't hold any grudges. I was the only Yankee he brought back to the Mets. By God, that should stop all this nonsense about he didn't like me, and I didn't like him.

In 1962 with the Mets, it was an entirely different situation than it was with the Yankees. There was nothing he could do about it. He was funny with the Mets. A good public relations man. Not with the Yankees, though. Casey and I argued with the Yankees. We never argued with the Mets. Casey summed up the difference beautifully one day: "He wanted to play every day with the Yankees. I want him to play every day with the Mets."

The 1949–53 Yankees were great. We didn't lose so we must have been the best. We had pitching. We had speed and defense. We kept out of the double play. We had contact hitters and we had long-ball hitters. Also, we were accustomed to a dividend in the fall. I don't know of too many corporations that pay that kind of dividend. It had a lot to do with our success. I know it opened a lot of doors for me.

I played with great guys. That's what you miss. That's why I like to go back to Old Timers' Day games. When I do, I'm glad to be able to say to myself that I made a contribution to those great teams.

Mel Allen called me "New Reliable." I was proud of that name. Tommy Henrich, of course, was "Old Reliable." But the ballplayers called me "Old Pro." They respected the way I was a bear-down player. The nicest thing that can happen to a ballplayer is to get such compliments from fellow ballplayers.

Once in a while, when I'm alone and driving a tractor on the farm, I look up at the sky and say, "How could I be so lucky? Baseball has given me everything." That's why I get so peeved at some of these owners and agents who are messing with the game.

And sometimes, when I'm on that tractor, I think about the 1952 World Series. That showed what kind of team we were. We were down three games to two and had to win two games at Ebbets Field. How'd we do it? They had *some* club. Geez, they were good! Hodges, Robinson, Reese, Cox, Campanella, Furillo, Snider, Newcombe, Erskine! And we beat 'em!

We had to be the best!

Tommy Byrne

Tommy Byrne says he could have been better than he was. The Yankees signed him for $10,000, the most money they had ever given a rookie up to that time. Clearly they expected great things from him.

But control problems proved to be his Achilles' heel. They called him "The Wild Man," and justly so. In 12 of his 13 major-league seasons, he walked more batters than he struck out. Considering his walk-strikeout ratio, an objective observer would have to conclude it was truly amazing that Tommy Byrne posted an 85–69 (72–40 with the Yankees) career record.

Tommy Byrne came up to the Yankees in 1943 as the heir apparent to Lefty Gomez, who had moved on to Washington. But, as Tommy said, he "walked the ballpark," so he was sent back to the minors. Five years later he returned to the Bronx for a four-year stay. A live arm compensated for an erratic one. He could have learned a lot from Eddie Lopat. But Byrne was not satisfied simply to get a batter out; he wanted to strike him out. In spite of back-to-back fifteen-win seasons in 1949–50, he was traded to the St. Louis Browns. Co-owner Dan Topping became frustrated *seeing Byrne run three-two counts on virtually every batter he faced.*

Overall, Tommy Byrne has good memories of his baseball career. He played under four managers—Joe McCarthy, Bucky Harris, Casey Stengel, and Rogers Hornsby—who are in the Hall of Fame. That is one of the reasons that he had a largely successful major-league career. Success breeds success, he says. In all, he played in four World Series. It could have been more, but the Yankees quit on him once.

Tommy Byrne remembers his live bat, too. In his sophomore year at Wake Forest, he batted .592. One year at Newark he batted .361. In the majors he batted .238 with fourteen home runs, many of which were in pinch-hitting situations. He also batted .300 in four World Series. Mel Allen called him "that good-hitting pitcher."

The Yankees brought Byrne back to New York, late in the 1954 season, when he had "learned how to pitch." Tommy proved it in 1955 when he won 16 games, lost 5, and led the league with a .762 winning percentage. In that year's World Series he pitched a complete-game victory over the Dodgers to become the only left-handed pitcher in 1955 to perform the feat.

When the Yankees traded Byrne in 1951, Casey said to Tommy, "Topping says you're too wild. But where am I going to find someone to win 15 games in your place?"

In 1955 Casey found the answer. He re-acquired Tommy Byrne to take Tommy Byrne's place. And Tommy Byrne went one win further. He won 16 games.

For some reason Tommy was a favorite of George Weiss's. Topping got rid of Tommy in 1951; Weiss brought him back late in 1954, and Tommy vindicated himself. He proved Topping was wrong to have traded him, and he proved that Weiss had been right to buy him back.

When I spoke to Tommy in the summer of 1987, he was the mayor of Wake Forest, North Carolina. Tommy Byrne's *roots are deeply imbedded in Wake Forest. Though he was born in Baltimore in 1919, he starred in baseball for the Deacons of Wake Forest University in the late 1930s. (Wake Forest University is in Winston-Salem, North Carolina; it is not the Wake Forest that Tommy has served for so long.) But many of his fond memories are of New York City. Tommy thinks that with his tools he should have done much better with the Yankees and in the majors than only 85 wins. Nevertheless, he is proud of his accomplishments and the role he played in the Yankees' success in the late 1940s and 1950s. And he wants to share them in print with his one daughter, three sons, and nine grandchildren. "Hey, listen," he said when we concluded the interview, "I want you to send me a copy of the book when it comes out." He paused. "No, wait, you better make that ten copies."*

When I was young, my parents were separated, and I spent quite a lot of time in an orphanage. We played a lot of baseball games against other orphanages. At age thirteen, I was a Yankee fan. My catcher said to me, "You'll be pitching for Detroit in 1937."

I replied, "No, I'll be pitching *against* Detroit in 1937."

Well, he was right. I was pitching *batting practice* in Detroit in 1937. The Tigers gave me a tryout. They offered me $4,000. But I signed with the Yankee for $10,000. That was the most they had ever given anyone. I told them what I wanted. They asked me to come up to New York to sign. Ed Barrow came into the office and walked out. I told him the A's had offered me $12,000. Ira Thomas, the scout for Philadelphia, was crazy about me. I told Ira, "I'll take your 12 if they don't offer me 10."

I was supposed to replace Lefty Gomez in the Yankee rotation. Lefty finished up in New York in 1942. The next year he was in Washington. That's the year I broke in with the Yankees. McCarthy said to me, "Tommy, you're my fifth starter." I got my first start in late May before 68,000 fans. Naturally I was excited. I got the first nine men out. Then I walked the ballpark. That's the type of season it was. I got only one more start and finished the season 2–1 with a 6.54 ERA.

McCarthy wanted me to switch to first base. I had hit .592 in my junior year at Wake Forest. In 1942 I batted .328 at Newark, where I had a 17–4 season. Mac wanted me to go back to Newark and work at first base. But I figured I had come too far as a pitcher to take a chance as a regular. The next two years I spent in the Navy. I played at Norfolk. When I came back in 1946, I was twenty-six. But I was still too wild. So I stayed in the minors. In 1947 I was 14–4 with Kansas City when the Yankees brought me back. I was 8–5 with New York in 1948. I didn't start until July when I shut the Tigers out. But I finally showed some consistency I completed five of 11 starts, won two games in the bullpen, saved two others, and posted a 3.30 ERA.

I was very fortunate that I played under a lot of good managers: Joe McCarthy . . . Casey Stengel . . . Bucky Harris . . . Rogers Hornsby . . . Paul Richards. McCarthy was a hard-nosed man who didn't say much, but he was a super guy. The Browns canned Hornsby in Boston. I was one of only two players who wouldn't sign the petition that Bill Veeck passed around to get rid of him. Casey liked me. I liked him. We couldn't have gotten along better. He was a left-hander, too. We understood each other.

One day we got into it on the mound, though. You

need five innings as a starter to get the win. But I walked three straight batters with two outs in the fifth inning. We were winning 5–2 at the time. But the bases were loaded and Gus Zernial was standing at the plate. Casey was storming in the dugout. Then he came out, and he waved to the bullpen before he got to the foul line. Well, I had the red-ass. "You're out of your mind," I said. "You know what the score is? Five-two. It was nothing-nothing when we started the game, and you had confidence in me *then*."

Casey snapped, "Give me the ball!"

"My ass!" I fired back, and I kicked the resin bag all the way to second base.

He followed me. "You know why I'm taking you out," he said. "I'm afraid you'll hit someone." I had already hit four batters. He brought Fred Sanford in. I threw the ball over Gerry Coleman's head at second. Sanford caught it coming in from the bullpen.

"See that!" I yelled at Casey. "It was a strike!"

I left the mound first. There were boos and aahs when Casey followed me. Then Zernial hit a double and the A's tied the game. We lost in 11 innings, 10–9. Everyone was mad in the clubhouse. Casey piped up, "When I make a pitching change, we'll walk to the dugout together. That way, if anyone gets booed, we'll get booed together." But Casey was in full control. That was just one of those situations where my *control* got to him.

When I threw balls, he got excited. I'd be missing by half an inch. The umpire would say, "Ball." I'd yell, "Call strikes or we'll be out here all day." Casey'd tell Collins, "Go over and talk to Byrne." Joe'd come over but he'd be embarrassed.

In the 1949 World Series Casey shouted to Coleman. That was a signal for Gerry to come to the mound. Casey was getting nervous.

"Whaddaya want?" I said.

"They told me to talk to you," he said.

"How're you getting along?"

"Fine. How are you?"

"I'm ready when you are."

"Let's go." On the second pitch to Hodges, Gil hit into a two-hop double play.

In 1949 and 1950 I won 15 games in each season. At one point in the two seasons, I was 17 and 2. But on June 15, 1951, when I got to the ballpark, Stubby Overmire's sitting in my locker. Casey told Pete Sheehey, the clubhouse man, to tell me to come to his office. Casey told me Dan Topping was upset about my bases on balls. But Casey was upset, too. "You won 30 games the last two years. Who's going to do that now?"

I was so shocked and surprised, I couldn't believe it. Every year I was getting better. It's an interesting game sometimes. But I figured I'd make a buck anyway. And I knew Topping had more problems than I did.

My control didn't get any better with the Browns. I walked more than twice as many batters as I struck out: 150 to 71. In one game I threw *248 pitches* in a 13-inning 3–2 loss. I walked 16 batters, a record for an extra-inning game. I remember another game with the Browns. I hit a home run against Sid Hudson of Washington with two strikes and two outs in the ninth inning to win the game. Al Evans was the catcher. Hudson threw a high fastball, and I hit it up through an exit in the right-field stands.

I spent two years in St. Louis. In 1953 I was with the White Sox. Chicago was a first-class operation. I started seven games and I was 2–0. Every game I pitched we won. In one of the games, I hit a grand slam in New York against Ewell Blackwell. But I was traded to Washington. The last game I pitched with the Senators, I struck out 12 batters in a 2–1 loss, but Clark Griffith sent me to Seattle in the Pacific Coast League *one day* before I became a ten-year man. Gerry Priddy was my manager there. I had a good year in Seattle in 1954. I was 20-10. At the plate I hit .295 with seven home runs and 45 runs batted in.

Well, Casey and George Weiss got me back. They called me up and said, "How're you feeling?"

I said, "I'm in good health. I'm breathing. Get me back." I was the first guy they brought back.

In my first start I beat Bob Turley in Baltimore. I hit a triple, a double, and walked. Who do you think met me when I arrived back at Yankee Stadium? Dan Topping. "I'm glad you're back," he said. The guy's in the cemetery now. He couldn't do anything about it. He was born with a silver spoon in his mouth.

But basically I feel very good about my Yankee experiences. Both before they traded me and after they brought me back. In 1949 I won 15 games. We had a lot of injuries that year. Tommy Henrich had a phenomenal year. Mel Allen gave him the nickname "Old Reliable." Tommy carried the club when Joe was out with his injury. Also in September, when the pennant was on the line. In the first game of the World Series, he gave us a lift, too, with that game-winning home run against Don Newcombe. He took his time at the plate and waited for his pitch. When he hit the home run, Newk didn't even twitch.

Joe's return in Boston gave us a lift, too. I remember the Red Sox had a hard-throwing young pitcher who stuck one in Joe's ribs with a base open. The next time there was no open base. The kid was wild, though. He couldn't—or wouldn't—put the ball over the plate. But Joe was mad. He swung at three bad balls away and fouled them off. He wouldn't take the walk. He finally hit one out of the ballpark and ran around the bases with the crowd going wild. The crowd wouldn't sit down for five minutes. And that was in Boston! But they're great fans. And they appreciated greatness when they saw it. They were cheering Joe's return. It was quite a sight to see.

The Red Sox had six guys who hit over .300 that year, and they had two 20-game winners. But they won only 35 games on the road. Still, they went down to the last game of the season before they were eliminated. The day before, things looked good for them. They were winning 4–0 when Birdie Tebbetts got to second. He said to Phil, "We're going to pitch Frank Quinn, a college kid, tomorrow. He's from Yale. He got $36,000 to sign."

Birdie was catching with Detroit when I was working out with them in 1937. In 1952 I said to him, "Did you say that to Rizzuto in 1949?"

"You know I wouldn't say something like that," he said. But I don't know. Phil wasn't that smart to make it up. Anyway everyone got off the bench and got on Birdie and said, "Let's go get them." The rest is history.

Ted Williams was some hitter for those Red Sox. He was so deliberate at the plate. He would come up to hit like he was the only man in town. I didn't like it. He wouldn't breathe until everything was all right. I'd say, "What are you hitting?" He wouldn't answer. "Don't you know?" I'd say. He'd snap, "Throw the ball!" But he could hit. He drove home 145 runs as a rookie.

I guess I angered some other hitters, too. I figured if I didn't throw the ball, they couldn't hit it. My teammates had trouble playing behind me. They couldn't get into a rhythm. But I figured we weren't going anywhere, and we were getting paid well.

Al Rosen didn't mind. He hit everything I threw. One day I told him what was coming. He couldn't believe it. And he couldn't hit it. That didn't work with Hank Bauer, though. One day we were winning 4–1 in the ninth, so I said, "Hank, how about a slider?" He fouled it off. But he hit the next one out of the park. When he got to third, I asked him, "Did it break?"

"It looked real good to me," he said.

As I said before, Casey and Weiss got me back in 1954. Both of them always backed me. And I proved to everyone that they were right. I won big in 1955. I was 16–5 with a league-leading winning percentage of .762. I didn't get my first start until May 30. They probably could have gotten rid of me. But Casey and Weiss had confidence in me. Then I kept on winning and no one could get me out of there. One day we're facing Dick Donovan. He had a sinker like Blackwell. Yogi won it with a home run in the eighth inning. I used to ride the trains at the time. I didn't fly my last three years in the majors. Before the game I was on the train for 33 hours. After the game Casey said in the clubhouse, "God-darn good thing Byrne took the train. Nice going, Byrne."

The Old Man used to play hunches once in a while. For example, we went into Detroit and one day we were tied 4–4 with two outs in the ninth. He brought me in to face a left-handed hitter, and I struck him out. I came up in the tenth with a run in, two on, and one out. They brought a left-hander in. It was a pinch-hit situation for Casey. I started to take one foot out of the box, but he let me hit. I hit the first pitch off the facing in right, and we won, 10–6. The pitcher threw me a fastball that sank. When I rounded the bases, the right fielder threw the ball in. I got the ball.

I got an Al Lopez story, too. One day I'm throwing junk and his guys are popping up. He's mad as hell. So he's vocalizing, calling me things he shouldn't have been saying. He tried to get to me. But I got to him instead. I needed rest. So I said to myself, *Instead of him using me, I'll use him.* I stalked toward the dugout. "What'd you say?" I challenged him. "I didn't hear you." Lopez got so red. He knew I wanted to hit him. But he was too deep in the dugout to get to. So I yelled to Dale Mitchell, who was sitting nearby, "What did he say? I couldn't hear him." Mitchell just shrugged, but I was rested. I went back to the mound and got the final out.

I was the only lefty to get a complete-game win against the Dodgers in 1955. They hadn't seen me pitch in some time, and I was pitching at the Stadium, so I figured I had a good chance. Billy Loes was pitching for them. It was Game Two of the World Series. We got all four of our runs in the first inning. I got a single with the bases loaded.

Not too many people remember my World Series win. But they remember my Series loss. That's the day Johnny Podres beat me 2–0. In the seventh game of the 1955 World Series. I gave up only three hits. In the fourth inning Campy doubled and Hodges singled him home. Later in the game Hodges hit a sacrifice fly against Bob Grim for the second run. Podres wasn't throwing hard that day but he had good control of his breaking ball, and he had a good straight change. Give him credit. He had to throw the ball. Give Campy credit, too. He called a great game. There were two key plays. Rizzuto got hit with a ball sliding into third, and Amoros made a catch that was out of this world.

In the 1957 World Series I figured in that controversial play with Nippy Jones. In Game Four we were up 5–4 when Jones batted for Warren Spahn. When I hit him with the ball, it rolled all the way back to the screen. I signaled to Yogi. I wanted him either to roll the ball back to plate umpire Augie Donatelli, or throw the ball to me. But the bat boy picked the ball up. Jones said, "Look at the ball." The wind was blowing in from left that day. I threw a curve and Jones raised his foot. If he didn't raise his foot, he wouldn't have gotten hit. Donatelli looked at the ball. I said, "That was there before I threw it." Well, Jones went to first and Felix Mantilla ran for him. Grim relieved me and Logan doubled Mantilla home. Everyone knows what happened then. We didn't put Mathews on to pitch to Aaron for the double play, and Eddie hit a game-winning homer.

After the 1957 season I retired. I wanted to come back but they wanted me to play the same role. If the opportunity to start games had been there, I never would have quit. No one loved the game more than I did. I went all the way to Florida in the spring of 1958 to tell Weiss I was hanging it up. He said, "I can give you more money but I can't give you more playing time." So I decided to get in some businesses and watch my children grow up.

I'm kinda disappointed that I didn't do better than I did with the talent God gave me. I should have been a phenom. We had a good defense and a good offense. There were always men on base and they always got you three runs. When I came up, it was hard to lose. But I didn't learn to pitch until I was thirty-four. My problem was, I didn't want the batters to even foul the ball off. I wanted to strike everyone out. Lopat would throw 85 pitches. I would throw 130. They hit more foul balls off me than fair ones. At age thirty-four it was different.

But I have no regrets. I'm satisfied. I'm in good health. I'll be sixty-eight the last day of this year. I've been the mayor of Wake Forest for a long time. If I run for another term and win, that will make twenty years. And I enjoy looking back.

For example, I got a big thrill in September of 1957. We were playing Kansas City and we had two on with none out. Lopat pinch hit and struck out. Then Collins pinch hit and struck out. Casey sent me up to hit for Turley. I hit one into the third deck to win the game. When I rounded the bases, I looked up into the boxes and saw Weiss cheering. He was one of my biggest boosters. That was a big thrill for me.

Another time, against Hal Newhouser, stands out in my memory. He struck me out the time before. I looked at a curve. The next time, he threw it again. I hit it out of the park in left field. He cursed me all the way around the bases.

Boy, those Yankee days were great ones. We won because we played harder than everyone else. We were always up because we were always going up against the other team's best pitchers. There were never any pushovers. We knew about Yankee tradition. We knew what the Yankees were all about. And we believed we could do what Yankee teams had done before. We were used to winning. After the 1955 season we were home for thirty days before we realized we had *lost* to the Dodgers.

Tom Ferrick

When Tom Ferrick was a young man, he wanted to pursue a religious life, to leave something behind him. But his natural father died and then his stepfather passed away, and he had to leave the Capuchin order to provide for his family. That's how Tom Ferrick became a ballplayer instead of a brother—and he has followed the path down which baseball has led him for more than fifty years.

In 1936 he signed with the New York Giants. But he hurt his arm, lost his fastball, and eventually became a finesse pitcher who relied on good control and ground balls to get batters out. Five years later he got to the major leagues with the Philadelphia Athletics. In between the start of his major-league career and the 36 years he has spent as a coach and a scout, Ferrick also pitched for the Indians, the Browns, the Senators, and the Yankees. Overall he both won and lost 40 games in his big-league career. He also picked up 56 saves and logged a 3.47 ERA, which was pretty respectable when one considers some of the clubs for which he played.

For one of his nine major-league seasons, he played with

the Yankees, who picked him up from the Browns just before the trading deadline in 1950 and dealt him to the Senators just before the deadline in 1951. Ironically, his 1950 season with the Yankees was his best year in the big leagues. Overall that year he won nine games, lost seven, and picked up a career-high 11 saves. With the Yankees he was 8–4. In that year's World Series he pitched one inning in relief and picked up a win in Game Three of the Yankees' four-game sweep of the Phillies.

The day the Yankees traded for Ferrick, they were in St. Louis. Tom switched clubhouses and uniforms, got Casey Stengel's call in relief that night, and picked up a save. Like most players, Ferrick has been on both sides of the winning and losing fence. He can readily pinpoint the differences between playing for a first-place and a seventh-place club. With the Yankees he could get two outs with one pitch; with the Browns he couldn't. Every game was a big one with New York; every game was the same with St. Louis. With the Yankees there was World Series money as an incentive; with the Browns there was little, if any, incentive.

In 1951 he was physically hurt when the Yankees traded him to the Senators. He was emotionally hurt by the trade, too, but he understood it. He was thirty-six years old at the time, and he wasn't contributing. He doesn't hold any grudges. In fact, his one regret in baseball is that he didn't get the chance to be Casey's pitching coach ten years later. Besides, it was good to be back in Washington with Clark Griffith and Bucky Harris. It was a good way to wrap up his major-league career

Tom Ferrick remembers the little things that were important in his life. When the Senators released him after he went 4–3 with one save in 1952, Griffith wrote him a letter, thanking him for his contributions. He's grateful that he got the chance to be a major-league pitcher; that he *played a part in the success of the 1949–53 Yankees; that he picked up some World Series money in 1950 to help with his mortgage; that Joe DiMaggio's fielding helped him to get a win in that year's World Series; that he made the scores of friendships he has in his many years in baseball; and that he and his wife were blessed with six children and eleven grandchildren.*

If Tom Ferrick had his life to live over, he says, he would live it the same way. He gave up his religious calling, but lived a religious life. And he has left something behind.

The last time I spoke with him, he was winding up his fiftieth year in baseball, scouting National League East clubs for the Kansas City Royals. Ferrick likes just about everyone, and just about everyone returns the favor. I've got an extra reason to like Tom, though.

When I had first spoken with him, he had taken an interest in my son Geoff. After a good high school baseball career, and with a lot of college coaches interested in him, Geoff was victimized by a wolf in sheep's clothing. An influential major-league baseball scout told me to use him as a reference for Geoff. He said that he would help Geoff, so we used his name on all of Geoff's college applications. But the scout gave Geoff a bad recommendation, without telling us, and killed all scholarship offers. Geoff ended up unhappy at the wrong school.

That's when Tom Ferrick helped him. Geoff was interested in transferring to Lynchburg College in Lynchburg, Virginia, a school that had a good baseball program. Ferrick didn't know the coach, Gerry Thomas, who had played in the Yankees' farm system, but nevertheless he wrote a strong recommendation on Geoff's behalf. Geoff didn't let Ferrick down. In his first season at Lynchburg, Geoff batted .451 and ended up fifth in the conference batting race.

This past fall, in his senior season, Geoff hit four home runs in two consecutive games against former Yankee Bobby

Richardson's Liberty University nine. In one of the games, Geoff hit two home runs in one inning. Richardson gave Geoff the game ball and autographed it. He added a postscript: "Would you be interested in a trade?"

Geoff got a second chance. But he might not have gotten it without Tom Ferrick's help. Thanks, Tom.

After my father died, I went to a Catholic grade school, the Glen Clyffe Seminary in Garrison, New York. The school was run by the Capuchin Brothers, who were connected to the Franciscans. It was a preparatory school for the seminary. They gave you a great education. I became interested in staying and going into the religious life. But in my fourth year my stepfather died, and since I was the oldest child, I had to go to work.

I signed with the Giants in '36. Willie Schroeder, who was a trainer with the Giants at the time, was a friend of my mother, and he got me to pitch batting practice for them. Teams are always looking for batting practice pitchers. Anyway I must have shown the Giants something, because they took me to spring training. Last year was my fiftieth consecutive year in baseball, excepting the three years I spent in the Navy during World War II.

In '41 I came up with the A's and had a pretty good year, I thought. I won eight games and saved seven others. But for some reason they didn't take me off the waiver list and Cleveland claimed me. In '42 I turned in a 1.99 ERA in 31 games, all but two out of the bullpen. After the war I returned to the Indians, but they sent me to the Browns in '46. From that time on, I jumped around a lot. In '47 and '48 I was with Washington. The following year, I returned to St. Louis for a year and a half. Just before the trading deadline in '50, Joe Ostrowski and I were sent to the Yankees in a mass transaction. The Browns got $50,000, too. The DeWitts needed the money. But it worked out well for me. I had my best year. Out of the bullpen I won nine games and saved 11. The next year I was back in Washington, and I closed out my career there in '52.

My second career began in '53 when I coached the Indianapolis Indians under Birdie Tebbetts. Then I went up with him to the Cincinnati Reds through '58. In '59 I coached the Phillies, under Eddie Sawyer; in '60 to '63, the Tigers, under Jimmy Dykes and Bob Scheffing; and in '64 and '65, the Kansas City Athletics, under Eddie Lopat. Midway through '65, Kansas City made me a scout. I moved with them to Oakland and stayed there through '69. Since that time I've been connected with the Royals. I'm a special assignment scout. I cross-check teams in the National League East. You know, see which players are coming on and which ones are slipping, in case we want to make a deal.

The day the Yankees traded for me, they were in St. Louis. I simply switched clubhouses on the same day. That night I relieved Vic Raschi and picked up a save in my first game for my new club. Every game was a big one with the Yankees. To St. Louis that night it was just another loss. I remember another save: Whitey Ford's first win in the majors. Against the White Sox.

When I came to the Yankees, I had been around. I was thirty-five. So I wasn't awed about joining the club. I'd been in the league six years, and I was near the end of my career. But it was nice to be on a pennant contender at last. Gerry Coleman and Phil Rizzuto made the double play. I wasn't used to getting two outs with one pitch. That helped me immensely, because I was a ground-ball pitcher.

After I hurt my arm in the Giants' farm system, I lost my velocity. I had to learn to pitch. I learned good control and I found out how to change speeds on my fastball. I studied hitters closely too. It was important to know who could run, steal, and hit-and-run. But, most importantly, I learned to keep the ball down.

There was one transition I had to make between St. Louis and New York, though. New York was more expensive than St. Louis. So I went to George Weiss and asked him for more money. I had nothing to lose. He gave me $1,000 more for living expenses. There was not much else he could do about it except put my mind at ease. He made the trade for me. And the people here weren't too happy with it.

I got a World Series win that year. In Game Three. Eddie Lopat came out after the eighth with the score tied at two. I came in, in the ninth. At Yankee Stadium. My first pitch was a high fastball to Granny Hamner, a good high fastball hitter. And I'm a low-ball pitcher. Hamner hit the ball up the alley and Joe got the ball on one bounce, and held it to a double. It turned out to be a big play. Andy Seminick bunted Hamner to third, and the next batter hit the ball to Joe Collins, who threw Granny out at the plate. In the bottom half Gerry Coleman singled home Gene Woodling with the winning run. For the third straight game, we won a one-run contest. But if Joe hadn't cut that ball off, it could have been a different game. The Yankees could beat you in a lot of ways. In that Series we had outstanding pitching and great defense. Of course, DiMaggio's homer made the difference in Game Two.

Joe was quiet. But he was the team leader. Everyone followed him along. He was a real model. He would play hurt so no one else could complain. That made everyone pull for each other. I remember one game in Washington he hit three home runs and a double in the first game of a doubleheader. That's when the fences were 400 feet in the corners. In the second game he flied out to the fence twice. With a little bit of luck, or in a different park, he could have had six home runs in a doubleheader. You have to believe a performance like that will rally a team together.

The day Casey put Joe at first, I came on in relief. I almost got him killed. It was a bright, sunny day. Someone hit a swinging bunt to first base. I fielded the ball and threw it into both the runner and the sun. I think I made up his mind to go back to the outfield.

Speaking of Casey though, he was a great manager. He knew how to handle young players. He was the first to perfect the platoon system. The way he handled Hank Bauer and Woodling was just great. He extended both of their careers. I had no problems with Casey at all. One day he came out to talk to me about Luke Easter. But he forgot to tell me what to throw him. Then Easter hit a home run. He was a dead low-ball hitter, and I was a low-ball pitcher. Casey just accepted it.

I roomed with Raschi. On the day of a game he was to pitch, he was all concentration. He was one of the most intense competitors I've ever seen. He was also one of the best money pitchers I've ever seen. One day in Detroit he gave up five runs in the first inning. Casey left him in. That showed the confidence Casey had in Vic's commitment. He knew Vic wouldn't give up just because he had gotten off to a bad start. Vic had the faculty, when he was in trouble, to throw his fastball a foot farther. And he got it over.

Casey's wife, you know, was a devout Catholic. He was a Baptist. One day they went to a Catholic church, and he noticed that there was a second collection. "Are they going to frisk us first?" he asked Edna. Another day she introduced him to a priest, and Casey quipped, "How much is this going to cost me?"

It was nice to be on a pennant winner and a World Series winner once in my life. I had finally reached the ultimate. It was my last hurrah. And from a financial standpoint, money was hard to come by at the time. My top salary was $11,500. So the winning share meant a little more money and an extra mortgage payment. It was a happy time.

Today's players, I call mercenaries. I can't blame them, but . . . I was really upset by what Gene Autry did last year. He picked up over two million dollars in salaries from other clubs. The owners are their own worst enemies. Buying pennants never did set well with me. I'd rather develop players, the Kansas City way. Television put us in this situation. In our day you could count the people. Today you don't know what the numbers are. In Kansas City our television and radio income is minimal compared to other clubs. So we stay away from free agency and train our players through the minors. Our ethics and principles are not distorted.

Just being in the major leagues was my big thrill. I wanted it since I was eight years dld. Having accomplished it was good enough. If I had to do it again, I would do it the same way. It allowed me to make a living and provide for my family. I've got a wife of forty-one years, six children, and eleven grandchildren. I'm glad I was born when I was, and did what I did.

I was hurt when I was traded. But I recognized it as a fact of life. I was thirty-six years old and I wasn't contributing. But I'm glad I was a part of their five world title teams. Luke Appling and Ernie Banks didn't even get a chance to play in the World Series. Even though I was only a small part of the Yankee success, I'm glad to be included. It was a baseball milestone for me.

So I went back to Washington and rejoined class people like Bucky Harris and Clark Griffith. A few things stand out about my last two years with the Senators. One day we had a big lead, and I was pitching to Ted Williams with a couple of runners on base. I called Al Evans, my catcher, out to the mound and told him, "Tell Ted I'm going to lay one in there. I want to see how far he can hit it." I could see Ted do a double-take when Al told him. I don't know if he believed Al, but I threw the next pitch right down the center of the plate. Ted hit the ball well but he hit it with top spin. Buddy Lewis, the right fielder, caught the ball, but it pinned him right to the wall.

Another day Tebbetts told Ted every pitch that was coming. He got upset. He didn't want to know. Some players are like that. Joe D was another one. When Charlie Dressen coached third base with the Yankees, he was great at stealing signs. But Joe didn't want to know what the pitches were, either. Ted and Joe didn't need to know.

Finally when Griffith released me in '52, he wrote me a letter to explain the move. "We're going with a youth movement," he said. "But I want you to know that I've appreciated your performance and effort. And I thank you for both." How many owners would do that today?

So it was time to hang up the spikes. But I had no regrets. Baseball was good to me. It still is. Twenty-three years after I retired, I received another big thrill from baseball. Bobby Brown, who is a great guy, was connected with the Rangers in '75. He brought back old Yankees and old Texas stars for a reunion. He invited me. Casey came down, too.

Casey told me, "You know, Tom, after the Yankees let me go, I almost took that Detroit job in '61. If I took the job, you were going to be my pitching coach." That was a great thrill for me: knowing that if Casey had had the chance, he would have picked me to work with him.

I said before that I have no regrets. I'm going to hedge just a little bit. Maybe I have that one.

Gerry Coleman

When Gerry Coleman came up to the Yankees in 1949, George Stirnweiss was the resident second baseman. But Gerry won the job and ultimately delivered the pennant-winning hit on the final day of the season.

During his tenure in the Bronx, he was challenged for the position by Billy Martin, Gil McDougald, and Bobby Richardson. Korea posed a challenge, too. But Gerry more than held his own. In his seven full seasons in New York, the Yankees won six pennants and four world championships. In his nine total seasons with the Yankees, they won eight pennants and six world titles.

The keys to Coleman were instruction and adjustment. When he was with the Newark Bears in 1948, he was persuaded by manager Bill Skiff to give up smoking and to choke up on the bat. The fences at Yankee Stadium were too far, Skiff said. Coleman decided to build himself up with weightlifting, but he concluded that he could make valuable contributions without hitting home runs. An example is the triple that he hit with the bases loaded on the final day of the 1949 season. It was a flare that he lobbed between Red Sox second baseman Bobby Doerr and right fielder Al Zarilla.

Gerry Coleman was only a .263 lifetime hitter, but he was a tough .263 hitter. He is proud of what they said about him: "He's only a one-for-four hitter. But that one hit will beat you."

Beat them is exactly what he did on the last day of the 1949 season. And what he did again in the 1950 World Series against the Phillies. The Yankees won the first three games of the four-game sweep by one-run scores. In Game One Coleman delivered the sacrifice fly that gave Vic Raschi a 1–0 win. In Game Three, in the bottom of the ninth inning, he singled home the winning run in a 3–2 victory.

Coleman also received good advice and examples from veteran Yankees. Frank Crosetti taught him how to improve his game. Joe DiMaggio, Charlie Keller, and Tommy Henrich showed him how to perpetuate the Yankees' winning tradition. There was an evolution of teaching going on, he says.

Gerry had his best year in 1950 when he batted .287, hit six home runs, and drove home 69 runs. After 1950 he was never again the same player. Injuries and Korea took their toll.

When he returned home from the Korean conflict, he had lost his dexterity, and his depth perception was impaired. But he endured and made adjustments. In the 1955 and 1956 World Series he had just five total at bats without a hit. But in 1957, his final season, he fought off a challenge by rookie Bobby Richardson, and hit a career-high .364 in the Fall Classic.

Then he retired as a player. It was Bobby Richardson's turn. The evolution of teaching continued.

Gerry Coleman played the game of baseball with intensity. The game was never fun for Gerry; the weight of Yankee tradition hung too heavily on his shoulders. Instead, the game was "satisfying," and the satisfaction came from winning, something the Yankees did in eight of Ger-

ry's nine years in the Bronx. I finally caught up with Gerry in Philadelphia, where he was working the broadcast of a Padre-Phillie game for San Diego. But he was catching a plane back to San Diego after the game, so he gave me his home telephone number in La Jolla, California, and urged me to call him soon. When I did, I said, "When can we talk?"

"How about right now?" he said. And for many hours we did.

When I last spoke with Gerry, he had a six-month-old daughter by his second wife. He has a grown daughter and son by his first marriage, which ended when his wife of thirty-five years died.

I'm intrigued by the fact that Gerry Coleman isn't living in the past and gives full credit to the talents of the modern-day ballplayer. For example, he thinks that the managerial job Dick Williams did with the 1984 Padres was equal to the best he's seen, and he believes the relieving that Goose Gossage gave that team was up there, too—with that of Joe Page in 1949. The essential drawback of the modern ballplayer, Gerry feels, is his unwillingness to play hurt, especially when he is in the first or second year of a multi-year contract. By way of contrast, Gerry says, Mickey Mantle could have been in the middle of a fifty-year contract, and he still would have played hurt—and all-out. There's a full-time intensity that's been lost.

In 1948, at the Yankees' spring training camp in St. Petersburg, I was the last man cut. I got a good look because I hit .280 for the Kansas City Blues the year before. The Blues had some team in 1947. Thirteen of us made it to the major leagues. Some of the players were Hank Bauer, Cliff Mapes, Steve Souchock, Ken Silvestri, and Bill Wight.

I got sent down to the Newark Bears in the International League. That was a break for me, even though I hit only .250. Bill Skiff, the manager, had a big influence on me. He turned my career around. He got me to quit smoking and to choke up on the bat. I started smoking in the service during World War II. But I quit the day after Skiff suggested it. My batting average had dropped 30 points. My career was hanging in the balance. No one ever said that. I just knew it.

At the plate I was swinging for the long ball. I was trying to hit home runs. But center field at Yankee Stadium was 461 feet. It was time to do some self-evaluation. I asked myself, *What are you trying to prove? Are you getting maximum results out of your talent? How are you going to get better? I think it's time you found out.*

I got a mirror and checked my hands. I decided to close my stance and choke up three to four inches on the bat. I also got on weights and got myself up to 180 pounds.

When I got to the Yankees in 1949, Frankie Crosetti, who was coaching then, exerted a great influence on me. I was switched to second base because Rizzuto was at short. Crosetti stayed with me and worked with me. He, Bobby Brown, and I would talk baseball for hours. Instruction was the key for me. He would never mention the right stuff, the things you could do. He would say, "Get the wrong stuff down." For example, I couldn't hit Bob Lemon, who would come sidearm at me. My body would be in the third-base dugout before I sat down on strikes. Crosetti would throw sidearm to me for hours. Finally, I was able to hit Lemon pretty well.

When I first got to Yankee Stadium, I looked up

at the triple-tier park. Then I looked at the fans. Both of them were intimidating. Actually, the fans are a harmless group. But they were a tremendous hurdle to me in the beginning. Then I saw Joe D in center field. I said, "Oh, my God!" I had an image built in my mind about Joe D. I was raised in San Francisco. So was he. He was God there.

The competition was intense. Tradition hung on your shoulders like an albatross at Yankee Stadium. Fun it never was. It was more satisfaction than fun. The satisfaction came from winning. I enjoyed winning. So did the Yankees. With them it was the bottom line.

I worried about a lot of things in those early days with the Yankees. Like Tommy Henrich, who was playing first base that first season. I feared him more than Casey. Tommy would snap at me, "We don't have any secrets on this club. If you want the ball, yell for it."

But I got a good break right off the bat. George Stirnweiss, the starting second baseman, got injured the first day of the season. I got a chance to play the second day and hit .400 for a month. Then I sat out 10 days with a sinus infection just as Stirnweiss got better. But they gave me the job anyway.

I played in 128 games in my rookie year and batted .275. In the World Series, against the Dodgers, I batted .250. I was pretty happy. Not with the numbers. I didn't give a damn about numbers. They used to say about me, "He only goes one-for-four, but that one hit will beat you." I was proud of that. It was exciting to win.

One of the things that I remember most about 1949 was Joe D's comeback in Boston. He missed the first 65 games of the season with a painful heel that didn't respond to an operation. But in a big series in Boston, he made a surprise start in the opening game of the three-game series. All he did was hit four home runs and drive home nine runs in those three games. When we came into Boston, we were eight games in front. We buried them. When we left, they were 11 games out. I still don't know how Joe did it.

But the Red Sox bounced back and took the lead in the last week of the season. Three days before the season ended, they could have clinched a tie for the pennant. But a wild pitch by Mel Parnell gave Washington an important win. For us. Ray Scarborough got the win for the Senators.

Then the Red Sox came into Yankee Stadium to close out the season with a two-game series. One win would have clinched the pennant for them. The Saturday game, October 1, was Joe D Day. We fell behind 4–0. Joe Page walked two runners home in relief. But we came back to tie the game and won it, 5–4, on Johnny Lindell's home run.

The Sunday game was sudden-death. Rizzuto hit a triple in the first inning. Red Sox manager Joe McCarthy played his infield back. Good thing for us. Phil scored on Henrich's weak ground ball to second. That run was the only one of the game until the bottom of the eighth, when we scored four times. Three of those runs scored on my bases-loaded triple. I didn't want to strike out in that situation. I wanted to make contact. I hit the ball over Bobby Doerr's head at second and in front of Al Zarilla in right. It was more luck than skill. But outside of the San Diego Padres' winning the pennant in 1984, that was my most outstanding moment. [Coleman announces the Padres' games.] McCarthy met me years later and said, "Way to go. You kept the ball in play." That meant a lot to me. As I said, numbers weren't important to me. Winning was.

In the World Series we took the Dodgers in five games. We beat them two more times during that five-year stretch, in 1952 and 1953. It's truly incredible the way we handled the Dodgers. They had a truly great team. Their first eight players were better than ours. But we had better pitching and better defense. Pee Wee Reese and Jackie Robinson worried us. They could do everything. We knew we could kay the other ones, though.

The Big Three made the difference. Allie Reynolds was the toughest clutch pitcher I've ever seen. When he struck out Stan Lopata to end the World Series in 1950, Lopata swung at three pitches that were in Yogi's glove. No one today has the arm that Reynolds did. Dwight Gooden doesn't even have it. Reynolds' stuff was incredible. Vic Raschi's arm was super, too. You can't buy arms like theirs. Eddie Lopat was easy to play behind, also. With a runner on first, you just knew he was going to throw a double-play ball.

Casey was smarter than all of us put together. He understood life. He grew up with John McGraw of the Giants. Everything McGraw did, Casey copied. Like platooning. McGraw kept Casey in the majors a few extra years by platooning him.

Casey was tough to play for, though. After he phased out Joe McCarthy's people, he demanded perfection. If you didn't perform, he would get you out of the lineup. His goal was to win. He had no friendships with the players. He liked Billy Martin and Mickey Mantle. But he went after them, too. I admired him. In my opinion, he was the perfect manager. He platooned, played the percentages, and handled the players, media, and fans well.

He and Joe D didn't get along. It was over a minor thing. One day Casey batted Johnny Mize fourth. Joe didn't speak to Casey again. Joe was bigger than life. Joe was the biggest name in sports, outside of Jack Dempsey and Joe Louis.

Joe was the greatest all-round player I ever saw. The way he handled himself, the team, and the game was impeccable. He understood his role thoroughly. He had an incredible mystique. No one else ever did it better. Every player is insecure. The pressure to succeed is great. But he wasn't the normal player. He had to be perfect every day. Joe was unhappy when he wasn't perfect. He had to be DiMaggio every day. And usually he was. As a result, he had a tremendous hold on people. You don't see them writing songs about anyone else. No one else ever emulated him.

My best year was 1950, when I batted .287. We had to beat out the Tigers, who had a good year. Whitey Ford came up to us late in the season and won nine of 10 decisions, including a clutch game against the Tigers in September. It gave us a half-game lead.

Three days before the season ended, Joe was hitting .301. It was a tense time for him. Everyone, especially the press, was wondering if he could keep his average above .300. Well, that afternoon Joe hit a screaming line drive at Eddie Joost, the A's shortstop. The ball handcuffed Joost but he made the play. After we made out, Joe went mumbling out to center. In the pre-inning warmups, Yogi overthrew me and the ball hit Joe in the heel. Already in a bad mood, he snapped at me, "You little banty rooster, can't you catch the ball!" Then he whipped the ball back at me, and it hit me in the knee. Both of us were limping around. In the meantime, Yogi, who had started the whole thing, was standing with his hands on his hips, like nothing had happened.

The 1950 World Series was a good one for me. Every time I came up, we had a chance to score. The runs were few and far between, but I was lucky enough to deliver three of them. With a fly ball, a ground ball, any way I could.

In Game One Raschi beat Jim Konstanty, 1–0. In the fourth inning Bobby Brown doubled, Hank Bauer got him to third with a 400-foot fly ball, and I scored him with a fly ball that wasn't quite so deep. Bauer's fly was the key to the victory.

In Game Three they played me out of position. Del Ennis played me toward the line in left, and Richie Ashburn shaded me to right center. In the bottom of the ninth, I lined a single to left center to score Woodling with the winning run. Tom Ferrick got the win in relief of Lopat.

Well, we swept the Series in four games. Whitey would have wrapped it up with a shutout, but Gene dropped that ball in left with two outs in the ninth. But you know that sun field in October. Casey was livid. He wanted the shutout. Now he wanted the sweep. So he called on Reynolds. As Casey returned to the dugout, he imitated Gene staggering under the ball. When he got back in the dugout, he paced up and down, pushing his hands up and pushing Woodling back. Gene never forgave him.

After 1950 something seemed to always get in the way. In 1951 I went well until June, when I got hurt. Then I went into a slump, and they brought Gil McDougald in. I ended up batting .249. It was my worst season pre-Korea.

In 1952 I started well. I was batting .405 after 11 games, but then I got called into the service for the second time. I was only seventeen when I got called up the first time. In World War II. I was at the University of Southern California on a basketball and baseball scholarship at the time. I was also in a Navy aviation program. In the service I became a second lieutenant in the Marines, assigned to dive bombers.

The Korean conflict—whoever would have dreamed it? When I got out in 1945, I was assigned to the reserves. Suddenly I was called up for six months. Then my tour of duty was extended to two-to-three years. They ran out of pilots. It didn't improve my career. I was twenty-eight, pushing twenty-nine, when I got out. I wasn't the hitter I was. I'd lost my dexterity. I felt no bitterness, though. I wasn't a professional Marine. But if they call you, you go. It's your duty. So you do it.

When I returned from the service, I had a depth perception problem. It stemmed from my flying days in Korea. One day when I was "joining up" the formation, making a turn on my own, I had trouble banking the plane.

The doctor asked, "Are you under pressure? Do you frown a lot?"

I said "yes" to both questions.

The problem was I was turning my eyes in. When they tested me on the 3-D machine, they found that my depth perception had dropped 50 percent. Too much work can go too far. It was a muscle thing. One day I kayed four times. That was the indicator. I didn't kay much. It was the pressure and the tension. When I got away from the pressure, the depth perception gradually came back. But 1954 was a lost season.

The following year was no better. In the third game of the season, when sliding home, I shattered my collarbone in twenty pieces. Later in the season Harry Byrd beaned me. I lost the ball.

In 1956 Phil wasn't hitting. He tried glasses but it wasn't the answer. They released him on Old Timers' Day. I ran into him before the game. He said, "I'm through. They just released me." He could play. He could do everything. But he never got over being released on Old Timers' Day. Casey moved me all over the infield that year. He did a lot of maneuvering in 1956. At various points of the season, he had a total of 20 infielders.

In 1957, my last year, I went from a starter to a reserve. It's not easy. It demands an adjustment. There was a lot of intense competition on the Yankees. No one wanted to be on the bench. Everyone wanted to be in there. But we all rooted for each other because, first and foremost, we all wanted to win. Bobby Richardson moved in at second that year. He was a young player who didn't make it, though, so I got my old job back in late July or early August. I played through the World Series, which was a good one average-wise for me. I hit .364 in seven games. It was obvious that Richardson was going to be the starting second baseman in 1958, though. He couldn't be denied. So when they offered me a job in the front office, I realized that I wasn't going to get any better, and I retired.

One play I'd like to have back took place in the bottom of the sixth inning of the fifth game of my last World Series. The Braves and the Yankees were tied at two games apiece with Lew Burdette and Whitey Ford hooked up in a scoreless duel. Eddie Mathews was up with two outs and no one on base.

He hit a bouncer to me that I didn't charge. I misjudged his speed and he beat my throw. I thought I had him all the way. The Braves followed with two more singles, the winning one by Joe Adcock, and we lost, 1–0. It wasn't a good play on my part. It blew the game and the World Series. But Whitey never said anything to me about my misplay.

In fact, he never said anything about any miscues. One day in 1950 he was pitching against Cleveland. Johnny Mize deflected a ball hit by Luke Easter to me. I threw the ball behind Whitey who was covering at first. Whitey got run over by Luke, all 240 pounds of him, but he never blinked. He got right up and threw out Al Rosen trying to advance to third. It was gratifying to be able to play with people like that.

Everyone on the Yankees got along. We liked each other. Everyone could be kidded. And that reminds me of a couple of stories.

One day in 1949 DiMag, Joe Page, and Lopat went deep-sea fishing. Page had had a rough night the night before. So he was sleeping in the cabin while the boat was trawling. While he slept, someone tied a bucket to his line and said, "Joe, you've hit one." He fought the "catch" for forty minutes. Finally, he saw the bucket. Boy, was he mad. Stirnweiss poured salt in the wound the next day when he walked into the clubhouse and said, "Hey, anyone want to go bucket fishing?"

Stirnweiss became the butt of the second story. Charlie Keller, Gus Niarhos, and he went hunting one off-season. They stayed at a hunting lodge. Every night Stirnweiss would relieve himself in the outhouse at the same time. One night Keller and Niarhos hung a bear skin on the door of the outhouse. When

Snuffy opened the door, the bear skin fell on him. He was so scared he ran right through the screen door.

My top salary was $19,000. But today's salaries don't bother me. Not if the players work hard. What does bother me is that some players hold back. They don't put out. I can see it from the booth every day. In the first year of a three-year contract, they might miss 30 to 40 games; in the second year, 20 games; and in the third year, three or four. Mickey Mantle could have had a fifty-year contract, he would still play the only way he knew how—a hundred percent, every day.

Back in our day, we had a more mature approach to the game. The Kellers, the Henrichs, the DiMaggios taught the younger players winning attitudes. As we grew up, we taught our young. An evolution of this teaching was always taking place. Consequently we were always winning. We thought it was our divine right. When Ceveland won in 1954, we said, "How'd that happen!"

We decided it wasn't going to happen again. In the years 1955–57 we built ourselves up for the challenge. The ingredients to win have to be right, though. You need to be with people who get along and people who think along. We did. Being Yankees was never our job. It was our religion!

APPENDIX

Hank Bauer

	G	AB	H	2B	3B	HR	R	RBI	BB	SO	SB	BA
1948 NY A	19	50	9	1	1	1	6	9	6	13	1	.180
1949	103	301	82	6	6	10	56	45	37	42	2	.272
1950	113	415	133	16	2	13	72	70	33	41	2	.320
1951	118	348	103	19	3	10	53	54	42	39	5	.296
1952	141	553	162	31	6	17	86	74	50	61	6	.293
1953	133	437	133	20	6	10	77	57	59	45	2	.304
1954	114	377	111	16	5	12	73	54	40	42	4	.294
1955	139	492	137	20	5	20	97	53	56	65	8	.278
1956	147	539	130	18	7	26	96	84	59	72	4	.241
1957	137	479	124	22	9	18	70	65	42	64	7	.259
1958	128	452	121	22	6	12	62	50	32	56	3	.268
1959	114	341	81	20	0	9	44	39	33	54	4	.238
1960 KC A	95	255	70	15	0	3	30	31	21	36	1	.275
1961	43	106	28	3	1	3	11	18	9	8	1	.264
14 yrs	1544	5145	1424	229	57	164	833	703	519	638	50	.277
WORLD SERIES												
1949 NY A	3	6	1	0	0	0	0	0	0	0	0	.167
1950	4	15	2	0	0	0	0	1	0	0	0	.133
1951	6	18	3	0	1	0	0	3	1	1	0	.167
1952	7	18	1	0	0	0	2	1	4	3	0	.056
1953	6	23	6	0	1	0	6	1	2	4	0	.261
1955	6	14	6	0	0	0	1	1	0	1	0	.429
1956	7	32	9	0	0	1	3	3	0	5	1	.281
1957	7	31	8	2	1	2	3	6	1	6	0	.258
1958	7	31	10	0	0	4	6	8	0	5	0	.323
9 yrs.	53	188	46	2	3	7	21	24	8	25	1	.245

Yogi Berra

	G	AB	H	2B	3B	HR	R	RBI	BB	SO	SB	BA
1946 NY A	7	22	8	1	0	2	3	4	1	1	0	.364
1947	83	293	82	15	3	11	41	54	13	12	0	.280
1948	125	469	143	24	10	14	70	98	25	24	3	.305
1949	116	415	115	20	2	20	59	91	22	25	2	.277
1950	151	597	192	30	6	28	116	124	55	12	4	.322
1951	141	547	161	19	4	27	92	88	44	20	5	.294
1952	142	534	146	17	1	30	97	98	66	24	2	.273
1953	137	503	149	23	5	27	80	108	50	32	0	.296
1954	151	584	179	28	6	22	88	125	56	29	0	.307
1955	147	541	147	20	3	27	84	108	60	20	1	.272
1956	140	521	155	29	2	30	93	105	65	29	3	.298
1957	134	482	121	14	2	24	74	82	57	25	1	.251
1958	122	433	115	17	3	22	60	90	35	35	3	.266
1959	131	472	134	25	1	19	64	69	43	38	1	.284
1960	120	359	99	14	1	15	46	62	38	23	2	.276
1961	119	395	107	11	0	22	62	61	35	28	2	.271
1962	86	232	52	8	0	10	25	35	24	18	0	.224
1963	64	147	43	6	0	8	20	28	15	17	1	.293
1965 NY N	4	9	2	0	0	0	1	0	0	3	0	.222
19 yrs.	2120	7555	2150	321	49	358	1175	1430	704	415	30	.285
WORLD SERIES												
1947 NY A	6	19	3	0	0	1	2	2	1	2	0	.158
1949	4	16	1	0	0	0	2	1	1	3	0	.063
1950	4	15	3	0	0	1	2	2	2	1	0	.200
1951	6	23	6	1	0	0	4	0	2	1	0	.261
1952	7	28	6	1	0	2	2	3	2	4	0	.214
1953	6	21	9	1	0	1	3	4	3	3	0	.429
1955	7	24	10	1	0	1	5	2	3	1	0	.417
1956	7	25	9	2	0	3	5	10	4	1	0	.360
1957	7	25	8	1	0	1	5	2	4	0	0	.320
1958	7	27	6	3	0	0	3	2	1	0	0	.222
1960	7	2	7	0	0	1	6	8	2	0	0	.318
1961	4	11	3	0	0	1	2	3	5	1	0	.273
1962	2	2	0	0	0	0	0	0	2	0	0	.000
1963	1	1	0	0	0	0	0	0	0	0	0	.000
14 yrs.	75	259	71	10	0	12	41	39	32	17	0	.274

Bobby Brown

	G	AB	H	2B	3B	HR	R	RBI	BB	SO	SB	BA
1946 NY A	7	24	8	1	0	0	1	1	4	0	0	.333
1947	69	150	45	6	1	1	21	18	21	9	0	.300
1948	113	363	109	19	5	3	62	48	48	16	0	.300
1949	104	343	97	14	4	6	61	61	38	18	4	.283
1950	95	277	74	4	2	4	33	37	39	18	3	.267
1951	103	313	84	15	2	6	44	51	47	18	1	.268
1952	29	89	22	2	0	1	6	14	9	6	1	.247
1954	28	60	13	1	0	1	5	7	8	3	0	.217
8 yrs.	548	1619	452	62	14	22	233	237	214	88	9	.279
WORLD SERIES												
1947 NY A	4	3	3	2	0	0	2	3	1	0	0	1.000
1949	4	12	6	1	2	0	4	5	2	2	0	.500
1950	4	12	4	1	1	0	2	1	0	0	0	.333
1951	5	14	5	1	0	0	1	0	2	1	0	.357
4 yrs.	17	41	18	5	3	0	9	9	5	3	0	.439

Tommy Byrne

	W	L	PCT	ERA	G	GS	CG	IP	H	BB	SO	ShO	SV
1943 NY A	2	1	.667	6.54	11	2	0	31.2	28	35	22	0	0
1946	0	1	.000	5.79	4	1	0	9.1	7	8	5	0	0
1947	0	0	–	4.15	4	1	0	4.1	5	6	2	0	0
1948	8	5	.615	3.30	31	11	5	133.2	79	101	93	1	2
1949	15	7	.682	3.72	32	30	12	196	125	179	129	3	0
1950	15	9	.625	4.74	31	31	10	203.1	188	160	118	2	0
1951 2 teams	NY A	(9G 2–1)		STL A	(19G 4–10)								
" total	6	11	.353	4.26	28	20	7	143.2	120	150	71	2	0
1952 STL A	7	14	.333	4.68	29	24	14	196	182	112	91	0	0
1953 2 teams	CHI A	(6G 2–0)		WAS A	(GG 0–5)								
" total	2	5	.286	6.16	12	11	2	49.2	53	48	26	0	0
1954 NY A	3	2	.600	2.70	5	5	4	40	36	19	24	1	0
1955	16	5	.762	3.16	27	22	9	160	137	87	76	3	2
1956	7	3	.700	3.36	37	8	1	109.2	108	72	52	0	6
1957	4	6	.400	4.36	30	4	1	84.2	70	60	57	0	2
13 yrs.	85	69	.552	4.11	281	170	65	1362	1138	1037	766	12	12
WORLD SERIES													
1949 NY A	0	0	–	2.70	1	1	0	3.1	2	2	1	0	0
1955	1	1	.500	1.88	2	2	1	14.1	8	8	8	0	0
1956	0	0	–	0.00	1	0	0	.1	1	0	1	0	0
1957	0	0	–	5.40	2	0	0	3.1	1	2	1	0	0
4 yrs.	1	1	.500	2.53	6	3	1	21.1	12	12	11	0	0

Gerry Coleman

	G	AB	H	2B	3B	HR	R	RBI	BB	SO	SB	BA
1949 NY A	128	447	123	21	5	2	54	42	63	44	8	.275
1950	153	522	150	19	6	6	69	69	67	38	3	.287
1951	121	362	90	11	2	3	48	43	31	35	6	.249
1952	11	42	17	2	1	0	6	4	5	4	0	.405
1953	8	10	2	0	0	0	1	0	0	2	0	.200
1954	107	300	65	7	1	3	39	21	26	29	3	.217
1955	43	96	22	5	0	0	12	8	11	11	0	.229
1956	80	183	47	5	1	0	15	18	12	33	1	.257
1957	72	157	42	7	2	2	23	12	20	21	1	.268
9 yrs.	723	2119	558	77	18	16	267	217	235	218	22	.263

WORLD SERIES

	G	AB	H	2B	3B	HR	R	RBI	BB	SO	SB	BA
1949 NY A	5	20	5	3	0	0	0	4	0	4	0	.250
1950	4	14	4	1	0	0	2	3	2	0	0	.286
1951	5	8	2	0	0	0	2	0	1	2	0	.250
1955	3	3	0	0	0	0	0	0	0	1	0	.000
1956	2	2	0	0	0	0	0	0	0	0	0	.000
1957	7	22	8	2	0	0	2	2	3	1	0	.364
6 yrs.	26	69	19	6	0	0	6	9	6	8	0	.275

Joe Collins

	G	AB	H	2B	3B	HR	R	RBI	BB	SO	SB	BA
1948 NY A	5	5	1	1	0	0	0	2	0	1	0	.200
1949	7	10	1	0	0	0	2	4	6	2	0	.100
1950	108	205	48	8	3	8	47	28	31	34	5	.234
1951	125	262	75	8	5	9	52	48	34	23	9	.286
1952	122	428	120	16	8	18	69	59	55	47	4	.280
1953	127	387	104	11	2	17	72	44	59	36	2	.269
1954	130	343	93	20	2	12	67	46	51	37	2	.271
1955	105	278	65	9	1	13	40	45	44	32	0	.234
1956	100	262	59	5	3	7	38	43	34	33	3	.225
1957	79	149	30	1	0	2	17	10	24	18	2	.201
10 yrs.	908	2329	596	79	24	86	404	329	338	263	27	.256

WORLD SERIES

	G	AB	H	2B	3B	HR	R	RBI	BB	SO	SB	BA
1950 NY A	1	0	0	0	0	0	0	0	0	0	0	–
1951	6	18	4	0	0	1	2	3	2	1	0	.222
1952	6	12	0	0	0	0	1	0	1	3	0	.000
1953	6	24	4	1	0	1	4	2	3	8	0	.167
1955	5	12	2	0	0	2	6	3	6	4	1	.167
1956	6	21	5	2	0	0	2	2	2	3	0	.238
1957	6	5	0	0	0	0	0	0	0	3	0	.000
7 yrs.	36	92	15	3	0	4	15	10	14	22	1	.163

Tom Ferrick

		W	L	PCT	ERA	G	GS	CG	IP	H	BB	SO	ShO	SV
1941 PHI	A	8	10	.444	3.77	36	4	2	119.1	130	33	30	1	7
1942 CLE	A	3	2	.600	1.99	31	2	2	81.1	56	32	28	0	3
1946 2 teams	CLE	A	(9G 0–0)		STL	A	(25G 4–1)							
" total		4	1	.800	3.58	34	1	0	50.1	51	9	22	0	6
1947 WAS	A	1	7	.125	3.15	31	0	0	60	57	20	23	0	9
1948		2	5	.286	4.15	37	0	0	73.2	75	38	34	0	10
1949 STL	A	6	4	.600	3.88	50	0	0	104.1	102	41	34	0	6
1950 2 teams	STL	A	(16G 1–3)		NY	A	(30G 8–4)							
" total		9	7	.563	3.79	46	0	0	80.2	73	29	26	0	11
1951 2 teams	NY	A	(9G 1–1)		WAS	A	(22G 2–0)							
" total		3	1	.750	3.52	31	0	0	53.2	57	14	20	0	3
1952 WAS	A	4	3	.571	3.02	27	0	0	50.2	53	11	28	0	1
9 yrs.		40	40	.500	3.47	323	7	4	674	654	227	245	1	56
WORLD SERIES														
1950 NY	A	1	0	1.000	0.00	1	0	0	1	1	1	0	0	0

Billy Johnson

		G	AB	H	2B	3B	HR	R	RBI	BB	SO	SB	BA
1943 NY	A	155	592	166	24	6	5	70	94	53	30	3	.280
1946		85	296	77	14	5	4	51	35	31	42	1	.260
1947		132	494	141	19	8	10	67	95	44	43	1	.285
1948		127	446	131	20	6	12	59	64	41	30	0	.294
1949		113	329	82	11	3	8	48	56	48	44	1	.249
1950		108	327	85	16	2	6	44	40	42	30	1	.260
1951 2 teams	NY	A	(15G–.300)		STL	N	(124G–.262)						
" total		139	482	128	26	1	14	57	68	53	49	5	.266
1952 STL N		94	282	71	10	2	2	23	34	34	21	1	.252
1953		11	5	1	1	0	0	0	1	1	1	0	.200
9 yrs.		964	3253	882	141	33	61	419	487	347	290	13	.271
WORLD SERIES														
1943 NY	A	5	20	6	1	1	0	3	3	0	3	0	.300
1947		7	26	7	0	3	0	8	2	3	4	0	.269
1949		2	7	1	0	0	0	0	0	0	2	1	.143
1950		4	6	0	0	0	0	0	0	0	3	0	.000
4 yrs.		18	59	14	1	4	0	11	5	3	12	1	.237

Bob Kuzava

	W	L	PCT	ERA	G	GS	CG	IP	H	BB	SO	ShO	SV
1946 CLE A	1	0	1.000	3.00	2	2	0	12	9	11	4	0	0
1947	1	1	.500	4.15	4	4	1	21.2	22	9	9	1	0
1949 CHI A	10	6	.625	4.02	29	18	9	156.2	139	91	83	1	0
1950 2 teams	CHI	A	(10G 1–3)		WAS	A	(22G 8–77)						
" total	9	10	.474	4.33	32	29	9	199.1	199	102	105	11	0
1951 2 teams	WAS	A	(8G 3–3)		NY	A	(23G 8–4)						
" total	11	7	.611	3.61	31	16	7	134.2	133	55	72	1	5
1952 NY A	8	8	.500	3.45	28	12	6	133	115	63	67	1	3
1953	6	5	.545	3.31	33	6	2	92.1	92	34	48	2	4
1954 2 teams	NY	A	(20G 1–3)		BAL	A	(4G 1–3)						
" total	2	6	.250	4.97	24	7	0	63.1	76	29	37	0	1
1955 2 teams	BAL	A	(GG 0–1)		PHI	N	(17G 1–0)						
" total	1	1	.500	6.25	23	5	0	44.2	57	16	18	0	0
1957 2 teams	PIT	N	(4G 0–0)		STL	N	(3G 0–)						
" total	0	0	–	6.23	7	0	0	4.1	7	5	3	0	0
10 yrs.	49	44	.527	4.05	213	99	34	862	849	415	446	7	13
WORLD SERIES													
1951 NY A	0	0	–	0.00	1	0	0	1	0	0	0	0	1
1952	0	0	–	0.00	1	0	0	2.2	0	0	2	0	1
1953	0	0	–	13.50	1	0	0	.2	2	0	1	0	0
3 yrs.	0	0	–	2.08	3	0	0	4.1	2	0	3	0	2

Ed Lopat

	W	L	PCT	ERA	G	GS	CG	IP	H	BB	SO	ShO	SV
1944 CHI A	11	10	.524	3.26	27	25	13	210	217	59	75	1	0
1945	10	13	.435	4.11	26	24	17	199.1	226	56	74	1	1
1946	13	13	.500	2.73	29	29	20	231	216	48	89	2	0
1947	16	13	.552	2.81	31	31	22	252.2	241	73	109	3	0
1948 NY A	17	11	.607	3.65	33	31	13	226.2	246	66	83	3	0
1949	15	10	.600	3.26	31	30	14	215.1	222	69	70	4	1
1950	18	8	.692	3.47	35	32	15	236.1	244	65	72	3	1
1951	21	9	.700	2.91	31	31	20	234.2	209	71	93	5	0
1952	10	5	.667	2.53	20	19	10	149.1	127	53	56	2	0
1953	16	4	.800	2.42	25	24	9	178.1	169	32	50	3	0
1954	12	4	.750	3.55	26	23	7	170	189	33	54	0	0
1955 2 teams	NY	A	(16G 4–8)		BAL	A	(10G 3–4)						
" total	7	12	.368	3.91	26	19	4	135.2	158	25	34	1	0
12 yrs.	166	112	.597	3.21	340	318	164	2439.1	2464	650	859	28	3

WORLD SERIES

1949 NY	A	1	0	1.000	6.35	1	1	0	5.2	9	1	4	0	0
1950		0	0	–	2.25	1	1	0	8	9	0	5	0	0
1951		2	0	1.000	0.50	2	2	2	18	10	3	4	0	0
1952		1	0	.000	4.76	2	2	0	11.1	14	4	3	0	0
1953		1	0	1.000	2.00	1	1	1	9	9	4	3	0	0
5 yrs.		4	1	.800	2.60	7	7	3	52	51	12	19	0	0

Cliff Mapes

		G	AB	H	2B	3B	HR	R	RBI	BB	SO	SB	BA
1948 NY	A	53	88	22	11	1	1	19	12	6	13	1	.250
1949		111	304	75	13	3	7	56	38	58	50	6	.247
1950		108	356	88	14	6	12	60	61	47	61	1	.247
1951 2 teams	NY	A	(45G-.216)		STL	A	(56G-.274)						
" total		101	252	66	10	3	9	38	38	30	47	0	.262
1952 DET	A	86	193	38	7	0	9	26	23	27	42	0	.197
5 yrs.		459	1193	289	55	13	38	199	172	168	213	8	.242

WORLD SERIES

		G	AB	H	2B	3B	HR	R	RBI	BB	SO	SB	BA
1949 NY	A	4	10	1	1	0	0	3	2	2	4	0	.100
1950		1	4	0	0	0	0	0	0	0	1	0	.000
2 yrs.		5	14	1	1	0	0	3	2	2	5	0	.071

Billy Martin

		G	AB	H	2B	3B	HR	R	RBI	BB	SO	SB	BA
1950 NY	A	34	36	9	1	0	1	10	8	3	3	0	.250
1951		51	58	15	1	2	0	10	2	4	9	0	.259
1952		109	363	97	13	3	3	32	33	22	31	3	.267
1953		149	587	151	24	6	15	72	75	43	56	6	.257
1955		20	70	21	2	0	1	8	9	7	9	1	.300
1956		121	458	121	24	5	9	76	49	30	56	7	.264
1957 2 teams	NY	A	(43G-.241)		KC	A	(73G-.257)						
" total		116	410	103	14	5	10	45	39	15	34	9	.251
1958 DET	A	131	498	127	19	1	7	56	42	16	62	5	.255
1959 CLE	A	73	242	63	7	0	9	37	24	7	18	0	.260
1960 CIN	N	103	317	78	17	1	3	34	16	27	34	0	.246
1961 2 teams	MIL	N	(6G-.000)		MIN	A	(108G-.246)						
" total		114	380	92	15	5	6	45	36	13	43	3	.242
11 yrs.		1021	3419	877	137	28	64	425	333	187	355	34	.257

WORLD SERIES

					2B	3B	HR	R	RBi	BB	SO	SB	BA
1951 NY A	1	0	0	0	0	0		1	0	0	0	0	—
1952	7	23	5	0	0	1		2	4	2	2	0	.217
1953	6	24	12	1	2	2		5	8	1	2	1	.500
1955	7	25	8	1	1	0		2	4	1	5	0	.320
1956	7	27	8	0	0	2		5	3	1	6	0	.296
5 yrs.	28	99	33	2	3	5		15	19	5	15	1	.333

Gil McDougald

	G	AB	H	2B	3B	HR	R	RBi	BB	SO	SB	BA
1951 NY A	131	402	123	23	4	14	72	63	56	54	14	.306
1952	152	555	146	16	5	11	65	78	57	73	6	.263
1953	141	541	154	27	7	10	82	83	60	65	3	.285
1954	126	394	102	22	2	12	66	48	62	64	3	.259
1955	141	533	152	10	8	13	79	53	65	77	6	.285
1956	120	438	136	13	3	13	79	56	68	59	3	.311
1957	141	539	156	25	9	13	87	62	59	71	2	.289
1958	138	503	126	19	1	14	69	65	59	75	6	.250
1959	127	434	109	16	8	4	44	34	35	40	0	.251
1960	119	337	87	16	4	8	54	34	38	45	2	.258
10 yrs.	1336	4676	1291	187	51	112	697	576	559	623	45	.276

WORLD SERIES

	G	AB	H	2B	3B	HR	R	RBi	BB	SO	SB	BA
1951 NY A	6	23	6	1	0	1	2	7	2	2	0	.261
1952	7	25	5	0	0	1	5	3	5	2	1	.200
1953	6	24	4	0	1	0	2	4	1	3	0	.167
1955	7	27	7	0	0	1	2	1	2	6	0	.259
1956	7	21	3	0	0	0	0	1	3	6	0	.143
1957	7	24	6	0	0	0	3	2	3	3	1	.250
1958	7	28	9	2	0	1	5	4	2	4	0	.321
1960	6	18	5	1	0	0	4	2	2	3	0	.278
8 yrs.	53	190	45	4	1	7	23	24	20	29	2	.237

Johnny Mize

	G	AB	H	2B	3B	HR	R	RBI	BB	SO	SB	BA
1936 STL N	126	414	136	30	8	19	76	93	50	32	1	.329
1937	145	560	204	40	7	25	103	113	56	57	2	.364
1938	149	531	179	34	16	27	85	102	74	47	0	.337
1939	153	564	197	44	14	28	104	108	92	49	0	.349
1940	155	579	182	31	13	43	111	137	82	49	7	.314
1941	126	473	150	39	8	16	67	100	70	45	4	.317
1942 NY N	142	541	165	25	7	26	97	110	60	39	3	.305
1946	101	377	127	18	3	22	70	70	62	26	3	.337
1947	154	586	177	26	2	51	137	138	74	42	2	.302
1948	152	560	162	26	4	40	110	125	94	37	4	.289
1949 2 teams	NY	N	(106G-.263)		NY	A	(13G-.261)					
" total	119	411	108	16	0	19	63	64	54	21	1	.263
1950 NY A	90	274	76	12	0	25	43	72	29	24	0	.277
1951	113	332	86	14	1	10	37	49	36	24	1	.259
1952	78	137	36	9	0	4	9	29	11	15	0	.263
1953	81	104	26	3	0	4	6	27	12	17	0	.250
15 yrs.	1884	6443	2011	367	83	359	1118	1337	856	524	28	.312

WORLD SERIES

	G	AB	H	2B	3B	HR	R	RBI	BB	SO	SB	BA
1949 NY A	2	2	2	0	0	0	0	2	0	0	0	1.000
1950	4	15	2	0	0	0	0	0	0	1	0	.133
1951	4	7	2	1	0	0	2	1	2	0	0	.286
1952	5	15	6	1	0	3	3	6	3	1	0	.400
1953	3	3	0	0	0	0	0	0	0	1	0	.000
5 yrs.	18	42	12	2	0	3	5	9	5	3	0	.286

Irv Noren

	G	AB	H	2B	3B	HR	R	RBI	BB	SO	SB	BA
1950 WAS A	138	542	160	27	10	14	80	98	67	77	5	.295
1951	129	509	142	33	5	8	82	86	51	35	10	.279
1952 2 teams	WAS	A	(12G-.245)		NY	A	(93G-.235)					
" total	105	321	76	16	3	5	40	23	32	37	5	.237
1953 NY A	109	345	92	12	6	6	55	46	42	39	3	.267
1954	125	426	136	21	6	12	70	66	43	38	4	.319
1955	132	371	94	19	1	8	49	59	43	33	5	.253
1956	29	37	8	1	0	0	4	6	12	7	0	.216
1957 2 teams	KC	A	(81G-.213)		STL	N	(17G-.367)					
" total	98	190	45	12	1	3	11	26	15	25	0	.237
1958 STL N	117	178	47	9	1	4	24	22	13	21	0	.264
1959 2 teams	STL	N	(8G-.125)		CHI	N	(65G-.321)					
" total	73	164	51	7	2	4	27	19	13	26	2	.311
1960 2 teams	CHI	N	(12G-.091)		LA	N	(26G-.200)					
" total	38	36	6	0	0	1	1	2	4	12	0	.167
11 yrs.	1093	3119	857	157	35	65	443	453	335	350	34	.275

WORLD SERIES													
1952 NY A	4	10	3	0	0	0	0	1	1	3	0	.300
1953	2	1	0	0	0	0	0	0	1	0	0	.000
1955	5	16	1	0	0	0	0	1	1	1	0	.063
3 yrs.	11	27	4	0	0	0	0	2	3	4	0	.148

Joe Ostrowski

	W	L	PCT	ERA	G	GS	CG	IP	H	BB	SO	ShO	SV
1948 STL A	4	6	.400	5.97	26	9	3	78.1	108	17	20	0	3
1949	8	8	.500	4.79	40	13	4	141	185	27	34	0	2
1950 2 teams	STL	A	(96G 2–4)		NY	A	(21G 1–1)						
" total	3	5	.375	3.65	30	11	3	101	107	22	30	0	3
1951 NY A	6	4	.600	3.49	34	3	2	95.1	103	18	30	0	5
1952	2	2	.500	5.63	20	1	0	40	56	14	17	0	2
5 yrs.	23	25	.479	4.54	150	37	12	455.2	559	98	131	0	15

WORLD SERIES													
1951 NY A	0	0	–	0.00	1	0	0	2	1	0	1	0	0

Vic Raschi

	W	L	PCT	ERA	G	GS	CG	IP	H	BB	SO	ShO	SV
1946 NY A	2	0	1.000	3.94	2	2	2	16	14	5	11	0	0
1947	7	2	.778	3.87	15	14	6	104.2	89	38	51	1	0
1948	19	8	.704	3.84	36	31	18	222.2	208	74	124	6	1
1949	21	10	.677	3.34	38	37	21	274.2	247	138	124	3	0
1950	21	8	.724	4.00	33	32	17	256.2	232	116	155	2	1
1951	21	10	.677	3.27	35	34	15	258.1	233	103	164	4	0
1952	16	6	.727	2.78	31	31	13	223	174	91	127	4	0
1953	13	6	.684	3.33	28	26	7	181	150	55	76	4	1
1954 STL N	8	9	.471	4.73	30	29	6	179	182	71	73	2	0
1955 2 teams	STL	N	(1G 0–1)		KC	A	(20G 4–6)						
" total	4	7	.364	5.68	21	19	1	103	137	36	39	0	0
10 yrs.	132	66	.667	3.72	269	255	106	1819	1666	727	944	26	3

WORLD SERIES													
1947 NY A	0	0	–	6.75	2	0	0	1.1	2	0	1	0	0
1949	1	1	.500	4.30	2	2	0	14.2	15	5	11	0	0
1950	1	0	1.000	0.00	1	1	1	9	2	1	5	1	0
1951	1	1	.500	0.87	2	2	0	10.1	3	8	4	0	0
1952	2	0	1.000	1.59	3	2	1	17	12	8	18	0	0
1953	0	1	.000	3.38	1	1	1	8	9	3	4	0	0
6 yrs.	5	3	.625	2.24	11	8	3	60.1	52	25	43	1	0

Allie Reynolds

			W	L	PCT	ERA	G	GS	CG	IP	H	BB	SO	ShO	SV
1942	CLE	A	0	0	–	0.00	2	0	0	5	5	4	2	0	0
1943			11	12	.478	2.99	34	21	11	198.2	140	109	151	3	3
1944			11	8	.579	3.30	28	21	5	158	141	91	84	1	1
1945			18	12	.600	3.20	44	30	16	247.1	227	130	112	2	4
1946			11	15	.423	3.88	31	28	9	183.1	180	108	107	3	0
1947	NY	A	19	8	.704	3.20	34	30	17	241.2	207	123	129	4	2
1948			16	7	.696	3.77	39	31	11	236.1	240	111	101	1	3
1949			17	6	.739	4.00	35	31	4	213.2	200	123	105	2	1
1950			16	12	.571	3.74	35	29	14	240.2	215	138	160	2	2
1951			17	8	.680	3.05	40	26	16	221	171	100	126	7	7
1952			20	8	.714	2.06	35	29	24	244.1	194	97	160	6	6
1953			13	7	.650	3.41	41	15	5	145	140	61	86	1	13
1954			13	4	.765	3.32	36	18	5	157.1	133	66	100	4	7
13 yrs.			182	107	.630	3.30	434	309	137	2492.1	2193	1261	1423	36	49

WORLD SERIES

			W	L	PCT	ERA	G	GS	CG	IP	H	BB	SO	ShO	SV
1947	NY	A	1	0	1.000	4.76	2	2	1	11.1	15	3	6	0	0
1949			1	0	1.000	0.00	2	1	1	12.1	2	4	14	1	1
1950			1	0	1.000	0.87	2	1	1	10.1	7	4	7	0	1
1951			1	1	.500	4.20	2	2	1	15	16	11	8	0	0
1952			2	1	.667	1.77	4	2	1	20.1	12	6	18	1	1
1953			1	0	1.000	6.75	3	1	0	8	9	4	9	0	1
6 yrs.			7	2	.778	2.79	15	9	5	77.1	61	32	62	2	4

Phil Rizzuto

			G	AB	H	2B	3B	HR	R	RBI	BB	SO	SB	BA
1941	NY	A	133	515	158	20	9	3	65	46	27	36	14	.307
1942			144	553	157	24	7	4	79	68	44	40	22	.284
1946			126	471	121	17	1	2	53	38	34	39	14	.257
1947			153	549	150	26	9	2	78	60	57	31	11	.273
1948			128	464	117	13	2	6	65	50	60	24	6	.252
1949			153	614	169	22	7	5	110	64	72	34	18	.275
1950			155	617	200	36	7	7	125	66	91	38	12	.324
1951			144	540	148	21	6	2	87	43	58	27	18	.274
1952			152	578	147	24	10	2	89	43	67	42	17	.254
1953			134	413	112	21	3	2	54	54	71	39	4	.271
1954			127	307	60	11	0	2	47	15	41	23	3	.195
1955			81	143	37	4	1	1	19	9	22	18	7	.259
1956			31	52	12	0	0	0	6	6	6	6	3	.231
3 yrs.			1661	5816	1588	239	62	38	877	562	650	397	149	.273

WORLD SERIES

			G	AB	H	2B	3B	HR	R	RBI	BB	SO	SB	BA
1941 NY	A		5	18	2	0	0	0	0	0	3	1	1	.111
1942			5	21	8	0	0	1	2	1	2	1	2	.381
1947			7	26	8	1	0	0	3	2	4	0	2	.308
1949			5	18	3	0	0	0	2	1	3	1	1	.167
1950			4	14	2	0	0	0	1	0	3	0	1	.143
1951			6	25	8	0	0	1	5	3	2	3	0	.320
1952			7	27	4	1	0	0	2	0	5	2	0	.148
1953			6	19	6	1	0	0	4	0	3	2	1	.316
1955			7	15	4	0	0	0	2	1	5	1	2	.267
9 yrs.			52	183	45	3	0	2	21	8	30	11	10	.246

Johnny Sain

			W	L	PCT	ERA	G	GS	CG	IP	H	BB	SO	ShO	SV
1942 BOS	N		4	7	.364	3.90	40	3	0	97	79	63	68	0	6
1946			20	14	.588	2.21	37	34	24	265	225	87	129	3	2
1947			21	12	.636	3.52	38	35	22	266	265	79	132	3	1
1948			24	15	.615	2.60	42	39	29	314.2	297	83	137	4	1
1949			10	17	.370	4.81	37	36	16	243	285	74	73	1	0
1950			20	13	.606	3.94	37	37	25	278.1	294	70	96	3	0
1951 2 teams	BOS	N (26G 5–13)				NY	A	(7G 2–1)							
" total			7	14	.333	4.20	33	26	7	197.1	236	53	84	1	2
1952 NY	A		11	6	.647	3.46	35	16	8	146.1	149	38	57	0	7
1953			14	7	.667	3.00	40	19	10	189	189	45	84	1	9
1954			6	6	.500	3.16	45	0	0	77	66	15	33	0	22
1955 2 teams	NY	A (3G 0–))				KC	A	(25G 2–5)							
" total			2	5	.286	5.58	28	0	0	50	60	11	17	0	1
11 yrs.			139	116	.545	3.49	412	245	140	2125.2	2145	619	910	16	51

WORLD SERIES

			W	L	PCT	ERA	G	GS	CG	IP	H	BB	SO	ShO	SV
1948 BOS	N		1	1	.500	1.06	2	2	2	17	9	0	9	1	0
1951 NY	A		0	0	–	9.00	1	0	0	2	4	2	2	0	0
1952			0	1	.000	3.00	1	0	0	6	6	3	3	0	0
1953			1	0	1.000	4.76	2	0	0	5.2	8	1	1	0	0
4 yrs.			2	2	.500	2.64	6	2	2	30.2	27	6	15	1	0

Frank Shea

		W	L	PCT	ERA	G	GS	CG	IP	H	BB	SO	ShO	SV
1947	NY A	14	5	.737	3.07	27	23	13	178.2	127	89	89	3	1
1948		9	10	.474	3.41	28	22	8	155.2	117	87	71	3	1
1949		1	1	.500	5.33	20	3	0	52.1	48	43	22	0	1
1951		5	5	.500	4.33	25	11	2	95.2	112	50	38	2	0
1952	WAS A	11	7	.611	2.93	22	21	12	169	144	92	65	2	0
1953		12	7	.632	3.94	22	23	11	164.2	151	75	38	1	0
1954		2	9	.182	6.18	23	11	1	71.1	97	34	22	0	0
1955		2	2	.500	3.99	27	4	1	56.1	53	27	16	1	2
8 yrs.		56	46	.549	3.80	195	118	48	943.2	849	497	361	12	5

WORLD SERIES

		W	L	PCT	ERA	G	GS	CG	IP	H	BB	SO	ShO	SV
1947	NY A	2	0	1.000	2.35	3	3	1	15.1	10	8	10	0	0

Charlie Silvera

		G	AB	H	2B	3B	HR	R	RBI	BB	SO	SB	BA
1948	NY A	4	14	8	0	1	0	1	1	0	1	0	.571
1949		58	130	41	2	0	0	8	13	18	5	2	.315
1950		18	25	4	0	0	0	2	1	1	2	0	.160
1951		18	51	14	3	0	1	5	7	5	3	0	.275
1952		20	55	18	3	0	0	4	11	5	2	0	.327
1953		42	82	23	3	1	0	11	12	9	5	0	.280
1954		20	37	10	1	0	0	1	4	3	2	0	.270
1955		14	26	5	0	0	0	1	1	6	4	0	.192
1956		7	9	2	0	0	0	0	0	2	3	0	.222
1957	CHI N	26	53	11	3	0	0	1	2	4	5	0	.208
10 yrs.		227	482	136	15	2	1	34	52	53	32	2	.282

WORLD SERIES

		G	AB	H	2B	3B	HR	R	RBI	BB	SO	SB	BA
1949	NY A	1	2	0	0	0	0	0	0	0	0	0	.000

Gene Woodling

		G	AB	H	2B	3B	HR	R	RBI	BB	SO	SB	BA
1943	CLE A	8	25	8	2	1	1	5	5	1	3	0	.320
1946		61	133	25	1	4	0	8	9	16	13	1	.188
1947	PIT N	22	79	21	2	2	0	7	10	7	5	0	.266
1949	NY A	112	296	80	13	7	5	60	44	52	21	2	.270
1950		122	449	127	20	10	6	81	60	69	31	5	.283
1951		120	420	118	15	8	15	65	71	62	37	0	.281
1952		122	408	126	19	6	12	58	63	59	31	1	.309
1953		125	395	121	26	4	10	64	58	82	29	2	.306
1954		97	304	76	12	5	3	33	40	53	35	3	.250
1955	2 teams	BAL	A	(47G-.221)		CLE	A	(79G-.278)					
"	total	126	404	104	21	3	8	55	53	60	33	3	.257
1956	CLE A	100	317	83	17	0	8	56	38	69	29	3	.262
1957		133	430	138	25	2	19	74	78	64	35	0	.321
1958	BAL A	133	413	114	16	1	15	57	65	66	49	4	.276
1959		140	440	132	22	2	14	63	77	78	35	1	.300
1960		140	435	123	18	3	11	68	62	84	40	3	.283
1961	WAS A	110	342	107	16	4	10	39	57	50	24	1	.313
1962	2 teams	WAS	A	(44G-.274)		NY	N	(81G-.274)					
"	total	125	297	82	12	1	10	37	48	48	27	1	.276
	17 yrs.	1796	5587	1585	257	63	147	830	830	920	477	29	.284

WORLD SERIES

		G	AB	H	2B	3B	HR	R	RBI	BB	SO	SB	BA
1949	NY A	3	10	4	3	0	0	4	0	3	0	0	.400
1950		4	14	6	0	0	0	2	1	2	0	0	.429
1951		6	18	3	1	1	1	6	1	5	3	0	.167
1952		7	23	8	1	1	1	4	1	3	3	0	.348
1953		6	20	6	0	0	1	5	3	6	2	0	.300
	5 yrs.	26	85	27	5	2	3	21	6	19	8	0	.318

INDEX

Boldface page numbers indicate interviews.

About the Author

Dom Forker is an award-winning sports editor and journalist, and a former featured monthly columnist for *Baseball Digest*. He has written seven other sports books, including *The Ultimate Baseball Quiz Book*, available in a revised Signet paperback edition. He lives with his family in Milford, New Jersey—just a long stone's throw from his beloved Yankee Stadium.